OTHELLO

Edited by

NORMAN SANDERS

Lindsay Young Professor of Humanities,
University of Tennessee

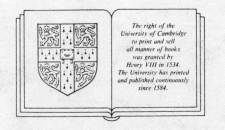

The right of the
University of Cambridge
to print and sell
all manner of books
was granted by
Henry VIII in 1534.
The University has printed
and published continuously
since 1584.

CAMBRIDGE UNIVERSITY PRESS

Cambridge
New York   Port Chester
Melbourne   Sydney

Published by the Press Syndicate of the University of Cambridge
The Pitt Building, Trumpington Street, Cambridge CB2 1RP
40 West 20th Street, New York, NY 10011, USA
10 Stamford Road, Oakleigh, Melbourne 3166, Australia

First published 1984
Reprinted 1985 1987 1988 1989

Printed in Great Britain by
the University Press, Cambridge

Library of Congress catalogue card number: 83–23195

British Library Cataloguing in Publication Data

Shakespeare, William
Othello.—(The New Cambridge Shakespeare)
I. Title   II. Sanders, Norman, 1929 Apr. 22–
822.3′3   PR2829

ISBN 0 521 22339 3 hard covers
ISBN 0 521 29454 1 paperback

THE NEW CAMBRIDGE SHAKESPEARE

The *New Cambridge Shakespeare* succeeds *The New Shakespeare* which began publication in 1921 under the general editorship of Sir Arthur Quiller-Couch and John Dover Wilson, and was completed in the 1960s, with the assistance of G. I. Duthie, Alice Walker, Peter Ure and J. C. Maxwell. *The New Shakespeare* itself followed upon *The Cambridge Shakespeare*, 1863–6, edited by W. G. Clark, J. Glover and W. A. Wright.

The New Shakespeare won high esteem both for its scholarship and for its design, but shifts of critical taste and insight, recent Shakespearean research, and a changing sense of what is important in our understanding of the plays, have made it necessary to re-edit and redesign, not merely to revise, the series.

The *New Cambridge Shakespeare* aims to be of value to a new generation of playgoers and readers who wish to enjoy fuller access to Shakespeare's poetic and dramatic art. While offering ample academic guidance, it reflects current critical interests and is more attentive than some earlier editions have been to the realisation of the plays on the stage, and to their social and cultural settings. The text of each play has been freshly edited, with textual data made available to those users who wish to know why and how one published text differs from another. Although modernised, the edition conserves forms that appear to be expressive and characteristically Shakespearean, and it does not attempt to disguise the fact that the plays were written in a language other than that of our own time.

Illustrations are usually integrated into the critical and historical discussion of the play and include some reconstructions of early performances by C. Walter Hodges. Some editors have also made use of the advice and experience of Maurice Daniels, for many years a member of the Royal Shakespeare Company.

Each volume is addressed to the needs and problems of a particular text, and each therefore differs in style and emphasis from others in the series.

PHILIP BROCKBANK
General Editor

CONTENTS

ILLUSTRATIONS

In the Textual Analysis, illustrations from the First Folio text (pp. 198–200) and that from the first quarto text (p. 196) are from copies in the Folger Shakespeare Library.

ACKNOWLEDGEMENTS

It is a pleasure to acknowledge various kinds of help received in the preparation of this volume. The staff of the Folger Shakespeare Library, Susan Brock and Robert Smallwood of the Shakespeare Institute, Sarah Hann of the BBC Hulton Picture Library, Jeanne Newlin of the Harvard Theatre Collection, and Mary White and Levi Fox of the Shakespeare Birthplace Library all gave much valued assistance with the illustrations; as did Raymond Mander and Joe Mitchenson and Angus McBean.

The Head of the English Department of the University of Tennessee, Joseph Trahern, and Dean Robert Landon of the College of Liberal Arts kindly arranged my teaching schedule to facilitate my work on the edition; and among other colleagues who helped with specific problems are Edward Bratton, Allen Carroll, Robert Mashburn and Charles Shattuck. It has been a delight to work with the General Editor of the series and an eagle-eyed Robin Hood who devoted their time quite unselfishly to ensure that my manuscript was as good as they could make it.

I am particularly grateful to the Mary Ellenberger Camp Foundation for the very concrete expression of confidence it has shown in my work. And as always my wife has worked with me on every aspect of the volume – quite literally in sickness and in health.

N.S.

Knoxville, Tennessee

ABBREVIATIONS AND CONVENTIONS

1. Shakespeare's plays

The abbreviated titles of Shakespeare's plays have been modified from those used in the *Harvard Concordance to Shakespeare*. All quotations and line references to plays other than *Othello* are to G. Blakemore Evans (ed.), *The Riverside Shakespeare*, 1974, on which the *Concordance* is based.

Ado	*Much Ado about Nothing*
Ant.	*Antony and Cleopatra*
AWW	*All's Well That Ends Well*
AYLI	*As You Like It*
Cor.	*Coriolanus*
Cym.	*Cymbeline*
Err.	*The Comedy of Errors*
Ham.	*Hamlet*
1H4	*The First Part of King Henry the Fourth*
2H4	*The Second Part of King Henry the Fourth*
H5	*King Henry the Fifth*
1H6	*The First Part of King Henry the Sixth*
2H6	*The Second Part of King Henry the Sixth*
3H6	*The Third Part of King Henry the Sixth*
H8	*King Henry the Eighth*
JC	*Julius Caesar*
John	*King John*
LLL	*Love's Labour's Lost*
Lear	*King Lear*
Mac.	*Macbeth*
MM	*Measure for Measure*
MND	*A Midsummer Night's Dream*
MV	*The Merchant of Venice*
Oth.	*Othello*
Per.	*Pericles*
R2	*King Richard the Second*
R3	*King Richard the Third*
Rom.	*Romeo and Juliet*
Shr.	*The Taming of the Shrew*
STM	*Sir Thomas More*
Temp.	*The Tempest*
TGV	*The Two Gentlemen of Verona*
Tim.	*Timon of Athens*
Tit.	*Titus Andronicus*
TN	*Twelfth Night*
TNK	*The Two Noble Kinsmen*
Tro.	*Troilus and Cressida*

Wiv.	*The Merry Wives of Windsor*
WT	*The Winter's Tale*

2. Editions

Cam.	*The Works of William Shakespeare*, ed. W. G. Clark, John Glover and W. A. Wright, 1863–6 (Cambridge Shakespeare)
Capell	*Mr William Shakespeare his Comedies, Histories, and Tragedies*, ed. Edward Capell, 1768
Delius	*Shakesperes Werke*, ed. Nicolaus Delius, 1872
Dyce	*The Works of William Shakespeare*, ed. Alexander Dyce, 1857
Dyce²	*The Works of William Shakespeare*, ed. Alexander Dyce, 2nd edn, 1864–7
Dyce³	*The Works of William Shakespeare*, ed. Alexander Dyce, 3rd edn, 1875–6
F	*Mr William Shakespeares Comedies, Histories, and Tragedies*, 1623 (First Folio)
F2	*Mr William Shakespeares Comedies, Histories, and Tragedies*, 1632 (Second Folio)
F3	*Mr William Shakespeares Comedies, Histories, and Tragedies*, 1664 (Third Folio)
F4	*Mr William Shakespeares Comedies, Histories, and Tragedies*, 1685 (Fourth Folio)
Furness	*A New Variorum Edition of Shakespeare: Othello*, ed. H. H. Furness, 1886
Hanmer	*The Works of Shakespear*, ed. Thomas Hanmer, 1744
Hart	*Othello*, ed. H. C. Hart, 1928 (Arden)
Johnson	*The Plays of William Shakespeare*, ed. Samuel Johnson, 1765
Keightley	*The Plays of William Shakespeare*, ed. Thomas Keightley, 1864
Knight	*The Pictorial Edition of the Works of Shakespeare*, ed. Charles Knight, 1841
Malone	*The Plays and Poems of William Shakespeare*, ed. Edmond Malone, 1790
Malone Var.	*The Plays and Poems of William Shakespeare*, ed. Edmond Malone [rev. J. Boswell], 1821
Muir	*Othello*, ed. Kenneth Muir, 1968 (New Penguin)
NS	*Othello*, ed. Alice Walker and J. Dover Wilson, 1957 (New Shakespeare)
Pope	*The Works of Shakespear*, ed. Alexander Pope, 1723
Q1	*The Tragœdy of Othello, The Moore of Venice...*, 1622 (First Quarto)
Q2	*The Tragœdy of Othello, The Moore of Venice...*, 1630 (Second Quarto)
Ridley	*Othello*, ed. M. R. Ridley, 1958 (Arden)
Rowe	*The Works of Mr William Shakespear*, ed. Nicholas Rowe, 1709
Steevens	*The Plays of William Shakespeare*, ed. Samuel Johnson and George Steevens, 1773
Steevens²	*The Plays of William Shakespeare*, ed. Samuel Johnson and George Steevens, 2nd edn, 1778
Steevens³	*The Plays of William Shakespeare*, ed. Samuel Johnson and George Steevens, 4th edn, 1793
Theobald	*The Works of Shakespeare*, ed. Lewis Theobald, 1733
Warburton	*The Works of Shakespear*, ed. William Warburton, 1747

3. Other works, periodicals, general references

Abbott	E. A. Abbott, *A Shakespearian Grammar*, 1869 (references are to numbered paragraphs)
Bailey	Samuel Bailey, *On the Received Text of Shakespeare's Dramatic Writings and its Improvement*, 2 vols., 1862–6
Bullough	Geoffrey Bullough (ed.), *Narrative and Dramatic Sources of Shakespeare*, 8 vols., 1957–75
Cinthio	Giraldi Cinthio, *Hecatommithi* (1566), Third Decade, Seventh Story; English translation in Bullough, VII, 239–52
conj.	conjecture
CQ	*The Critical Quarterly*
ELH	*ELH: A Journal of English Literary History*
ELR	*English Literary Renaissance*
Fortescue	J. W. Fortescue, *Shakespeare's England*, 2 vols., 1916, I, 132–3
Heath	Benjamin Heath, *Revisal of Shakespeare's Text*, 1765
Hulme	H. M. Hulme, *Explorations in Shakespeare's Language*, 1962
Jourdain	M. Jourdain, in *Transactions of the Philological Society*, 1860, p. 139
lit.	literally
McKerrow	R. B. McKerrow, *Printers' and Publishers' Devices in England and Scotland 1485–1640*, 1949
N&Q	*Notes and Queries*
Nicholson	Originator of textual conj. in Cam.
OED	*Oxford English Dictionary*
Onions	C. T. Onions, *A Shakespeare Glossary*, 1911; rev. edn, 1953
Partridge	Eric Partridge, *Shakespeare's Bawdy*, 1948
Pliny	Pliny, *Naturalis Historia*, trans. Philemon Holland (1601)
PMLA	*Publications of the Modern Language Association of America*
SB	*Studies in Bibliography*
Schmidt	Alexander Schmidt, *Shakespeare-Lexicon*, 2 vols., 1874–5
SD	stage direction
SEL	*Studies in English Literature*
SH	speech heading
SQ	*Shakespeare Quarterly*
S.St.	*Shakespeare Studies*
S.Sur.	*Shakespeare Survey*
subst.	substantively
Tilley	M. P. Tilley, *A Dictionary of the Proverbs in England in the Sixteenth and Seventeenth Centuries*, 1950 (references are to numbered proverbs)
TLS	*The Times Literary Supplement*
Tollet	Originator of textual conj. in Furness
Upton	John Upton, *Critical Observations on Shakespeare*, 1746
Walker	*see* NS
Wilson	*see* NS

INTRODUCTION

Date

The earliest evidence of the date of *Othello* is the record of a performance at court found in the Accounts of the Master of the Revels of the time, Edmund Tilney, for the year 1604:

By the Kings Maiesties plaiers. Hallamas Day being the first of Nouembar. A play in the Banketinge house att Whithall called The Moor of Venis. Shaxberd.

This account book, discovered by Peter Cunningham, was obtained by the British Museum in 1868, and may well have been known to Edmund Malone, who in the notes to his edition of 1790 and in the Variorum edition of 1821 records that he had 'indisputable evidence' that the play was acted in 1604. Despite Malone's supporting testimony, the manuscript entry was suspected of being a forgery (by Richard Grant White and others in the nineteenth century and by Samuel Tannenbaum in the twentieth) until it was authenticated by A. E. Stamp in 1930.[1] During Shakespeare's lifetime the play was again performed at court in 1612/13 as part of the celebrations marking the marriage of Princess Elizabeth to the Elector Palatine; and it was acted publicly by the King's Men's company at the Globe Theatre in April 1610, and at Oxford in September of the same year. There were other early-seventeenth-century productions: at Blackfriars Theatre in November 1629 and May 1635, and at Hampton Court in December 1636.[2]

The play was first printed, in quarto format (Q1), by Nicholas Okes for Thomas Walkley who published it in 1622, having entered the title in the Stationers' Register on 6 October the previous year. A year later, in 1623, it was published with a fuller text in the First Folio (F), and again in quarto in 1630 (Q2). The present text is based upon both early editions, those readings being adopted which can be defended as the nearest to Shakespearean usage and intention.[3]

Evidence based upon probable sources used and on changes detected in Shakespeare's style during his career generally buttress the indication given by the Revels Accounts that the play was probably written *circa* 1602–4. It is fairly clear that some passages in the play were written under the influence of Philemon Holland's translation of Pliny's *Naturalis Historia*, which was published in 1601; and Shakespeare may also have relied upon Richard Knolles's *General History of the Turks* (1603) for details of the Venetian–Turkish wars found in 1.3, 2.1 and 2.2.[4] The metrical tests applied by F. G. Fleay and the tabulations of weak and light endings by J. K. Ingram, while

---

[1] *The Disputed Revels Documents*, 1930.
[2] See E. K. Chambers, *William Shakespeare*, 2 vols., 1930, II, 336, 343, 352, 353, and G. Tillotson, *TLS*, 20 July 1933, p. 494.
[3] See Textual Analysis, pp. 193–207 below.   [4] See below, p. 10.

not carrying the weight among modern scholars that they had in the nineteenth century, separately put the play at about the same period of Shakespeare's career.[1] A. Hart's detection of echoes from *Hamlet*, if not particularly persuasive, at least does nothing to affect a post-1602 dating; and the phrase 'more savage than a barbarous Moor', found in Dekker and Middleton's *Honest Whore*, Part One (after April 1604), 1.1.37 (ed. F. Bowers, 1955), while not specific enough to be a definite allusion to *Othello*, may be evidence of the play's existence and popularity.[2]

The possibility that Shakespeare's handling of some of his dramatic materials may be connected with royal tastes and interests may point to an early-Jacobean date. James I, who came to the throne in 1603, was known to be fascinated by Turkish history and had written a poem called *Lepanto*, which was published originally in 1591 and republished in England on his accession. There are many references to this poem by English writers at the time, including Ben Jonson and Knolles, whose *History* was dedicated to the king. It is possible that a play set among the events and naval actions which led ultimately to the Battle of Lepanto may have been written with an eye to the intellectual interests of the King's Men's new royal patron.[3] And it may be more than a coincidence that it was for the winter season's festivities of 1604 that Queen Anne desired Ben Jonson to devise a splendid masque specifically about Moors, which led to the mounting of *The Masque of Blackness*, in which she herself appeared in dusky make-up.[4]

There has been an enormous amount of discussion of Warburton's suggestion that the lines 'The hearts of old gave hands; / But our new heraldry is hands, not hearts' (3.4.42–3) are a topical allusion to the baronetage, the new titled order – ranking below peers and above knights – instituted by James I in 1611, which bears the red hand of Ulster as its badge. But the passage does not merit serious consideration as evidence for a late date for the play's composition; and it is impossible to accept as an interpolation made some eight years after the play's original writing.[5]

We may conclude, then, that *Othello* must have been written after 1601 and before autumn 1604, with late 1603 to early 1604 being the most likely time of its completion.

Sources

The principal narrative source for the play was the seventh novella in the third decade of Giraldi Cinthio's *Hecatommithi*. This collection of tales within a framework, first published in Venice in 1566, was used by a number of Elizabethan and Jacobean dramatists in their search for plots. The fact that it provided the source for *Measure*

[1] See Chambers, *Shakespeare*, I, 255–69; and Furness, p. 255.
[2] *TLS*, 10 October 1935, p. 631. As supporting evidence for a post-1601 dating E. Jones suggests that the name Othello may have been partly modelled on Thorello, a jealous husband in Ben Jonson's *Every Man in His Humour* (1598), and that Brabantio's name and character may have been influenced by the Duke of Brabant in the anonymous play *The Weakest Goeth to the Wall* (1600); see Jones, *Scenic Form in Shakespeare*, 1971, pp. 149–51.
[3] See E. Jones, '*Othello, Lepanto*, and the Cyprus wars', *S.Sur.* 21 (1968), 47–52. *Macbeth* may also have been written with James's interests in mind – in that case Scotland and witchcraft.
[4] See M. Rosenberg, *The Masks of Othello*, 1961, p. 200.
[5] See Commentary at 3.4.42–3.

for Measure, which was also performed at court at the end of 1604, may suggest that Shakespeare had discovered its professional usefulness about this time. No sixteenth-century English translation of Cinthio's work has survived, although the book was known in England soon after its first publication;[1] and it is difficult to determine with any finality whether Shakespeare used the Italian original or the French translation of Gabriel Chappuys, published in his *Premier Volume des Cents Excellentes Nouvelles* (1584).

There are four verbal links that draw the play and the Italian version together. Othello's demand, 'Give me the ocular proof...Make me to see't' (3.3.361–5) is closer to Cinthio's 'se non mi fai...vedere co gli occhi' than to Chappuys's 'si tu ne me fais voir'. Q1's use of the unusual word 'acerbe' (F 'bitter') at 1.3.338 may be an echo of Cinthio's 'in acerbissimo odio'; just as Iago's gloating 'I do see you're moved' (3.3.219) is nearer to the Italian 'ch' ogni poco di cosa voi moue ad ira', where the French verb used is 'inciter'. Also, the unique Shakespearean usage 'molestation', describing the enchafed flood at 2.1.16, may have been influenced by Cinthio's Moor who speaks of the sea in a similar way in a passage omitted by Chappuys: 'ogni pericolo, che ci soprauenisse, mi recherebbe estreme molestia'.

Evidence that it was the French version Shakespeare used is of the same kind. The words 'if it touch not you, it comes near nobody' (4.1.187) seem to echo Chappuys's 'ce qui vous touche plus qu'à aucun autre', where the Italian verb is 'appartiene'; and Iago's emphasis on the importance of Cassio's 'gestures', as Othello spies on them in 4.1, is nearer to the French 'gestes' than the Italian 'atti'. Perhaps more substantial than these verbal similarities, however, is one of Chappuys's additions to the original text. In the lines of the play concerning Cassio's request that Bianca copy the embroidery of the handkerchief, the phrase 'take out the work' (or a variant of it) is used three times (3.3.298, 3.4.174, 4.1.145) – a sense of 'take out' found nowhere else in Shakespeare. No similar phrase occurs in Cinthio; but Chappuys adds to the Italian passage dealing with Cassio's decision the phrase 'tirer le patron' (copy the pattern).

In view of the evidence, therefore, one can only say that Shakespeare may have used Cinthio's original or Chappuys's translation or both of them, while making due allowance for the possibility of a no longer extant English translation based on them.[2]

Cinthio claimed that his tales were taken from real life, and although this is demonstrably not true of some of his stories, the stark realism of his narrative of the Moor and his Venetian wife has sent scholars to Italian history in the search for parallel tragedies of human jealousy. Most of those suggested do have details in common with the play, with one concerning a member of the Moro family, and another featuring a captain nicknamed 'Il Moro'; but none of them strikes one as necessarily having been in Shakespeare's mind at the time of the play's composition.[3]

---

[1] Some stories were used by William Painter in his *Palace of Pleasure* (1566–7), and Robert Greene used one story as a source for his play, *James the Fourth* (1590).

[2] For a full description of these details, see K. Muir, *The Sources of Shakespeare's Plays*, 1977, pp. 182–96, and E. A. J. Honigmann, '*Othello*, Chappuys, and Cinthio', *N&Q* 211 (1966), 136–7.

[3] For details of these, see Bullough, VII, 195–6.

Of the principal characters in Cinthio's story only Disdemona is named; Othello is called simply 'Capitano Moro' or 'Moro', Cassio is designated as a 'Capo di Squadra' (Captain or low-ranking officer), and Iago is an 'Alfiero' (Ensign or standard-bearer). The Moor is a distinguished soldier highly valued by the Signory of Venice, and Disdemona falls in love with him for his fine qualities and despite his looks. In defiance of her family's efforts to make her wed another man, she marries the Moor and they live happily in Venice for some time. When her husband is ordered to take command of the garrison in Cyprus, she pleads eagerly that she may accompany him; and despite his misgivings about the dangers of the voyage, the Moor allows her to sail with him in his command ship.

In Cyprus, as in Venice, Disdemona's best friend is the Ensign's wife, with whom she spends most of her time. The Ensign himself is high in the Moor's favour, although he is actually a villain with great skill in concealing his true nature beneath a manner that strikes everyone as being soldierly and noble. He passionately desires Disdemona, but is unable to woo her openly because of his fear of the Moor. When she gives no encouragement to his advances, he convinces himself that she is in love with the Captain, who is a great friend of the Moor and a frequent visitor to his house. He tries to formulate a plan by which he may satisfy the hatred he begins to feel for Disdemona in his disappointment; and he decides to accuse her of adultery with the Captain.

A chance to put this plan into action offers itself when the Captain wounds another soldier while on guard-duty and is dismissed by the Moor. Disdemona frequently begs her husband to reinstate the Captain, and the Ensign suggests to his commander that she is so importunate only because she has become disgusted with his looks and his black skin and is sexually attracted to the Captain. The Moor is deeply troubled by the Ensign's insinuations, and is so violently angry with his wife that she is afraid to persist with her intercession for the Captain.

The Moor demands from the Ensign ocular proof of his wife's infidelity. So one day while Disdemona is visiting his wife and playing with his child, the Ensign steals from her girdle an embroidered handkerchief which was her husband's wedding gift to her, and drops it in the Captain's bedroom. The Captain, recognising it as Disdemona's property, goes to the Moor's house to return it; but finding the Moor at home and unwilling to risk his displeasure, he runs away. The Moor believes he recognised the Captain in the vicinity of the house and asks the Ensign to find out all he can about the Captain's relationship with Disdemona.

The Ensign arranges to talk with the Captain while the Moor can observe them but not hear what they are saying. During the conversation the Ensign acts as though he is amazed at what he is being told, and later tells the Moor that the Captain admitted to adultery with Disdemona and confessed that she had given him her handkerchief the last time they slept together.

When the Moor questions his wife about the loss of the handkerchief, she is so embarrassed in her behaviour and so confused in her attempts to find it that he takes her reactions to be a proof of her guilt. He becomes obsessed with the idea of killing his wife and the Captain; and he behaves so out of character that Disdemona confides

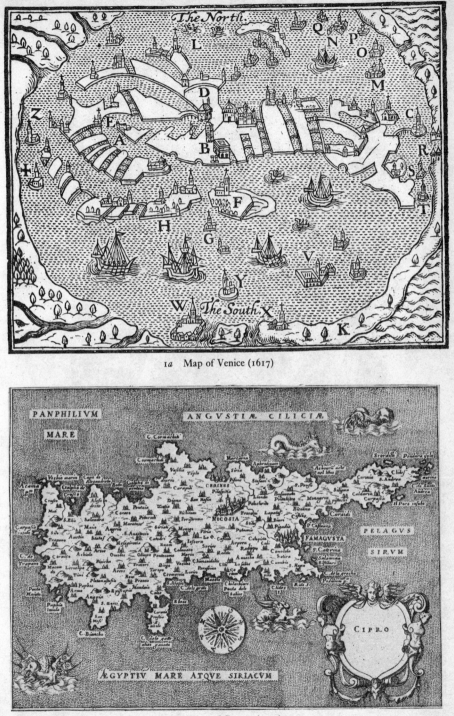

1*a*   Map of Venice (1617)

1*b*   Map of Cyprus (1590)

2a A Venetian officer (1609)

her troubles to the Ensign's wife, who knows all about her husband's plans but dare not speak about them because she is afraid of him.

The Captain has in his house a woman very skilled in embroidery who, recognising the handkerchief as Disdemona's, decides to copy the pattern before returning it. The Ensign spots the woman at this work sitting in her window, and so brings the Moor to see her that he may be convinced of his wife's guilt. At the Moor's request and after having been paid a large sum of money, the Ensign waylays the Captain on his way from a prostitute's house. However, he botches the murder attempt, succeeding only in cutting off his victim's leg.

The Moor first considers killing his wife by stabbing or poison; but finally works out with the Ensign a plan which will enable them to murder her and escape detection. One night while in bed with his wife he orders her to investigate a noise he has heard in the adjoining room. When she does so, the Ensign, who is hiding in a closet, beats her to death with a stocking filled with sand. In order to make the murder appear

2*b*   The Duke (Doge) of Venice (1609)

to be an accident the two men effect the collapse of part of the ceiling on her body.

Soon after Disdemona's funeral, the Moor, distraught at her loss and repenting of his crime, cashiers the Ensign who thereupon tells the Captain that it was the Moor who attacked him. The Captain duly indicts the Moor before the Signory, who sentence him to be tortured. He persists in denying all knowledge of the crime and is released but banished from Venice. After some time, Disdemona's family have him murdered in exile. The Ensign later commits another crime for which he is imprisoned; and after his release he dies from the tortures inflicted on him during his incarceration.[1]

Even from this summary it is obvious that Shakespeare took a great deal from

[1] For a modern translation of Cinthio's tale, see Bullough, VII, 239–52.

Cinthio. The play like the story has two geographical locations: Venice, providing the social and military context in which the characters originate; and the garrisoned island of Cyprus where the principals are isolated and the personal tragedy develops. Cinthio's conception of the Ensign, with his convincing admirable exterior successfully concealing an enormous native evil, is expanded to become the most credible and frightening of Shakespeare's villains. The levels of affection between Othello, Desdemona and Cassio grow out of flat statements in the source. It is the Captain's cashiering that offers the Ensign his chance to sow the seeds of doubt in the Moor's mind. And in both play and tale it is the handkerchief that provides the crucial 'evidence' of adultery which precipitates the tragedy. Everywhere in Cinthio's narrative also one lights upon small details, words and ideas which are the germs of so many aspects of the play's totality.

More striking than such similarities, however, are the changes made by Shakespeare as he refashioned the tale. It is noticeable that there is no close following of the source in the first two acts. Rather the emphasis of the original is altered, new characters are created, and mere hints and phrases are developed into speeches and even parts of scenes. A sentence in Cinthio to the effect that Disdemona's family wished her to marry another man is the seed that produced Desdemona's noble birth, her elopement, and her distraught and racially prejudiced father – indeed much of the material contained in the first three scenes of the play. The Capo di Squadra, the well-loved visitor to the house of the Moor and Disdemona, becomes Cassio, Othello's best friend and companion in his wooing, whose promotion to lieutenant alienates the vicious Ensign. This addition to the source in turn gives Iago the professional and personal motivation for his hatred of Othello, which is far stronger than the sexual lust for Disdemona that drives Cinthio's character.[1] The need for the audience to plumb Iago's complicated and twisted psyche requires the creation of Roderigo, whose intimacy with the villain enables us to learn much that we may add to the information provided by his soliloquies. Perhaps most remarkable of all are the breathtaking addresses to the Senate by Othello and Desdemona which Shakespeare conjures out of one bald statement of the Italian original:

It happened that a virtuous Lady of wondrous beauty called Disdemona, impelled not by female appetite but by the Moor's good qualities, fell in love with him, and he, vanquished by the Lady's beauty and noble mind, likewise was enamoured of her.[2]

In the later acts of the play Cinthio's narrative line is followed much more closely; but significant changes are also made here. Iago, with Roderigo's help, plans Cassio's disgrace and dismissal specifically to further his plot against Othello. On Iago's advice Cassio actively solicits Desdemona's help for his reinstatement. The circumstances surrounding the handkerchief are deliberately changed: Cassio, unlike the Captain, is ignorant of Desdemona's ownership; Emilia, a waiting-woman rather than the intimate friend of the source, is innocent of any knowledge of her husband's designs and thus becomes an unwitting provider of the ocular proof. The Captain's

---

[1] But note the remnant of this in Iago's lines at 2.1.272–4.   [2] Bullough, VII, 242.

needlewoman and the prostitute he visits are combined in the play to become Bianca, Cassio's mistress; and the handkerchief itself is made to figure prominently in the overhearing scene. And, of course, the play's tragic ending is quite different from Cinthio's sequence of plotted murders, trials, imprisonments and torturings.

No such cataloguing of specific plot and character changes can convey the way in which the sordid story of Italian intrigues became the greatest domestic tragedy in the English language. For it takes no account of the immensely rich poetic texture, the means by which an exotic past impinges on the dramatic immediacy, the relentless emotional grip the play exercises upon the audience in the theatre, and the psychological accuracy with which the characters are conceived and the complexity with which they are imbued. Most of all it does nothing to account for the miracle by which Cinthio's Moor – 'a very gallant man...of great prudence and skilful energy' – becomes Othello, a character who contains such mighty oppositions that he stands second only to Hamlet in his capacity to provoke the widest critical disagreements.

Although Cinthio is the primary source, a number of other influences have been detected. The fourth story of Geoffrey Fenton's *Certain Tragical Discourses* (1567), which was translated from Belleforest's *Histoires Tragiques* (1561), contains in its tale of jealousy and murder details similar to those found in the play and not present in Cinthio. Don Spado, the Othello figure, has a spasm of physical frenzy resulting from his jealous obsession; and his tragedy is set against a background of the Turkish wars. His murder of his wife in their bedroom has a good deal in common with 5.2 of the play – such details as the maid's calling for help from neighbours who break into the room; the wife's revival and attempt to exonerate her husband; the final kiss; and the husband's suicide across the body of his wronged wife.[1]

In the earlier section of the play it is possible that Shakespeare also drew some details from the second tale of Barnabe Rich's *Farewell to Military Profession* (1581), which he had earlier used as a source for *Twelfth Night*. There are suggestive parallels between Rich and Shakespeare in the handling of such matters as the Christian ruler who must meet the alarming threats from the invading Turks and the storm which separates the defending fleet. But more interesting are the correspondences between Rich's story and 1.3 of the play, including the Duke's appointment of a famous military leader, the clandestine courtship of the general appointed, the pursuit of the revenge-bent father, the father's demand for justice, the senators' sympathy for the eloping couple, the summons of the daughter to give her own testimony, and the Duke's futile attempt to comfort the stricken father.[2]

In building up the character of his noble Moor Shakespeare may also have recalled items from his other reading. There are some interesting similarities between aspects of Othello's military and personal life and Plutarch's *Life of Cato Utican*.[3] In the story of Procris and Cephalus in George Pettie's *A Petite Palace of Pettie his Pleasure* (1576)

[1] P. N. Siegel, 'A new source for Othello?', *PMLA* 75 (1960), 480, and W. E. McCarron, '*Othello* and Fenton: an addendum', *N&Q* 211 (1966), 137–8.
[2] See *Rich's Farewell to Military Profession*, ed. Thomas Cranfill, 1959, pp. l–lii.
[3] W. Graves, *SQ* 24 (1973), 181–7.

he may have found the idea of a girl's being won by her lover's story-telling powers. There are some remarkable similarities between Othello's account of his adventures and the description of John Leo's career given by John Prory in the preface to his translation of Leo's *The History and Description of Africa* (1600).[1] Shakespeare also clearly used Philemon Holland's translation of Pliny's *Naturalis Historia* (1601) for some exotic allusions in Othello's speeches: the cannibals, anthropophagi, hollow caves, mines of sulphur, gum-dropping Arabian trees, chrysolite, mandragora, colloquintida; the movement of the Pontic and the Propontic and the Hellespont waters; and possibly his reply to Brabantio's charge of seducing his daughter by means of witchcraft.[2] The magical origin of Desdemona's handkerchief may be based on Ariosto's account of Cassandra's supernatural weaving in *Orlando Furioso*, 46, 64–5; and some persuasive verbal parallels have been adduced between the play and Apuleius's *Golden Ass*.[3]

Materials for the Venetian setting and the context of the Turkish wars Shakespeare drew from various sources. For information about the Venetian government and the city, he was apparently indebted to William Thomas's *History of Italy* (1549) and Lewes Lewkenor's translation *The Commonwealth and Government of Venice* (1599) of G. Contarino's *De Magistratibus et Republica Venetorum* (1543). The doubts about the strength of the Turkish forces expressed at the opening of 1.3 could have been suggested by more than one episode in Richard Knolles's *General History of the Turks* (1603) – to which we may also owe the presence of the mysterious 'Signior Angelo' at 1.3.16 as well as some details of the watch on the Cyprus cliffs in 2.1.[4]

Othello's race

The dramatic emphasis placed on the racial difference between Othello and the other characters in the play is one of Shakespeare's most striking departures from Cinthio's tale. The very idea of the hero's alienation from his society is implicit in the subtitles of both Q1 and F texts; it appears in the choice of identification seized upon by the anonymous clerk who made the entry in the Revels Accounts; and it was at the heart of at least one playgoer's recollection of Burbage's portrayal of the 'grieved Moor'.[5] Yet despite the theme's obvious centrality in the play, there is no agreement about which race exactly it was that Shakespeare had in mind for Othello.

For Cinthio and his readers, as for the Venetians in the play, the spectacle of a foreign commander of Italian forces was nothing remarkable. Indeed, according to Contarino's study of the Republic,[6] by long custom the city 'held it a better course to defend their dominions upon the Continent with foreign mercenary soldiers, than with their homeborn citizens'; and there was even a law that ensured that the general of the army was always foreign born.[7] It is noticeable that it is no part of even Iago's

[1] L. Whitney, 'Did Shakespeare know Leo Africanus?', *PMLA* 37 (1922), 470–88.
[2] Muir, *Sources*, pp. 182–96.
[3] J. M. Tobin, 'Apuleius and the Bradleian tragedies', *S.Sur.* 31 (1978), 33–43.
[4] Bullough, VII, 211–14. [5] *The Shakespeare Allusion-Book*, 2 vols., 1909, I, 272.
[6] See above. [7] Bullough, VII, 235.

huge racial antagonism to Othello that his commanding officer is not a Venetian; and Brabantio, before the play begins, viewed the Moor only as a distinguished soldier and honoured guest. It is only when race is connected with miscegenation that it becomes a highly-charged emotional issue for the internationally-minded Venetians; and it was probably more so for the insular theatregoers of Jacobean England.

The origins of popular English knowledge of Africa and its inhabitants may be traced to *Mandeville's Travels*, which discussed such topics as racial characteristics and geographical locations of the varying degrees of blackness possible in the human race. By 1555, in books like Richard Eden's *Decades*, which included accounts of voyages to the dark continent, there were available first-hand descriptions of 'Moors, Moorens, or Negroes' and evidence that some could be of noble and even royal blood. And in 1601 Africans were to be seen in sufficient numbers in London for Queen Elizabeth to be 'discontented at the great numbers of Negars and blackamoors which are crept into the realm'.[1]

As the knowledge of the dark continent became more widespread, under the influence of Hakluyt's *Principal Navigations* (1589), distinctions drawn between various African peoples were possible. For example, George Abbott, in *A Brief Description of the Whole World* (1599), separated 'blackish Moors' from 'exceedingly black Negroes... than whom no men are blacker'; and Leo Africanus underlined the difference with his 'white or tawny Moors' from the Mediterranean coast and the southern 'Negroes or black Moors'.[2] That Shakespeare was aware of such distinctions as these is obvious from the stage direction to 2.1 of *The Merchant of Venice*, which signals the entrance of the Prince of Morocco as 'a tawny Moor all in white'. Also, like his fellow Londoners, he could compare visually the 'Negars and blackamoors', which so troubled the queen, with the sixteen members of the embassy from Barbary who, led by Abd el-Ouahed ben Messaoud, were in the city between August 1600 and February of the following year. During their stay, their dress, customs and behaviour caused a scandal which must have caught the attention of all Londoners; and there is still extant the official portrait of the ambassador himself, showing a bearded, hawk-faced, cunning Arab complete with turban, flowing robes, and elaborately ornamented scimitar (illustration 3a).[3]

The only other Moor in Shakespeare's works is Aaron, the villain in *Titus Andronicus*, who is clearly conceived as a woolly-haired, thick-lipped 'coal-black Moor' (3.2.78) in the play, and is represented as such in Henry Peacham's drawing of a sixteenth-century production of it.[4] Aaron too is apparently aware of colour differences, for he explicitly remarks on the tawny hue of the child he has fathered on the white empress Tamora, 'half me and half thy dame' (5.1.27).

The evidence for the kind of Moor Othello is in the play is far more difficult to interpret; and this has led to the widely different costumes and make-up that actors have adopted for the role (illustrations 7 and 8).[5] At first sight the references to his colour seem straightforward, with the words of many of the characters being very

[1] See E. Jones, *Othello's Countrymen*, 1965, pp. 1–26.   [2] *Ibid*.
[3] See B. Harris, 'A portrait of a Moor', *S.Sur.* 11 (1958), 89–97.
[4] See *S.Sur.* 1 (1948), 17–22 and Plate I.   [5] See pp. 40–7 below.

3*a* Abd el-Ouahed ben Messaoud ben Mohammed Anoun, Moorish Ambassador to Queen Elizabeth (1600–1)

specific for us today. The Duke assures Brabantio that his 'son-in-law is far more fair than black' (1.3.286); Iago toasts the health of the 'black Othello' (2.3.27); Brabantio finds it incredible that his daughter would cleave to a 'sooty bosom' (1.2.70); Emilia, rising to the defence of her mistress, sees the Moor as a 'blacker devil' (5.2.132); and Othello himself laments, 'haply for I am black' (3.3.265) and sees Desdemona's supposedly besmirched honour as being 'begrimed and black' as his own face (3.3.388–9). But we know that Shakespeare did use the word 'black' to mean 'brunette' (as opposed to 'blonde') or merely 'dark-complexioned' (as opposed to 'fair-skinned, not sun-tanned'), usually in an uncomplimentary sense; though it should be noted that, of some fifty-six occasions on which he uses the word, in only about seven does it have this connotation.

All of the other indications of Othello's race amount to an awareness that his

3*b* Frontispiece to *Othello* in Nicholas Rowe's edition of Shakespeare's works (1709)

features are strikingly at odds with white Venetian standards of good looks. To the jealous rival, Roderigo, he is a 'thick-lips' (1.1.67); he is a 'devil' to Emilia (5.2.132); Iago envisions him as 'an old black ram' (1.1.89), and as someone at whom the typical Venetian gorge heaves with disrelish (2.1.221–2). Desdemona herself feels obliged to account for her rejection of the racial norms of appearance in her choice of a husband by telling the Senate that she 'saw Othello's visage in his mind' (1.3.248); even as one element in her father's disbelief is the conviction that her nature could not err so preposterously as to wed 'what she feared to look on' (1.3.98). Perhaps most surprisingly of all, Iago, believing sincerely that Desdemona must grow to see that her husband is defective in loveliness of favour (2.1.218–20), is actually able to get Othello to accept without demur that it proves her unnatural that she refused 'many proposèd matches/Of her own clime, complexion, and degree' (3.3.231–2), in order to wed someone whose looks made her shake with fear (3.3.209).

For the modern reader all of these indications of colour and race would almost certainly point to a Negro; but for the seventeenth-century Londoner they could apply equally well to an Arab. Iago's derogatory comparison of Othello to a 'Barbary horse' (1.1.111–12) would not be taken by any member of the Blackfriars audience to be other than to an Arabian steed; and his scornful use of the term 'barbarian' (1.3.343) is exactly that used by Elizabeth's courtiers to refer to Abd el-Ouahed and his entourage.[1] Even in the lie he tells Roderigo about Othello's demotion, it is Mauritania (i.e. the land of the Moors) he selects for the imaginary posting (4.2.217). More generally, it was the north African races that were popularly associated with the kinds of reactions that Othello manifests in the play: as Leo Africanus writes of the Moors of Barbary,

No nation in the world is so subject unto jealousy; for they will rather lose their lives, than put up any disgrace in the behalf of their women.[2]

There is, then, no way of saying with absolute certainty how Shakespeare conceived Othello racially. A black/white opposition is clearly built into the play at every level: factually, physically, visually, poetically, psychologically, symbolically, morally and religiously. This is ultimately the only important theatrical fact. And being so, it is probably true that, regardless of how such an effect could have been created on the Jacobean stage, only a Negroid Othello can produce the desired responses in the theatres of the Western world, at present and in the foreseeable future.

The plot and its inconsistencies

Shakespeare's dramatic fashioning of Cinthio's story has long raised problems of interpretation because of the large number of inconsistencies between what is said or implied in some parts of the play and information given on the same subjects at others. In *Othello*, these cannot be put down to a characteristic untidiness about detail to which we attribute such things as the conflicting evidence of Hamlet's age or the apparent confusion about Viola's musical role in *Twelfth Night*. Rather they are an integral part of any understanding of the theme of marital jealousy and the psychological credibility of the characters and their actions.

As long ago as 1850 John Wilson ('Christopher North') pointed out the discrepancies caused by Shakespeare's management of time in the play,[3] and developed his theory of the 'double-time scheme'. The first two acts present us with no difficulties in this regard. Indeed Act 1 dramatises events that require little more time than they would do to act on the stage. The opening scene is almost exact in its equation of stage time and 'real' time. Iago's trip from Brabantio's house to seek Othello at the Sagittary is covered adequately by the exchanges following his exit at line 159; just as the time taken by Brabantio to rouse his kindred and follow Iago is represented on stage by the first 54 lines of 1.2. In a similar way the discussion of the intentions of the Turkish

---

[1] e.g. John Chamberlain and Dudley Carleton in Harris, 'A portrait of a Moor', p. 94.
[2] Bullough, VII, 209.
[3] *Blackwood's Magazine*, November 1849; April and May 1850.

fleet by the senators in the opening lines of 1.3 account for the time taken by Othello and Brabantio to move from the Sagittary to the council chamber. In fact, the only obvious theatrical telescoping Shakespeare employs is in making Othello's speech describing his wooing equal the time taken by Iago to fetch Desdemona from the inn. However, even here the leisurely narrative movement of the lines, and their convincing poetic evocation of years passed and their geographical spread endow them with a theatrical length far in excess of the two minutes they take to deliver.

The length of the interval between Acts 1 and 2 is whatever it took to sail from Venice to Cyprus, and the opening alarms and arrivals leading up to the entrance of Othello at 2.1.173 credibly convey the division of the ships by the storm and their staggered making of landfall. The guard is mounted and Cassio is made drunk and cashiered during the same night. The next morning he petitions Desdemona, Iago begins his temptation of Othello, and the deaths of the supposedly guilty lovers are plotted.

It is possible to imagine a break in the action between Acts 3 and 4, but we receive a powerful theatrical impression that 4.1 is practically a continuation of 3.3. From the beginning of Act 4 to the end of the play the action is continuous. Lodovico arrives from Venice and is invited to dinner the same evening; and it is immediately after this, between midnight and one o'clock, that Roderigo waylays Cassio and meets his own death at Iago's hands. The events leading to the catastrophe in the bedroom follow without a break.

All of the specific references to the passage of time in the text are reinforced by the strong sense of fast movement as events crowd on each other. We recognise subconsciously that Othello's irrational descent into jealous obsession must be one continuous sweep, even as Iago himself is aware that one moment's pause for thought might lead the Moor to 'unfold' him to Cassio (5.1.20–1) and that the epileptic fit is but a fortunate occurrence out of his control which prevents the confrontation that could wreck his plans.

At odds with this impression of speed are a large number of allusions which imply that the events we witness on stage are happening over a much longer spread of time. For example, Emilia assures us that Iago has implored her to steal Desdemona's handkerchief 'a hundred times' (3.3.294–5); Othello's torment seems to be based upon the thought of Desdemona's many 'stolen hours of lust' (3.3.339) and his own many nights of ignorance (3.3.340–2). Iago's account of his night spent with Cassio, although fictitious, needs time to have happened in order to be credible (3.3.414). Emilia and Desdemona both speak as though the marriage took place some time ago: ''Tis not a year or two shows us a man.... Nay, we must think men are not gods, / Nor of them look for such observancy / As fits the bridal' (3.4.97–144). The way Othello questions Emilia about her mistress's doings (4.2.1–10), his conviction that his wife has committed 'the act of shame / A thousand times' (5.2.210–11), and his report of seeing Desdemona at her bedtime prayers (4.2.22) all suggest a longer experience of married life than that allowed by the play. Bianca's reproaches to Cassio for his long absence are more specific: 'What! Keep a week away? Seven days and nights?' (3.4.167); and the treatment of their relationship generally suggests that it was of long standing. Finally, the disappearance of the Turkish threat to Cyprus, the informing of the Venetian Senate, the decision to replace Othello with Cassio, and Lodovico's diplomatic mission all require more time than the play supplies.

John Wilson's explanation of this temporal confusion was that Shakespeare was working with two time-schemes: 'short time' which depicts the actions taking place on stage as an unbroken sequence of events; and simultaneously the provision of sufficient indications to set them in a larger context which reminds the audience of 'longer time'. This double-time scheme was proof to Wilson and to many subsequent scholars of Shakespeare's dramaturgical mastery in adapting Cinthio's more leisurely narrative for the stage. As such it was to be placed alongside the brilliant transformation of the lengthy trials, imprisonments and drawn-out deaths of the source into the tragic concentration of the two final scenes of the play.

It is, however, not possible to consider the inconsistencies of time on their own; they are clearly connected with many contradictions in other aspects of the play. The character of Cassio is something of a puzzle. At 1.1.21 he is said to be a man 'almost damned in a fair wife', while in Acts 3–5 he is depicted as a sexually active bachelor. At 1.2.51–2 he appears to be completely ignorant of Othello's interest in Desdemona, whereas later we are informed that he went wooing with his captain (3.3.70–1) and was very often a go-between for them (3.3.95–9). And his elevation to the governorship of Cyprus from his status as disgraced and cashiered officer strikes one as odd sometimes even in performance. There is a similar uncertainty about Roderigo. In 1.1 he is quite clearly a well-known, if unwelcome, suitor for Desdemona's hand and is therefore presumably one of the 'wealthy curlèd darlings' of Venice whom she rejected for Othello. Yet later he threatens Iago that he will make himself known to her (4.2.193–5) in order to claim back the jewels he seems to have been giving Iago for her over a long period of time.

Ned B. Allen[1] has drawn together all of the inconsistencies in the play and argued that they are the result of Shakespeare's having written the play in two parts: first Acts 3–5, where he followed Cinthio closely and took over the long time-span of the tale; and later Acts 1–2, in the composition of which he recalled the details of the source far less accurately, intending to revise the later acts so that they would coincide with the earlier ones but not managing to do so. While Allen's marshalling of his evidence is exemplary, he does play down some of the connections between the play's 'two parts', and there is no real pointer that the acts were written in the order he suggests. We know that Shakespeare did revise the play;[2] and it is hard to believe that he would have allowed the inconsistencies to stand if he had thought that they would seriously affect its theatrical impact.

We cannot remind ourselves too frequently that the play does work in the theatre – indeed, that it is notorious for its power to make audiences lose control of themselves. This being so, we should perhaps give less weight to the study-produced 'problems' of the play. The kind of minutely accurate dovetailing of theatrical plots we have been trained to expect since the eighteenth century sometimes makes the

[1] 'The two parts of *Othello*', *S.Sur.* 21 (1968), 13–29.
[2] See Textual Analysis, pp. 201–5 below.

modern mind dissatisfied with some aspects of Renaissance drama: the widely allusive exploration of a dramatic idea, the frequent loose ends, and fierce concentration on the truth of the immediate moment. Like his contemporaries, Shakespeare often worked using large impressionistic effects and his delving into the depths of the human spirit always recognises the futility of any effort to pluck out its mystery completely.

When he addressed himself to the topic of sexual jealousy, he knew he was entering a realm where reason has no place, where concepts like evidence, ocular proof, observable fact, and demonstrable truth are merely pathetic echoes from a hoped-for world of Baconian clarity. The plot of *Othello*, with all its inconsistencies, its lack of perfect orderliness, its blurring of chronological time, and its frightening picture of a mind defining existence in terms of its twisted ideals, is the perfect vehicle for conveying the experience of obsessive jealousy. Any attempt to impose intellectual neatness on the play's distillation of raw passion in action leads to a denial of the profundity of its truth – and to an imitation of Iago, the blinkered rationalist and failed playmaker.

The play and its critics

During the seventeenth century *Othello* was one of the most frequently performed of Shakespeare's plays, and, if we are to judge from the number of allusions to it, one of the most highly esteemed.[1] Its power clearly fascinated other dramatists, for John Webster, Francis Beaumont, John Ford, Philip Massinger and John Fletcher all imitated its effects in their own work. From the Restoration to the present day it has had an unbroken stage history, never suffering from the cycles of popularity and neglect that have been the fate of other plays in the Shakespeare canon. The two main roles have always offered actors of very different kinds irresistible challenges to their art, and the play has exercised on theatre audiences a uniquely powerful impact obviously based on a deeply-felt involvement with the characters and their relationships. From the tears shed by the Oxford audience at Burbage's performance to the pretty lady who sat next to Pepys and cried out to see Desdemona smothered, from the fainting ladies of Betterton's productions to the Victorian playgoer who loudly urged Macready to 'choke the devil!', the play's theatrical grip has never been less than remarkable.

The setting undoubtedly played its part in the original success. For Shakespeare's contemporaries Italy had long possessed a double image. It was the land of romance, pleasure and refinement; the country of Ariosto, Petrarch and Castiglione; the Renaissance model for less civilised northern lands. It was also the sump of sophisticated vice, the birthplace of the atheistic politician Machiavelli, a country made up of the courts of vicious princelings where poisoning, whoredom and sodomy abounded. Venice of all Italian cities was almost a type-name for the commercial republic, raised to grandeur on dynamic, international and unscrupulous capitalism. It was the free state of Europe, a racial and religious melting-pot which had

[1] See G. E. Bentley, *Shakespeare and Jonson*, 1945, p. 113–14.

successfully challenged the great European monarchies, and which gazed in two directions: towards civilised Christianity and towards the remote eastern world of pagan infidels, the Turks, and the mighty power of Islam. As William Shute,[1] the English translator of the first history of Venice put it,

Italy is the face of Europe; Venice the eye of Italy. It is not only the fairest but the strongest and activest part of that beautiful and powerful nation.

But as such it was also the exemplar of all those exotic vices against which men as unlike as Thomas Nashe and Roger Ascham warned the youth of England.

Around 1599 there had developed a craze for drama with an Italian setting; and for Jacobean theatregoers Italy had become almost the accepted site of the more sensational tragedies of the period. John Marston in his *Antonio and Mellida* (*c.* 1599) was perhaps the first to see its possibilities; but they were soon explored in plays such as Webster's *The White Devil* and *The Duchess of Malfi*, Tourneur's *The Revenger's Tragedy* and Ford's *'Tis Pity She's a Whore*. And, of course, Shakespeare himself five years before writing *Othello* had availed himself of a Venetian locale for *The Merchant of Venice*, the comedy of his other great outsider, Shylock the Jew.

Shakespeare could therefore rely upon the ready acceptance by his audience of Venice as an appropriate place for his story of an exotic Moorish general, a Turkish invasion threat, a poisonous Machiavellian villain, an irate whore, powerful magnificoes, a carpet knight and a courtly lieutenant, with its hints of witchcraft and magic, and its violence, cruelty and sexual passion. The fact that the hero was a Moor would have had some additional associations for the Blackfriars playgoers. They would have had an automatic insular distrust of the alien, would have made the connection, natural to an Englishman of the time, between him and barbarism, and would have linked him vaguely with magic, lewdness and proneness to jealousy. If Burbage did play the role as Negroid, then he may well have been viewed initially as 'of all that bears man's shape, likest a devil', a creature 'fearful in sight and bearing'. Yet, even though Shakespeare availed himself of such racial, historical and geographical associations, he in no way simply adopted them. In fact, it is the ways in which he manipulated them for his own tragic purposes that in part give the play its extraordinary grip on audiences.

It is noticeable that every effort is made to circumscribe the effects and implications of the characters' actions. For example, while Venice and its political importance provide the credible seed-bed of the tragedy, the actual working-out of the situation takes place in Cyprus. This shift from the great influential commercial city to a beleaguered Mediterranean island is motivated on the narrative level by the continuing Christian crusade against the Turks; but this matter is hurried from the audience's attention in a couple of scenes. Its dramatic value lies largely in enabling Shakespeare to have the ideal conditions for his domestic drama. The new wife is thereby isolated from the family and friends she has alienated by her choice of a husband, who himself is busy with a command that makes him responsible for the welfare of others. The villainous ancient is moving in the world of military campaign

[1] Quoted in J. R. Brown, *Shakespeare in Performance*, 1973, p. 292.

4   A possible staging of Act 1, Scene 3, as at the Blackfriars Theatre, by C. Walter Hodges. *Brabantio*:
Here is the man: this Moor. See p. 191 below

that is most familiar and congenial to him. These are the conditions that give
believability to such things as Iago's management of Cassio's disgrace among soldiers
celebrating a recent escape from battle but remaining edgy about its still-felt threat;
and to a middle-aged general's reactions to the familiar circumstances of his profession
complicated by the presence of a woman he views as its crowning glory.

This geographical narrowing of focus is reinforced by the absence of the allusive
widening of scope normally present in Shakespearean tragedy. There is no metaphorical
creation of a surrounding universe. There is no choral commentary to give a context
to the lovers' fate such as we find in *Romeo and Juliet*, no vast world history that affects
and is affected by the doings of an Egyptian queen and one of the triple pillars of
Rome as in *Antony and Cleopatra*. We find no rich pattern of reference to an other-world
like that provided by the witches in *Macbeth*, or the ghosts in *Hamlet*, *Julius Caesar*
and *Richard III*, or by the easy conjuring of elemental gods in *King Lear*. And despite
the Turkish invasion and the Venetian origin of the action, there is established no
vital connection between private decision and public event such as that made by

Fortinbras's presence in *Hamlet* or the Volscian–Roman conflict in *Coriolanus*. As A. C. Bradley puts it: '*Othello* has not...the power of dilating the imagination by vague suggestions of huge universal powers working in the world of individual fate and passion.'[1]

The whole movement of the action is that of a narrowing gyre. After 2.2 the people of Cyprus are forgotten; and by Act 4 the doings of the great world have become so distant from Othello's concerns that he hardly reads the dispatch from the Senate, for there can be no real competition between the orders of his Venetian masters and his obsessive desire to hear Desdemona's conversation. In fact, the last three acts make us concentrate on a purely personal world created by Iago and Othello until we are locked physically and symbolically into the claustrophobic bedroom–tomb of the doomed pair.

The hero's mental path contributes to this sense of contraction. The breadth of his character and the scope of his imagination shrink to a single obsession which usurps the government of his whole being. Moreover, this state is arrived at not by voluntary action but by a robot-like response to another's suggestions. Alone among the tragic heroes, Othello is a patient rather than an agent, worked on by forces outside himself, as total a victim of deception as any character in the Shakespearean canon.

It is the ending of the play that separates it most strikingly from the other tragedies. In the first place, there is no emphatic re-establishment of public order such as Malcolm's prognostication of a healthier Scotland after Macbeth's death, or the powerful entrance of Fortinbras as Hamlet's heir, or even the gesture of picking up the pieces by Albany and Edgar after Lear's purgatory. The tragic loading of Othello's bed does not affect anyone, Venetian or Cypriot. All we hear is Gratiano's arrangements for Desdemona's estate, with Cassio's lip-service remark, 'For he was great of heart', standing for the final panegyric that other tragic heroes receive. The real emphasis is on the punishment of the villain; there is no effort to understand the nature of the catastrophe, no attempt to ritualise the hero's end. The impulse of the finale is the very human one of personal dissociation from the inexplicable pain of other people's lives – let the curtains be drawn round the bed, for the object poisons sight.

Such features of the work as these have led many critics to find the nature of its tragic vision indefinable, so that there is no consensus of opinion whatever. At one end of the scale we find Granville-Barker's[2] claim that it is 'a tragedy without meaning', and at the other G. R. Elliott's[3] eulogy: '*Othello* is...surely the world's supreme *secular* poem of "human love divine".' Between these two extremes lie innumerable variants of them; but even the most adulatory are haunted by the idea that in some way or another we are dealing with a masterpiece *manqué*, whose very perfection of form and theatrical effectiveness make it a lesser artistic experience than its great competitors.

The critical dissatisfaction with the play as a whole may be represented by the two

[1] *Shakespearean Tragedy*, 1904 (1941 edn), p. 185.
[2] *Prefaces to Shakespeare*, fourth ser., 1946 (1978 edn), p. 114.
[3] *Flaming Minister*, 1953, p. xxxiv.

main views of the hero himself, which interestingly reflect the two main stage Othellos to one or other of which actors seem naturally drawn. The first of these – the traditional – is the heroically noble soldier–lover calling for an admiration and sympathy that survive the hideous descent into cruelty and violence. Dr Johnson summed up well the qualities that so many writers have seen in this Moor and elaborated with great subtlety: 'magnanimous, artless, and credulous, boundless in his confidence, ardent in his affection, inflexible in his resolution, and obdurate in his revenge'.[1] Perhaps the most unreservedly committed exponent of this view is J. Dover Wilson.[2] He believes, as Coleridge put it, that natural inclination to jealousy is not the main point of Othello's character; it is

rather an agony that the creature, whom he had believed angelic, with whom he had garnered up his heart and whom he could not help still loving, should be proved impure and worthless. It was the struggle *not* to love her. It was a moral indignation and regret that virtue should so fall.[3]

This is what makes him 'one of the great lovers in the literature of the world, the greatest lover in Shakespeare'.[4]

The quality of love that has stirred critics to such encomia is seen to be one of a rare sublimity. In it there is a perfect balance of the spiritual and the physical. Desdemona's appreciation of her husband's mind is coupled with her desire to experience those rites for which she married him (although some of the more old-maidish of these critics do find these desires, apparently permissible in the fourteen-year-old Juliet, difficult to accept in a young Venetian noblewoman). Othello's palpable physical delight is similarly blended with his enjoyment of his wife's 'conversation' and his recognition that the value of his whole life and even the universe itself finds its incarnation in her. The very sight of her after the small death of their parting can produce a perfect ecstasy in him:

> It gives me wonder great as my content
> To see you here before me. O, my soul's joy...
>   If it were now to die,
> 'Twere now to be most happy; for I fear
> My soul hath her content so absolute
> That not another comfort like to this
> Succeeds in unknown fate.   (2.1.175–85)

And this in turn confirms his faith in a divine universal harmony comparable with that of the world's creation:

>   Perdition catch my soul
> But I do love thee; and when I love thee not,
> Chaos is come again.   (3.3.90–2)

The rarity of such affection as this (and its possible danger) has been rightly described by Helen Gardner,[5] another of the Moor's defenders, as an 'attempt to found

---

[1] *Samuel Johnson on Shakespeare*, ed. W. K. Wimsatt, 1960, p. 114.   [2] In NS, pp. xxi–lvi.
[3] *Coleridge's Shakespearean Criticism*, ed. T. M. Raysor, 2 vols, 1930, II, 350.   [4] NS, p. xxii.
[5] '*Othello*: a retrospect, 1960–67', *S.Sur.* 21 (1968), 10.

the social bond of marriage on passionate love...a great adventure of the human spirit...that brings with it a possibility of agony that those who seek for no such unity in their experience do not risk'.

Total erotic commitment is inextricably linked with that other centre of Othello's being out of which it grew and which it ultimately replaced: his pride in the exercise of his profession of arms. Educated opinion about war has changed during the present century, as a result of two World Wars, the fighting in Vietnam and the use by terrorists of a perverted military code. These things have made it difficult to see the soldier as the traditional symbol of uncomplicated masculine virtue, and critical response to this aspect of Othello's character has been greatly affected in consequence.

Othello is pre-eminently a soldier in the classic mould. He is, as John Bayley has demonstrated,[1] a man of achievement, aware of his supremacy in his profession. This accounts for the immense 'positional assurance'[2] he displays in the moments of crisis he has to face. It lies behind his crushing scorn of civilian streetbrawlers:

> Keep up your bright swords, for the dew will rust them...
> Were it my cue to fight, I should have known it
> Without a prompter. (1.2.59–84)

And it is responsible for his angry assertion of power when the order of Cyprus is threatened:

> Zounds, if I stir,
> Or do but lift this arm, the best of you
> Shall sink in my rebuke. (2.3.188–90)

Whether he is facing Desdemona's irate father and her armed relatives, or answering the accusation of witchcraft before the full Senate, or dealing with a disciplinary problem on the watch, he demonstrates a capacity for swift decision, a monumental authority and a calm self-confidence that are characteristic of his kind. Unless we give the fullest emphasis to the ideal that lies behind these qualities and accept as valid Othello's view of himself as military man, the great farewell speech to his profession, with its spectacular sense of the glory and grandeur of war, becomes merely a mindless exercise in the glamorising of a peculiarly beastly job.

Growing out of the hero's idea of his self is the play's stress on 'reputation', which is the reflection of this self in others' eyes. His speeches are littered with references to the way 'estimation', 'report' and 'opinion' amount to a proof of worth, which in turn is given a wider context by the implications of these same concepts as they are discussed in their different ways by Cassio, Iago, Emilia and Desdemona. This urge in Othello for verbal definition is one part of the style of speech that Shakespeare fashioned for him, one that has no parallel in the whole canon. Wilson Knight,[3] its best analyst, calls it the '*Othello* music' – a 'highly-coloured...stately' idiom, 'rich in sound and phrase'. It is characterised by 'visual or tactile suggestion...the slightly overdecorative phrase...the presence of simple forward-flowing clarity of dignified

---

[1] *The Characters of Love*, 1960.   [2] R. B. Heilman, *Magic in the Web*, 1956, p. 138.
[3] 'The *Othello* music', in *The Wheel of Fire*, 1930.

statement'. It has 'a unique solidity and precision of picturesque phrase or image' and 'a peculiar chastity and serenity of thought'. The power of such poetry is what defines Othello as both soldier and lover. For despite his apologies to the Senate that he is 'rude' in his speech, he is in fact very self-conscious about his rhetorical skill. He knows it is the vehicle for his majestic authority as well as the source of his power to win Desdemona, which he redisplays in the plain unvarnished tale of the whole course of his love.

Any opinion of Othello's idiom and of his whole bearing must also take into account the normal Renaissance expectations of such a man. Because he is 'a prince by his birth and only one below a prince by his office' he is obliged not to forget his place and should never act like an ordinary man. Except under Iago's influence, Othello never does; and John Holloway[1] has produced evidence to suggest that in attitude, manner and speech he may be considered to be acting strictly in accordance with the most famous sixteenth-century conduct manuals on how a prince should behave.

For the defenders of the 'Noble Moor', the terrible fall of the play's middle scenes is testimony to Iago's power of manipulating and perverting Othello's positive strengths. All his soldierly qualities are rechannelled so as to be used destructively in an erotic sphere rather than appropriately in a military one. Power of immediate decision becomes rash and thoughtless response; clarity of objective turns into ruthless pursuit of an obsession; awareness of a deserved reputation is transformed into a monomaniacal concentration on himself as an object of universal scorn; and his electric blend of thought and action is placed at the service of a heartless revenge. By such means does a sublime and idealising love become its own disease, jealousy. Once this hell is passed through, the traditionalists' Othello is seen to rise in the final scene above his former degradation. The tears he sheds at his wife's death-bed are tears of joy at the new realisation that 'the devil has been proved false and she true, that her soul is in bliss, that she had loved him after all'.[2]

However, in the accounts of even the most ardent of the 'Noble Moor's' advocates, there runs a thread of reservation. For some the character is the product of a confined imagination; for others he lacks the visionary dimension of the other tragic heroes, and for many there is a lack of inwardness in his creation, as though Shakespeare's shaping mind were not wholly engaged. It is just this kind of reservation that is the clue to the whole character and the play itself for those critics who hold the second view of Othello. These may be represented by F. R. Leavis,[3] whose essay on the play has had far too much influence owing to his great authority as a critic of poetry and the novel, and despite the fact that his remarkable gifts are clearly of the type that makes him about as naturally incapable of appreciating drama as it is possible to be. Leavis's Othello 'has from the beginning responded to Iago's "communications" in the way Iago desired and with a promptness that couldn't be improved upon', and he does so because his love is 'composed very largely of ignorance of self as well as ignorance of [Desdemona]...it [is] much more a matter of self-centred and self-

[1] *The Story of the Night*, 1961, pp. 37–56.   [2] NS, p. lvi.
[3] 'Diabolic intellect and the noble hero', in *The Common Pursuit*, 1952.

regarding satisfactions – pride, sensual possessiveness, appetite, love of loving'. With varying degrees of stridency others have developed this picture of an easily-duped, egregiously egocentric Moor. His majestic idiom itself is viewed as incontrovertible evidence of his proclivity for self-dramatisation, his romantic capacity for self-delusion, his inability to cope with life, his flair for the picturesque and the histrionic. His soldierly authority is to such writers a façade masking a psychological need to rely upon position because he is secretly unsure of himself and hypersensitive to all challenge. And his deep erotic commitment is really an indication of his inexperience in giving, the hallmark of a middle-aged man disqualified for a demanding personal relationship by a life in the camps.[1]

It is the ending of the play that provokes the greatest disagreement in accounts of the two Othellos. For the traditionalists his last great speech (5.2.334–52) re-elevates the hero to his former grandeur and nobility because he realises the truth and can justify his deliberate act of self-punishment. For those who consider the Moor merely credulous and foolish, T. S. Eliot may speak in his notorious condemnation of the death speech:

What Othello seems to me to be doing in making this speech is *cheering himself up*. He is endeavouring to escape reality, he has ceased to think about Desdemona, and is thinking about himself...dramatising himself against his environment. He takes in the spectator, but the human motive is primarily to take in himself.[2]

It is obvious that the two main views of Othello are based as much on the ideals of the critics themselves as on their reading of the play. Johnson's picture of the Moor is clearly that of the sedentary intellectual who elsewhere said, 'Every man thinks meanly of himself for not having been a soldier, or not having been at sea.'[3] Similarly, the version of Leavis and Eliot is that of all people for whom introspection, self-awareness, deliberate thought, balanced judgement and the contented inhabitation of a dilemma are more congenial than a life of action and passionate involvement. As the play in the theatre draws the audience emotionally into its world, so the play in the study challenges the reader's own intellectual convictions and assumptions.

The character of Iago has occasioned far less critical disagreement than that of Othello. Because there is no possibility of any difference in the moral judgement to be passed on his nature and his behaviour, the innumerable studies of him tend to elaborate aspects of the negation he embodies – materialism, perversion, hatred, bestialism, destruction, doubt, satanic glee and death. His two faces have fascinated literary critics every bit as much as the problems of conveying them credibly on stage have taxed the actor's art. Bradley was at his very best on the subject, and many of his ideas have been elaborated by his successors, notably W. H. Auden,[4] in his picture of the satanic practical joker *par excellence*, and William Empson,[5] who saw him as a critique of an unconscious pun on the word *honest*.

[1] e.g. A. Nicoll, *Studies in Shakespeare*, 1931; L. Kirschbaum, 'The modern Othello', *ELH* 2 (1944), 283–96; D. A. Traversi, *Approach to Shakespeare*, 1938; R. B. Heilman, *Magic in the Web*, 1956.
[2] 'Shakespeare and the stoicism of Seneca', in *Selected Essays*, 1932 (1949 edn), pp. 130–1.
[3] J. Boswell, *Life of Johnson*, ed. G. B. Hill and L. F. Powell, 1924, III, 265–6.
[4] 'The joker in the pack', in *The Dyer's Hand*, 1962.
[5] '*Honest* in Othello', in *The Structure of Complex Words*, 1951.

The total credibility of his villainy has rightly been seen to come from the complete imaginative involvement of the dramatist, the inwardness that seems to have gone into his creation; and from the perfectly judged fashioning of an idiom and imagery and vocabulary that convincingly embody his brutish vision of the world and that infect Othello's own quite different speech during the middle scenes of the play.[1] This achievement has been attributed to Shakespeare's unconscious recognition of a similarity between his own playwright's art and Iago's thought processes as the 'amateur of tragedy', as Hazlitt called him. In Bradley's words, there is a

curious analogy between the early stages of dramatic composition and those soliloquies in which Iago broods over his plot, drawing at first only an outline, puzzled how to fix more than the main idea, and gradually seeing it develop and clarify as he works upon it or lets it work.[2]

However, this *aperçu* can be (and has been) taken too far if it is not remembered that there is a wide divergence between Shakespeare's and Iago's achievements: the play is a success owing to total artistic control by the dramatist, whereas Iago's plot is a failure by a miscalculating improviser.

The two main areas of dispute about the character concern his motivation and the real nature of his psychological make-up and what it represents symbolically. Interpreters have puzzled over Coleridge's phrase describing the apparently passionate origin of Iago's motives and the detached intellectual coolness with which he formulates them in his speeches: 'the motive-hunting of a motiveless malignity'.[3] In disagreeing, some have argued that, because we learn of his jealousy, professional disappointment and personal hatred of Cassio from his soliloquies, we must accept them 'not of course as true, but as the expression of his actual feelings'.[4] Others, also relying on theatrical convention, have explained away the nature of his evil and his justifications of it by drawing attention to his descent from earlier stage types. It has been strongly argued, for example, that his theatrical ancestor is the old Vice of the Morality plays, who as the agent of Satan was obliged to declare himself malign even while he uttered accurate assessments of the human virtues it was his mission to pervert and destroy.[5] But it has also been pointed out that he has as many features of the stage representations of the Devil himself as of his dramatic surrogates.[6]

The attempts to describe the actual configuration of Iago's psyche have been as various as the interests and private bugbears of the critics writing them. As the type of amoral artist he is found to be fashioning a world in his own image; as the classic stage Machiavel he personifies rationality, self-interest, hypocrisy, cunning, expediency and efficient 'policie'. Latent homosexuality and deep-rooted misogyny have been cited as the real driving forces of his nature; and he has not escaped identification with other twentieth-century bogeymen: the amoral experimental scientist and the omnipresent death-wisher.

[1] See S. L. Bethell, 'The diabolic images in *Othello*', *S.Sur.* 5 (1952), 62–80; and M. M. Morozov, 'The individualization of Shakespeare's characters through imagery', *S.Sur.* 2 (1949), 83–106.
[2] Bradley, *Shakespearean Tragedy*, p. 231.
[3] *Coleridge's Shakespearean Criticism*, I, 49.   [4] Muir, p. 16.
[5] B. Spivack, *Shakespeare and the Allegory of Evil*, 1958.
[6] L. Scragg, 'Iago – vice or devil?', *S.Sur.* 21 (1968), 53–65.

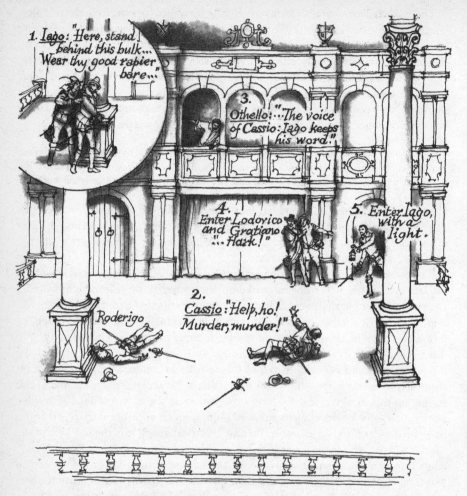

1. Iago: "Here, stand behind this bulk... Wear thy good rapier bare..."

3. Othello:..."The voice of Cassio: Iago keeps his word."

4. Enter Lodovico and Gratiano ..."Hark!"

5. Enter Iago, with a light.

Roderigo

2. Cassio: "Help, ho! Murder, murder!"

5   A possible staging of Act 5, Scene 1, as at the Globe Theatre, by C. Walter Hodges. Successive events, shown here simultaneously, are numbered in sequence. See p. 191 below

Of course, all views of Iago will be influenced by the opinions their holders have of Othello, because the source and direction of his terrifying power over the Moor are, as even Thomas Rymer[1] perceived, a crucial critical issue of the play. The 'Noble Moor' implies a villain of almost supernatural powers; whereas an easily credulous ass makes for merely a pathological liar putting in train an action that moves out of his control during the last two acts. Obviously Iago is parasitic on Othello; and there have not been lacking voices to push this fact to its logical conclusion by claiming that the two men are dramatised aspects of the human condition, or symbolic representatives of the conflicting forces in a single psyche; as J. I. M. Stewart has it,

[1] See N. Alexander, 'Thomas Rymer and *Othello*', *S.Sur.* 21 (1968), 67–77.

Othello *is* the human soul as it strives to be and Iago *is* that which corrodes or subverts it from within...It is as if Iago only wins out because of something fundamentally treacherous in time, some flux and reflux in it which is inimical to life and love.[1]

It is only relatively recently that the character of Desdemona has been accorded the kind of critical attention always received by the two leading male roles. During the eighteenth and nineteenth centuries there were many who shared Thomas Rymer's distaste at the very fact of her marrying a blackamoor. Even Coleridge was taken aback by a noble Venetian lady's choice of 'a veritable negro' for a husband;[2] and other critics, less restrained, were convinced that she was 'little less than a wanton', or 'strumpet-like', or a moral coward lacking in any self-respect.[3] Modern versions of such disapproval have been less extreme and range from B. Spivack's[4] odd conviction that Cassio and Desdemona are really in love with one another to Auden's belief that 'given a few more years of Othello and Emilia's influence...she might well, one feels, have taken a lover'.[5]

However, such anti-Desdemona impulses are the exception rather than the rule. As Marvin Rosenberg[6] has noticed, she has more frequently during the present century been 'in grave danger of being canonized'. As early as 1904 A. C. Bradley[7] had started the dehumanising trend with his opinion that she is 'ardent with the courage and idealism of a saint'; and others have followed his lead, transforming her variously into the world of the spirit that Iago wishes to destroy,[8] or a life-force for order, community, growth and light,[9] or goodness and purity personified,[10] or the supreme value of love.[11]

In a general way all these opinions depend on our seeing Desdemona's life in the play as being dependent on how we view Othello – on our assuming that she is, although in a very different way, as dramatically parasitical on the hero as Iago is. But, as a recent writer has put it, 'the significance of the play is deepened by what it shows her individual inner experience to be – especially what it shows in her love for Othello and her ways of responding to him throughout the action'.[12] When taken as a person in her own right, Desdemona may be seen to have a more complex character than she was credited with in earlier criticism, the principal lineaments of which are already clear. Her sexuality is squarely faced and emphasis is laid upon 'her sensual attraction to Othello, which she never thinks of denying' and which is the part of her nature that makes her powerfully attractive to all the men in the play. The independence of spirit that leads her to defy society's conventions, to be half the wooer, and to beg before the full Senate for permission to accompany her husband to Cyprus is seen to be the same strength that 'enables her to bear the public

[1] *Character and Motive in Shakespeare*, 1949, pp. 107–8.
[2] *Coleridge's Shakespearean Criticism*, I, 47.
[3] See Rosenberg, *Masks of Othello*, pp. 207–8.   [4] Spivack, *Allegory of Evil*, p. 12.
[5] 'The alienated city: reflections on *Othello*', *Encounter* 17 (August 1961), 13.
[6] *Masks of Othello*, p. 208.   [7] Bradley, *Shakespearean Tragedy*, p. 201.
[8] Heilman, *Magic in the Web*.
[9] A. Kernan, '*Othello*: an introduction', in A. Harbage (ed.), *Shakespeare: The Tragedies*, 1964, p. 80.
[10] Spivack, *Allegory of Evil*.   [11] Knight, *The Wheel of Fire*.
[12] J. Adamson, '*Othello' as Tragedy*, 1980, p. 215.

humiliation of a blow, to insist to a raging Othello that she is indeed honest, and to argue her innocence with considerable passion'.[1] Even her ability to deceive her father is interpreted as evidence of the remarkable control over her true feelings which she later exercises on the beach, and on public occasion and in private encounter in the final scenes.

The two chief aspects of this 'new' Desdemona that force a reconsideration of her role in the moral scheme of the play are the particular qualities of her innocence and her love. Both are connected with a sexual unself-consciousness which is 'neither an ignorant nor a repressed state of mind' but is 'the mark of her absolutely positive moral standing when contrasted with the sexually self-conscious, self-torturing and destructive personalities of her persecutors'.[2] Her love is something larger than the helpless affection found in most traditional accounts. Her relationship with her husband is every bit as all-embracing as his love for her. It is 'more crucial to her than her life; and in recognising that she cannot exist without his love, accepting her death is the only way she has of being circumstanced, shutting herself up to Fortune's alms, by a kind of suicide'.[3] For this seventeenth-century feminist a tragic death is preferable to relinquishing responsibility for her own life.

In the mass of criticism devoted to the play one can find illuminating analysis of almost every aspect of it; what one cannot find is any consensus about the nature of its unique world or the ordering of its moral landscape. Perhaps such a consensus should be sought in the one area about which even critics furthest apart agree: namely, its success as a work for the theatre. Older scholars like Levin Schücking and Elmer Stoll[4] have given primacy to dramatic values; but because they were applying a corrective to what they saw as Bradley's novelistic approach to the play, they both overstressed the mere reaching for sensational effect by devices of bold unrealism. More recently, critics have focused on a rather different aspect of the play's theatrical existence – the audience's reaction to it. The spectator, being a part of the dramatic event Shakespeare designed, is himself invited 'to enter the world of *Othello* and its rhythms, not only through imagining himself into the world on stage but through his own responses to that imagined world'.[5]

What must be faced in any future critical account is what the stage history makes quite clear: that completely satisfying performances can be given which have at their heart quite different readings of the central character and his true nature. The savage animalism of Salvini's performance on the nineteenth-century stage was recalled vividly long after he had ceased to play; and Godfrey Tearle's gentleman-poet, created at Stratford-upon-Avon in 1948, has remained definitive for many a still-living playgoer. This must mean that both elements of the character are deeply written into the role. Naturally, the actor has to make a single choice and stick with it – such is

[1] A. J. Cook, 'The design of Desdemona: doubt raised and resolved', *S.St.* 13 (1980), 192.
[2] W. Adamson, 'Unpinned or undone?: Desdemona's critics and the problem of sexual innocence', *S.St.* 13 (1980), 183. [3] Adamson, '*Othello*' as Tragedy, p. 263.
[4] L. Schücking, *Character Problems in Shakespeare's Plays*, 1922; E. E. Stoll, *Othello: An Historical and Comparative Study*, 1915.
[5] R. Hapgood, 'Othello', in S. Wells (ed.), *Shakespeare: Select Bibliographical Guides*, 1973, pp. 165–6; see also Adamson, '*Othello*' as Tragedy, on this topic.

the nature of his medium. But the literary critic is not obliged to ignore the multiple levels of the part that the performer cannot simultaneously represent on stage. In fact, criticism which settles for a single definition is aping the mental processes of Iago instead of attempting to appreciate the supreme artistry of Shakespeare's manipulation of the series of dichotomies on which the play is based and which enable the audience to respond to the experience it offers with a complexity not possible for the characters themselves.

Visually and metaphorically the opposition of black and white is at the heart of the work. And this is explored in all its variants: evil and good, deceit and truth, illusion and reality, ignorance and knowledge, dishonesty and honesty, hate and love, death and life. These polarities, however, are not offered us as the series of clearly defined alternatives that this listing suggests; rather, all the terms are dramatically and poetically redefined. Iago is perceived by everyone as 'honest' which in his case actually means 'dishonest'; Desdemona appears to Othello to be 'unchaste' but is in truth 'honest'. Physically Othello is black like the devil, yet it is beneath the white skin of Iago that the real devil lurks. But then Desdemona's whiter skin than alabaster is not the sepulchre concealing her dishonour but the symbol of her purity and truth. Iago's seductive display of rationalism is not the divine function of the mind, it is a perversion. It is instead Othello's instinctive response to life that is always more 'reasonable'.

Just as such usually accepted absolutes are questioned by a profound mental quibbling so that the distinctions between them become blurred, so the characters are seen as being not made up of well-defined strengths and weaknesses. Their personal qualities are good or bad, strong or weak only in accordance with the way they are used. Othello's immense capacity for total personal commitment to an ideal leads him to make romantic love the cornerstone of his marriage and his existence; but this same characteristic causes him to react violently to the belief that he was wrong in so doing. All his outstanding professional virtues become parodies of themselves when he draws on them to solve problems of a personal relationship. Decisiveness becomes rash action; emotional engagement turns into ruthless obsession; automatic active response to crisis is transformed into a capacity for murder. Similarly with Desdemona: independence of mind emerges as stubborn persistence; joyful erotic confidence leads to dangerous interference in her husband's professional life; innocent conviction precludes any apprehension of evil until it is too late; assumption of responsibility for her own fate turns into something perilously close to masochism; and, most horrifying of all, a love that transcends all ordinary limits results in the passive acceptance of death at its loss.

The whole play is founded on the different ways a single object may be viewed because of divergent human perspectives, interpretations and natural predilections. In ordinary lives it is difficult to maintain black-and-white divisions in any of those beliefs by which we order our existence. Circumstances demand the modification of our ideals, conditions force upon us reduced aspirations and narrowed expectations. We know that each time we make such an adjustment we are parting with the better part of ourselves. Yet we hope even as we make the inevitable compromise that it does not entail the destruction of the value involved. But the tragic hero is not ordinary. He is someone who is willing to live out the truth of his being regardless of the consequences; and for this attempt he pays the full price.

The subject of *Othello* is the possibility of full self-realisation within the context of personal relationships. This is what makes it the most private of the great tragedies and ultimately accounts for an audience's sense of involvement in it of the sort that the stage history illustrates. To complain of its lack of supernatural reference or its limited metaphysical range is to miss the point. Lodovico's command – 'The object poisons sight; / Let it be hid' – is the only possible end, because the arena for the struggle the protagonists have lived through is best symbolised by the curtained bed. The complex relationship between Othello, Iago and Desdemona unleashes the creative and destructive forces inherent in the human condition; but it does so in a way that affects no one but themselves.

The language of the play

One of the more interesting developments in the criticism of Shakespeare in recent years has been the emphasis laid on the purely theatrical aspects of his plays. John Russell Brown[1] and others have drawn our attention to the ways in which drama can make its impact by non-verbal means and to the wealth of action that lies between the lines, in the sub-text. As a result we can see that weight must be given to such symbolic effects as the physically conveyed emblem of a cowardly Falstaff carrying the misplaced honour of Hotspur bodily from the battlefield at Shrewsbury, or the apparently infinite possibilities in delivery, costume, movement and gesture offered the actors by the Folio and quarto texts.[2]

Because of the obvious value of this kind of criticism, we should not forget that it is, however, the text alone that demands some stage business and offers possibilities for others. All theatrical contrivance must either grow directly out of or be legitimately suggested by the received text; if it does not, we find ourselves with a travesty of the play – of which there have been far too many in the twentieth-century theatre. The blueprint Shakespeare passed to his fellows was invariably a highly-wrought verbal construct, and it is from this that our experience of the work – like theirs – must begin. This is especially true of *Othello*, in which Shakespeare seems to have used so many of the resources of the language as vehicles for deliberately designed dramatic effects.

Most immediately striking are the carefully-fashioned and quite distinct idioms he invented for his two main characters. At the most obvious level we notice that Iago uses more prose than Othello. Further, this prose is characterised by the stylistic patterns typical of Euphuism,[3] one example of which is this:

---

[1] For example, in *Shakespeare's Dramatic Style*, 1971, and in his 'theatrical' edition of *Othello* in *Shakespeare in Performance*, 1973.

[2] J. R. Brown, 'The study and practice of Shakespeare production', *S.Sur.* 18 (1965), 58–69.

[3] Wolfgang Clemen has brilliantly isolated this aspect of Iago's dialogue in *The Development of Shakespeare's Imagery*, 1951, ch. 13.

'Tis in ourselves that we are thus or thus. Our bodies are our gardens, to the which our wills are gardeners. So that if we will plant nettles or sow lettuce, set hyssop and weed up thyme, supply it with one gender of herbs or distract it with many, either to have it sterile with idleness or manured with industry, why the power and corrigible authority of this lies in our wills.

(1.3.313-19)

Such a style is intellectually generated; it is ingenious speech – the result of a conscious calculation of effect rather than an instinctive utterance springing unbidden from the subconscious. The parallelism and antithesis, the symmetrically balanced sentences and phrases are an exact measure of the cool self-awareness that typifies all Iago says and does. It is syntactically the style of Janus, the two-faced god by whom he swears (1.2.33).

Exactly the same qualities are to be found in his venture into improvised verse to entertain Desdemona after she has landed in Cyprus:

> She that was ever fair, and never proud,
> Had tongue at will, and yet was never loud;
> Never lacked gold, and yet went never gay;
> Fled from her wish, and yet said 'Now I may'...   (2.1.145-8)

Here, of course, Iago is deliberately acting the role of male cynic expected of him; but the poetic vehicle for his performance is ironically a true reflection of the habit of thought natural to him. It also echoes the sententious couplets of facile comfort the Duke offers to Brabantio at 1.3.200–7, the hollowness of which the distraught father easily sees through and mimics, in order to apply them to the national emergency so seriously viewed by the Venetian Senate (1.3.208–15).

A similar self-consciousness is observable in Iago's blank verse speeches. Whenever he resorts to metaphor there is always a strict control of the image, a closed quality, whereby a static mental picture is evoked rather than any dynamic imaginative propulsion into some wider topic; for example:

> but indeed my invention
> Comes from my pate as birdlime does from frieze...   (2.1.124-5)

> the thought whereof
> Doth like a poisonous mineral gnaw my inwards...   (2.1.277-8)

Perhaps the best illustration of such imagistic narrowness occurs at the moment he reaches the peak of his control over Othello, and is moved in his triumph to attempt an imitation of the Moor's own soaring cosmic allusiveness. But all he manages to produce is this:

> Witness you ever-burning lights above,
> You elements that clip us round about,
> Witness that here Iago doth give up
> The execution of his wit, hands, heart,
> To wronged Othello's service.   (3.3.464-8)

Even when we turn to the material content of Iago's verse, we are struck by the same impression of blinkered vision. His military profession is the 'trade of war'

(1.2.1), which can be demonstrated in the personalised brutality of warfare when a man might yerk his enemy under the ribs (1.2.5) and which he believes can best be organised by a pedestrian system of advancement, 'the old gradation, where each second / Stood heir to the first' (1.1.37–8). The images he draws from the sea and commerce are equally unromantic: with an emphasis on the common sailor's handling of ropes (1.3.328–9) or an insistence on seeing Othello's winning of Desdemona as the action of a freebooter who has 'boarded a land carrack' he hopes to make 'lawful prize' (1.2.50–1).

This capacity in Iago to reduce imaginatively all he contemplates is most vividly seen in those lines which convey his view of humanity. All spiritual values are debased. Love is merely an anatomical function – 'carnal stings...a lust of the blood and a permission of the will' (1.3.322–36); reputation is 'an idle and most false imposition, oft got without merit and lost without deserving' (2.3.247–8); Cassio's modern military skills which earned him quick promotion are reduced to the activities of a grubbing book-keeper (1.1.31); Othello's romantic vision of his profession is really only a love of 'pride and purposes' manifesting itself in 'bombast circumstance, / Horribly stuffed with epithets of war' (1.1.12–14); loyalty and service are 'obsequious bondage' like that of an ass (1.2.45–8); women are things (3.3.304), guinea-hens (1.3.309), and wild-cats (2.1.109).

These last two comparisons are examples of perhaps the most repulsive aspect of Iago's vocabulary: namely his tendency to depict the world as a 'stable or malodorous menagerie'.[1] His speech habitually degrades human activities to the level of the doings of despicable animals: he himself is a spider who will 'ensnare as great a fly as Cassio' (2.1.164) and Roderigo becomes his hunting dog to be loosed on the lieutenant (2.1.284–5); married men are but yoked beasts of burden (4.1.64–5); Othello is a Barbary horse (1.1.111–12) and an old black ram tupping the white ewe Desdemona (1.1.89–90); and the act of love is a making of a 'beast with two backs' (1.1.116).

It is, however, quite another kind of reference that moves Iago's speech from the merely psychopathic to the metaphysical plane. All of his real life is inward. Driven by a Machiavellian materialism and self-interest, he values only those who 'Keep yet their hearts attending on themselves' (1.1.51) and considers 'soul' to be the possession only of men who 'do themselves homage' (1.1.54). As he tells us himself, he is not what he is (1.1.66): not the 'honest' blunt-spoken soldier that most characters in the play attest to his being, but rather a devil creating his own hell on earth and effecting the damnation of others. Darkness is his natural element and he dominates the three night scenes (1.1, 2.3, 5.1). He calls easily on the powers of blackness, on the 'Divinity of hell' (2.3.317); his success in trapping Cassio is recognised, as the warning bell proves his skill, with 'Diabolo, ho!' (2.3.142); 'Hell and night' form the climate that will bring his 'monstrous birth to the world's light' (1.3.385–6). He really believes that he can turn Desdemona's virtue into pitch (2.3.327), make human love into the prey of 'the green-eyed monster' of jealousy (3.3.168), and Cassio's quality of daily beauty into crass irresponsibility.

[1] See Morozov's analysis of this in 'Individualization of Shakespeare's characters', pp. 87–9.

He can, of course, do none of these things; but he has the ability to do something much worse: he can make them seem to be true. This Ensign who does not show the flag of his real nature (1.1.155–6) is the master stage director who can manage his cast of players so that two nocturnal broils are enacted without the participants realising they are not acting spontaneously; he can verbally create a scene of adultery which can set Othello on the rack (4.1.1–34); he can put on 'heavenly shows' which are actually devilish entertainments (2.3.318–20). Even his props are not what they seem to be: the handkerchief, so emotionally loaded by Othello, is simultaneously the precious gift to Desdemona and yet a trifle light as air (3.3.323), which Cassio's possession transforms into what it is not. That which Othello does not even see clearly in Cassio's hand – 'Was that mine?' (4.1.166) – becomes the ocular proof of adultery. 'Honesty' itself is in him a guise of dishonesty; and a particular kind of honesty (i.e. chastity) in Desdemona appears to be begrimed and black as Othello's face (3.3.387–9).

One of the means which Shakespeare employs to indicate the gradual hold Iago develops over Othello's mind is the growing infection of his speech by Iago's vocabulary.[1] The villain's bifurcated vision is impossible for the hero. Whereas the former delights in the dualities of saint and devil, beauty and dishonesty, alabaster skin and the possibility of concealed rottenness, the latter finds such insecurity unbearable. For him 'to be once in doubt / Is once to be resolved' (3.3.181–2) – that is, to be certain of the opposite of the quality so doubted. This transference of manner of thought from man to man is commenced in an exchange in which the words heard are only the tips of the psychological action taking place in the sub-text:

IAGO   My noble lord –
OTHELLO What dost thou say, Iago?
IAGO   Did Michael Cassio,
        When you wooed my lady, know of your love?
OTHELLO He did from first to last. Why dost thou ask?
IAGO But for a satisfaction of my thought;
        No further harm.
OTHELLO   Why of thy thought, Iago?
IAGO I did not think he had been acquainted with her.
OTHELLO O yes, and went between us very oft.
IAGO Indeed?
OTHELLO Indeed? Ay, indeed. Discern'st thou aught in that?
        Is he not honest?
IAGO Honest, my lord?
OTHELLO Honest? Ay, honest.
IAGO My lord, for aught I know.
OTHELLO   What dost thou think?
IAGO Think, my lord?   (3.3.92–106)

Iago's habitual conception of man as animal produces in Othello's mind a hideous vision of a bestial world inhabited by goats, monkeys, toads, crocodiles, blood-sucking flies and poisonous snakes. The distant romantic world filled with anthropophagi and

---

[1] See Bethell, 'The diabolic images in *Othello*'.

headless men that was so integral a part of Othello's courtship is recreated in his marriage bed with horned men and green-eyed monsters for its inhabitants. Iago's Scarfe-like view has become for Othello a nightmare of Hieronymus Bosch.

Ironically the Moor takes over too the Venetian's diabolic vision. The mental hell he creates for himself with Iago's assistance has at its centre the 'devil' Desdemona. The prayer for perdition to catch his soul (3.3.90–1) in his last moment of perfect erotic security is answered by his ensign. Desdemona becomes in his eyes a 'fair devil' (3.3.479) with a demonically sweating palm (3.4.38), who must be 'double damned' (4.2.36) because she is 'false as hell' (4.2.38), and whose fate must be determined by 'black vengeance' called from its 'hollow cell' (3.3.448) for the purpose. Her bedroom is the inferno itself at the door of which stands her maid Emilia as portress (4.2.89–91) and in which she must be killed lest, Satan-like, 'she'll betray more men' (5.2.6). When we thus consider the dimensions of the horrible conceit wrought by Iago's suggestions in Othello's imagination there can be no greater irony in the play than what he says just prior to his total collapse: 'It is not words that shakes me thus' (4.1.40).

Othello's idiomatic norm which Iago so perverts is far different from this animalistic, monstrous, diabolic universe. It is in fact one of the glories of English dramatic poetry. So much has been written about it that it is sufficient here to instance some of the characteristics of the '*Othello* music'.[1]

The first point to be made about it is that this stately, formal, slow-moving poetry, so heavily loaded with vividly realised physicality, is the perfect vehicle for conveying to the audience the cast of mind, character and powerful emotion of this hero who is 'in life', as he tells us, rude in his speech and 'little blessed with the soft phrase of peace' (1.3.81–2). He is no more a 'poet' than any other verse-speaking character in the play; it is merely that this eloquent verbal music best exhibits the nature of the man his experience has made him. As G. Wilson Knight[2] has sensitively observed, there is an inward aloofness, a separation of image from image and word from word, seen clearly in a passage such as this:

> O heavy hour!
> Methinks it should be now a huge eclipse
> Of sun and moon, and that th'affrighted globe
> Should yawn at alteration. (5.2.99–102)

Here, as elsewhere, the machinery of the universe is vividly juxtaposed with human experience. In a similar manner geographical spread and adventurous travel are compared, at length but distantly, with moments of powerful emotion and states of being: in the great aria describing his wooing (1.3.127–69) and in the assertion of his unswerving will (3.3.454–63). Even as he comes to face the truth in his haunting final lines, there is the same non-fusion of images, as the medicinal gum of the Arabian trees is set against the non-curative tears Othello sheds; as another ignorant pagan unknowingly throws away great wealth; and as one kind of state traitor, 'a malignant

---

[1] G. Wilson Knight in *The Wheel of Fire*, 1959 edn, pp. 97–119.   [2] *Wheel of Fire*, pp. 97–8.

and a turbaned Turk', simply parallels the Moor himself, a far worse traducer who struck down the loveliest of all Venetians (5.2.334–52).

In the theatre, the voices of Robeson or Tearle in our own day have projected movingly the most remarkable quality of Othello's speech: its romantic, heroic, picturesque, adventurous, exotic nature. For him life is highly coloured, euphemistically elevated. War is not, as it is for Iago, a trade, but a glorious world of tented fields, plumed troops, neighing steeds, shrill trumps, spirit-stirring drums, and cannons which rather 'th'immortal Jove's dread clamours counterfeit' (3.3.349–58) than kill messily. Every facet of his life that is susceptible to an enhancing inflation is emphasised, even as those which cannot are relegated to being of minimum influence and small memory. His being sold into slavery and his redemption thence are quite overwhelmed poetically by his recollections of cannibals, blemmyae, heaven-touching hills, vast antres and arid deserts (1.3.139–44). Every line Othello utters in his normal manner illustrates how all he has experienced has been related to himself with a breathtaking egocentricity which is clearly signalled by the grammatical focus of his avowal of the sincerity of his love for Desdemona: 'She loved me for the dangers I had passed, / And I loved her that she did pity them' (1.3.166–7).

When Othello, late in life, finds in Desdemona the erotic equivalent of his military profession, he transfers on to her all the imaginative appreciation which had formerly been lavished on his career. She becomes his 'fair warrior' (2.1.174), his 'captain's captain' (2.1.74) and his camp companion. But more significant, and fatal, than this verbal militarising of his wife is his insistence on making her the sole object of his full powers of romantic projection. She is not only his love but Love itself which banished chaos from the universe at the beginning of the world (3.3.90–2). Meeting her after a frightening absence is quite literally for him the equivalent of heaven:

> If it were now to die,
> 'Twere now to be most happy; for I fear
> My soul hath her content so absolute
> That not another comfort like to this
> Succeeds in unknown fate.   (2.1.181–5)

Just how totally unsuitable a character for the burden of such idealisation Desdemona actually is finds expression in her horrified response to this:

> The heavens forbid
> But that our loves and comforts should increase,
> Even as our days do grow.   (2.1.185–7)

However, the poetry in the play is not merely a device for individualisation of character. The large language patterns interweave themselves across character, mental state and particular situation. Deceitful appearance is not linked exclusively with 'honest Iago'. Honest (i.e. chaste and truthful) Desdemona did deceive her father in wooing and marrying Othello, she does attempt to conceal from her husband the loss of the handkerchief, and she even dies with a charitable lie upon her lips about the manner of her death. Emilia's assumption of the façade of moral cynicism (4.3.60–99) is as false as her husband's exterior and conceals a love that makes her

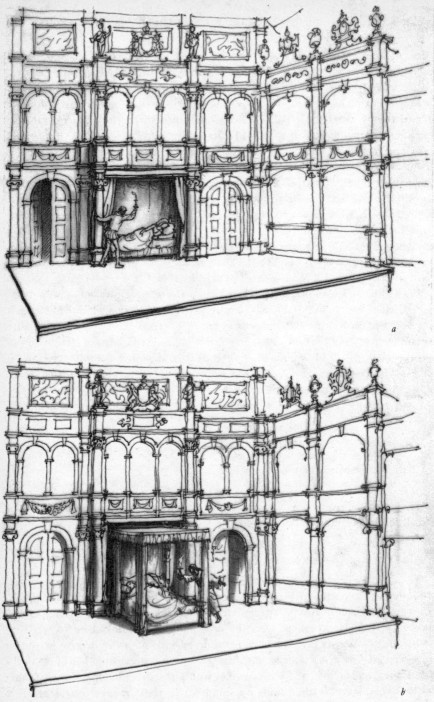

a

b

6 Possible ways of staging Act 5, Scene 2, by C. Walter Hodges. Two methods (adapted from (*a*) Ross and (*b*) Hosley) conjectured for the original staging of Desdemona's bed at the Blackfriars Theatre. See p. 191 below

prepared to die in the defence of truth and goodness. Othello's black countenance is to Desdemona the unattractive casing of a beautiful mind, whereas to Roderigo, Brabantio and Iago it is the proper colouring for the devil Iago ensures he becomes. And Iago's own whiteness, quite different from the alabaster skin of Desdemona, hides a soul as black as any in the literature of the world.

This dichotomy between being and seeming is reflected in the language of blackness and whiteness, dark and light, hell and heaven that touches so many aspects of the play: the fact of miscegenation and the varied responses it provokes; the night hours in which Iago creates his discord and violence; and the hell of doubt and jealousy that is set against the lovers' celestial vision of their world.

Growing out of the geographical position of Venice as Europe's gateway to the exotic eastern lands is the thread of magic and witchcraft that surfaces at various points in the play. For Iago, of course, these things mean diabolic conjuring and devilish spirits to twist and pervert others. For Othello the magic in the web of the handkerchief is a symbol of the binding power of marital love (3.4.51–72), of the extent to which the gentle Desdemona has transformed his whole existence. It was by means of the witchcraft of his words that he was able to win her love, a form of enchantment her father took to be of a malignant nature (1.3.60–4, 99–106).

Naturally, none of the language in the play works in isolation, and many of its effects in their rich interrelationships can only be seen to the full when in production. Lighting, costume, sound-effects, blocking, actors' appearance, gesture and movement are all available to reinforce and develop the implications found in the verbal texture. No reading of the play, for example, can hold in the mind the blackness of Othello at *every* entrance, which a stage production conveys effortlessly with the simple application of make-up. The iterated vocabulary and imagery of trial and legal process become visually and positionally realised when we view the Senate scene (1.3) with the Duke as judge, the senators as jury, Brabantio as accuser, Othello as defendant and Desdemona as expert witness. The reader's silent registering of the exotic ambience of the play cannot have the ocularly induced excitement provided by the lavish 'discoveries' in Zeffirelli's production at the beginnings of 1.3 and 2.1, which were virtually animated Tintorettos. The authority and resonance of 'Keep up your bright swords, for the dew will rust them' (1.2.59) are given an extra dimension when spoken by a white-gowned Paul Robeson with the swords pointed at his breast and the torchlight glistening on his black skin. The sheer alienation of Othello from his society will be held forever in the mind of the audiences who saw Laurence Olivier's cat-like, sensuous, Caribbean walk. The awful vulgarity of Iago's mind (a rarely noticed trait) was made actual when Leo McKern sat gleefully and gloatingly across the chest of the insensible Anthony Quayle; even as Iago's underlying twisted psyche was transmitted silently in the tiny betraying gestures of Jose Ferrer as he taunted the blundering Robeson.

Many similar theatrically conveyed meanings were obviously present in productions now out of living memory: Irving's slow revelation of Iago's diabolic countenance as he conceived his plan; Salvini's display of sexual savagery and hatred; Barry's physical projection of passion destroying reason; Quin's visual isolation of the black and white dichotomy by the spotlighted peeling of a very white glove from a very black hand. All these effects, which struck the actors' contemporaries so forcibly, clearly grew out of the play's verbal patterns and yet elicited the kind of response of which we are incapable in the study.

Of course, no single production can hope to do more than realise some aspects of the drama's totality; even as no critical reading can attempt to do more than offer a simplified version of the original. Both the literary and the theatrical approaches are thus necessary and interrelated; for just as no production can convey the intellectual grasp of the poetic machinery of *Othello* that one can derive from Wilson Knight's essay on the '*Othello* music', so no essay can burn into the mental ear for a lifetime Godfrey Tearle's delivery of 'My wife, my wife! What wife? I have no wife' (5.2.98) with its huge freight of the despairing futility of all human aspiration.

Stage history

Among actors *Othello* has always been one of the most admired of Shakespeare's plays. During the eighteenth century it was generally considered the greatest of the tragedies both for the regularity of its structure and the truth of its characterisation. Admiration was just as high in the nineteenth century, though there was more effort at this time to define the nature of the work as a whole, by taking into account its eloquence, romance and passion, and the strong character oppositions. In the present century, while there has been much theatrical discussion of these same aspects of the play, more emphasis has been placed on the ways in which it differs radically from the other tragedies. However, one reaction that actors over the years seem to have in common is their ready appreciation of the theatrical difficulties and opportunities presented by the title role – one that, as Colley Cibber put it, the 'Master Actor would delight in'.

In the early-seventeenth-century performances by the King's Men, Burbage and Swanston played Othello; and from contemporary testimony the former's interpretation was apparently remembered vividly alongside his Hamlet. There is some evidence that Taylor, who acted Iago, was aware of the humorous ingredient in the part; for Charles Guilden complained

I'm assur'd, from very good hands, that the person that acted Iago was in much esteem of a comedian which made Shakespear put several words and expressions into his part, perhaps not agreeable to his character, to make the audience laugh.[1]

At the company's performance at Oxford in 1610, however, while all the actors were capable of drawing tears from the crowd, it was the boy who impersonated Desdemona who, as one spectator reported, 'moved us especially in her death when, as she lay on her bed, her face itself implored the pity of the audience'.[2]

The play's popularity on the Restoration stage is amply attested by the number of performances. Even in opposition, Thomas Rymer provided supporting evidence:

[1] *Reflections on Rymer's Short View of Tragedy* (1694), in Furness, p. 397.
[2] Tillotson, *TLS*, 20 July 1933, p. 494.

'From all the tragedies on our English stage, *Othello* is said to bear the bell away';
and it is significant that it is this play that came most readily to Aphra Behn's mind
in defending the decency of her own works. Pepys saw the play twice: first, on 11
October 1660 at the Cockpit Theatre with Burt as the Moor and Clun as Iago. During
this performance the final scene made the same impact as it had in Oxford fifty years
earlier; for 'a pretty lady' sitting next to the diarist 'called out, to see Desdemona
smothered'. In a second viewing at the Theatre Royal on 6 February 1669, Pepys
thought that Burt's performance had deteriorated, and that the Iago of Mohun was
inferior to Clun's. Later in the century Burt was superseded by Hart (a celebrated
Cassio) and the strikingly handsome Kynaston assumed Cassio's role.

It was during the Restoration that performances of *Othello* took on a dimension
they had not previously possessed; for it was at this time that an actress first played
Desdemona. If the illustration for Nicholas Rowe's edition really does reflect
contemporary stage practice (see illustration 3*b*), then the highly sexual verbal content
of the play was given a visual equivalence not possible in Shakespeare's day. It is
perhaps a testimony to the play's popularity that this first appearance of an actress
in the leading female role was the subject of a special, rather leering, prologue:

> I saw the lady dressed.
> The woman plays today: mistake me not;
> No man in gown, or page in petticoat;
> A woman to my knowledge, yet I can't
> (If I should die) make affidavit on't.[1]

There is no detailed account of any Restoration production; but one may speculate
that the general impudicity and stress on lascivious behaviour rife in the comedies
of the time must have influenced the portrayal of Othello's and Desdemona's love.

Yet, in keeping with the growth of neo-classical literary theory, the theatrical texts
for *Othello* were undergoing a change at odds with some aspects of probable stage
practice. The version of the play prepared for the Smock Alley Theatre, Dublin,
displays numerous cuts aimed at 'refinement' of the original text in the interests of
Decorum. Othello's lines suffer most, with a view to emphasising his nobility, dignity
and heroic stature. The Smock Alley Moor is not allowed to wish that housewives
make a skillet of his helm or for his nature to be exchanged for that of a goat. It is
beneath his dignity to set Emilia to spy on Desdemona; and the final lines of his
farewell to his profession apparently struck the Rymerish adapter as smacking too
much of extravagant self-pity. Gone too is the obsessive visual sexuality of his lines
at the beginning of 4.1; and he goes to his death without his tears like Arabian gum.
Desdemona's occasional domestic allusions are excised in the interests of ladylike
behaviour and speech; and her Willow Song apparently affronted the Restoration
image of a tragic heroine. Iago's part suffers least, though some pruning was thought
necessary in the more conspicuous examples of his hypocrisy.[2]

This refining process continued during the eighteenth century, typified by the texts

---

[1] Thomas Jordan, *Royal Arbor of Loyal Poesie* (1664), pp. 24–5.
[2] *Shakespearean Prompt-Books of the Seventeenth Century*, ed. G. B. Evans, vol. VI, part 1, 1980.

produced by Francis Gentleman. But although there were versions like those of Ducis in France and Schröder in Germany, in which the ending was altered so that Othello and Desdemona might be saved, in England the play was never the mangled victim that *King Lear* became in the hands of Nahum Tate.

There are only seven years during the whole century in which there is no notice of a production of *Othello* in the London theatres. During the early period Betterton was the outstanding performer of the leading role, with Mrs Bracegirdle and Mrs Bradshaw as his Desdemonas. He probably acted the part as early as 1683, but his succession of great productions stretched from that of 21 May 1703 at Lincoln's Inn Fields to his farewell to the part on 15 September 1709 at the Queen's Theatre. Betterton's great strength lay in the subtlety with which he conveyed the awful agony of the victim of jealousy and lost love, and this is the quality of his playing that Richard Steele seized upon in his obituary of the actor:

the mixture of love that intruded upon his mind upon the innocent answers Desdemona makes, betrayed in his gesture such a variety and vicissitude of passions, as would admonish a man to be afraid of his own heart, and perfectly convince him, that it is to stab it, to admit that worst of daggers, jealousy.[1]

Barton Booth, who was Betterton's Cassio in his final appearance, took over the main role and acted it until 1727. He stressed the hero's moving struggles to keep powerful inner emotions under iron control, and managed the difficult blending of a tenderness that turns to pathos without weakness and a grandeur that becomes lost in fury without brutality. However, it was Quin who was Betterton's real successor. He was monumentally heroic in the neo-classical style, and his speaking gave the great lines every ounce of grandeur. His naturally striking presence was enhanced by his stately, slow-moving gait and the all-white uniform he adopted. While it was generally agreed that his interpretation lacked tenderness, pain and inner fire, he was immensely popular and some of the stage business he invented became famous – notably the slow peeling off of one white glove to reveal the black hand beneath it. He played the role for some twenty years, his final performance being at Covent Garden in 1751. Ryan and Cibber were the most frequent Iagos at this period, both of whom tended to project an impression of Machiavellian 'policie' in action with every line and gesture.

Despite Garrick's dominance of the English stage at this time, his Othello was a failure. His new 'natural' style of acting, which he had pioneered with Macklin, was at the opposite pole from Quin's old-fashioned heroic manner. Like all his acting, his performance was original in its conception, daring in execution, and based on a text in which many of the typical eighteenth-century cuts had been restored, most notably the epileptic fit in Act 4. But his small stature, his 'little wincings and gesticulations of body' and his high emotionalism alienated the age's standards of Decorum. His stark black make-up and high oriental turban provoked Quin's cruel jest that he looked exactly like the little black boy carrying the tea-kettle in Hogarth's *Harlot's Progress*. Through even his friends' comments there runs the idea that his whole conception of the part was too strange, violent and undignified for the age of

[1] *The Tatler*, 4 May 1710.

elegance. His Iago was better received and was, like Macklin's, a masterly portrait in the 'natural' manner, with most of the villainy being conveyed during the soliloquies. He tried the main role for the last time at Covent Garden on 20 June 1746, with Macklin as Iago and Mrs Cibber as one of the best Desdemonas of the period.

Part of the reason for Garrick's abandonment of the play may well have been the accepted supremacy of Spranger Barry in the leading part. After his first performance at Drury Lane in October 1746, Barry was to be *the* Othello in twenty revivals for the next thirty years. Accounts of his playing are universally adulatory, and are matched only by Kean's notices in the next century. He possessed a marvellously mellifluous voice and a striking figure, both of which he used to project what seemed to his contemporaries the perfect fusion of dignity and love which grew under Iago's influence to a tempest of bloody passion, in which

you could observe the muscles stiffening, the veins distending, and the red blood boiling through his dark skin – a mighty flood of passion accumulating for several minutes – and at length, bearing down its barriers and sweeping onward in thunder, love, reason, mercy all before it.[1]

Towards the end of the century another great actor, like Garrick, failed in the main role. John Philip Kemble's first Othello was at Drury Lane on 8 March 1785, with his sister Mrs Siddons as Desdemona, and his last was at Covent Garden in May 1805. With too much 'philosophy in his bearing and reason in his rage'[2] all his great strengths as a heroic actor seemed to count against him in this part. His looks and stature, his bodily mien and his rectilinear style were quite unsuited for the grieved Moor, whom he 'wrapped in a mantle of mysterious solemnity awfully predictive of his fate'.[3] The real surprise of the Kemble production was the Desdemona of Mrs Siddons who, being the greatest Lady Macbeth, was never expected to produce her gracious, sympathetic, strong, dignified and sweetly tender Venetian girl.

During the nineteenth century the text of *Othello* underwent extensive bowdlerisation in the theatre as in the printed versions. There were two main types of stage interpretation of the title role: the restrained, dignified, deeply troubled and sometimes intellectual Moor; and the blazing portrait of torrential sexual passion and wild jealousy. Macready, Fechter and Irving all offered variants of the quiet Othello. Macready's playing oscillated between the old grand manner and the new 'naturalistic' modern style that was becoming popular under French influence. It was with an Othello acted exclusively in this French style that Fechter amazed London audiences. His deliberately assumed conversational tone, his monotonous delivery and his obtrusive theatrical tricks militated against any real grasp of the massive passion that the role requires.

Irving's attempts at the part, particularly the production with Ellen Terry as a brilliant Desdemona and Booth as Iago, were a resounding commercial success, but he himself knew that the role had defeated him. Like Garrick, his appearance was

---

[1] Rosenberg, *Masks of Othello*, pp. 45–6.
[2] J. Boaden, *Memoirs of the Life of John Philip Kemble*, 2 vols., 1825, I, 292.   [3] *Ibid.*

against him. Slight of build, weak of voice and delicately featured, he replaced the grandeur and dignity of the original with domestic detail; and he tried to convey passion and grief by outbursts that struck his fellow-actors as petulant ranting. As Ellen Terry remarked, his reading of the character had no emotional centre, no build-up of passion, no strength.

The best Moor in the 'restrained' tradition during the nineteenth century was probably Edwin Booth. Using the most expurgated of texts, he created a simple-hearted noble black gentleman, burying his palpable torment and occasional violent outbursts under waves of remorse and humane feeling. There was no animal fury or jealous rage even in the final scene, just a musically-voiced sacrificial priest tenderly punishing an errant soul.

None of these stars could begin to rival the two great Othellos of the period: Kean and Salvini. Kean's performance was universally admired and is the first of which we have a detailed contemporary analysis. He adopted a tawny rather than black make-up and managed to combine heart-breaking grief with jealousy amounting to insanity. For William Hazlitt it was 'the finest piece of acting in the world', and many other contemporaries were struck by the fact that it was not like acting at all: not simulation but revelation:[1]

there was all the fitful fever of the blood, the jealous madness of the brain: his heart seemed to bleed with anguish, while his tongue dropped broken, imperfect accents of woe.[2]

The role was notoriously interwoven with Kean's personal life. On 28 January 1825, only eleven days after his appearance as co-respondent in Alderman Cox's sensational divorce case, he appeared in the play and was hooted by the audience as he lamented Desdemona's supposed infidelity. And it was as Othello that he made his last exit on 25 March 1833. Mortally ill, he managed to get through the first two and a half acts up to the 'Farewell' speech, when he collapsed in the arms of his son Charles, who was his Iago, and was carried from the stage for ever.

Another actor's personal life was entangled with the main role in a rather more emotionally immediate fashion. Edwin Forrest, the American tragedian, based his whole conception and playing of the character on the extent to which it mirrored his own emotional state. In 1848, after ten years of marriage, he discovered that his wife was having an *affaire* with one George Jamieson and immediately started divorce proceedings. At the trial Mrs Forrest was found innocent and Forrest himself was convicted of adultery and ordered to pay alimony. He appealed against this judgement in vain for some eighteen years and became an embittered social outcast. Clearly he channelled this experience into his playing of Othello. A man of massive physique, he alternated the extraordinary power of his rages with a tender affectionateness, which became in the last act a self-pitying wavering between desire for revenge and longing for a lost love that apparently characterised his own life.

Kean's only real rival appeared later in the century in the person of the Italian Tommaso Salvini. His Moor was characterised by a frank erotic sensuality in the early

[1] B. Cornwall, *The Life of Edmund Kean*, 1835, pp. 85–6.
[2] W. Hazlitt, *Works*, ed. P. P. Howe, 1930–4, XVIII, 332.

a   Edmund Kean (1814, 1832–3)   *b*   Paul Robeson with Peggy Ashcroft (1930)

c   Frederick Valk (1942)   *d*   Laurence Olivier (1964)

7   Some 'Negro' Othellos

scenes, which was replaced by an overwhelming grief, which was in turn succeeded by despair, agony and a final cataclysm of violence. The savagery he displayed in the murder scene scandalised English audiences of the 1870s:

he pounced upon [Desdemona], lifted her into the air, dashed with her...across the stage and through the curtains, which fell behind him. You heard a crash as he flung her on the bed and growls as if of a wild beast over his prey.[1]

But for Henry James it was 'impossible to imagine anything more living, more tragic, more suggestive of a tortured soul and of a generous, beneficent strength changed to a purpose of destruction. With its tremendous force, it...has not a touch of rant or crudity.'[2] The first naturally black Othello appeared about this time, Ira Aldridge, an American Negro who was in real life married to a white woman. Rather against the general expectation that he would be barbaric and primitive, he was actually solemnly intense and was often condemned as too intellectual, though he did emphasise his colour, as in his famous point of slowly enclosing Desdemona's white hand in his dark one.

The role of Iago received more attention in the Victorian period than it had previously, and much thought was given to his motivation and the ways in which his inner villainy and outer honesty could be made plausible on the stage. Kean had stressed the villain's jocular, hearty, likeable exterior but managed to suggest also

an overactivity of mind that is dangerous to himself and others; that so far from hating his fellow-creatures, he is perfectly regardless of them, except as they may afford him food for the exercise of his spleen.[3]

The failed Othellos – Fechter, Macready and Irving – were also notable Iagos. The first two followed Kean's conception, with Fechter using a great deal of stagy business to show the two faces of a polished Venetian courtier, and Macready combining bluff soldierliness with a vigorous, many-sided deviltry. Irving's performance was considered one of his best for the stark contrast he managed between the outer heartiness and the inner vindictiveness. He never failed to thrill audiences with his celebrated piece of business when he covered his face completely with his hands and then slowly drew them downwards to reveal an expression of satanic glee as his plot takes shape in his brain. Booth was the most widely admired Iago of his time. He somehow convinced the spectators of his intangible glow of evil, while being outwardly gravely sympathetic and respectfully watchful. The force of his wickedness accumulated slowly, almost completely concealed, until it finally burst out in demonic joy as he pointed at the dead bodies on the bed.

At the start of the present century two actors played the leading role with great commercial success. Forbes-Robertson, despite the admiration he commanded, was thought to fall short of the power that Kean and Salvini brought to the part, and he acted in the play only twice in his career. Oscar Ashe's Othello had more animal fury, but the poetry and spiritual agony that Robertson so markedly possessed quite eluded

[1] J. R. Towse, *Sixty Years of the Theatre*, 1916, p. 163.
[2] *The Scenic Art*, 1957, p. 189.   [3] Hazlitt, *Works*, XVIII, 201.

a Spranger Barry (*c.* 1775)   *b* Tommaso Salvini (1875)

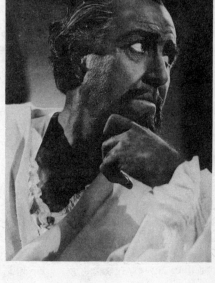

c Johnston Forbes-Robertson (1901)   *d* Godfrey Tearle (1948–9)

8 Some 'Arab' Othellos

him. Most of their successors were lacking in passionate intensity and murderous violence. The words 'Northern' and 'intellectual' were the ones used to describe a number of performances of the 1920s and 1930s which struck spectators as being reductive of the stature of the hero: they were of small ordinary men in distress rather than of giants under torture.

Some of the best-remembered Othellos of the first half of the twentieth century were those who conveyed the majestic, dignified and romantic aspects of the character: they were the deeply-grieved and highly-civilised gentlemen-poets. Abraham Sofaer's Moor at the Old Vic in 1935 is described in terms that would have amazed the fans of Salvini:

At first what he seeks is lucidity and a firm establishment of Othello as a man of tenderness and reason...not wishing to foam at the mouth, he is a little too cold...His performance is masterly, alike in its unsurpassed use of language and in the flowing urgency of its thought.[1]

Wilfred Walter's portrayal at Stratford-upon-Avon and London was in the same mould: dominating nobility and beautiful tenderness in the early scenes and a plunge into degradation that is preceded by a hesitation as he realises with horror what he is doing, and then a return to love at the end.

It was, however, Godfrey Tearle who between 1921 and 1950 perfected this reading of the character. His immensely dignified stage presence, consummate classical technique and emotional power all impressed audiences and critics alike. His Moor was a natural leader whose graceful movements and musical rendering of the great set speeches drew sympathy and admiration. While he passed rapidly from strong masculine tenderness to deadly rage, he

holds what is savage in the Moor severely in check and when he comes to smother Desdemona compels us to the Coleridgean view that jealousy is less the point of Othello's passion than an agony that the creature whom he believed angelic should prove impure and worthless.[2]

The most recent example of the 'Tearle Othello' was John Neville's civilised, intellectual performance which was remarkable for the poignancy of his grief and the haunting way in which he evoked the sweetness of his love with the pain of his recollections. He alternated the main role with Richard Burton, who was able to develop an energy that suggested a barbaric and uncontrolled passion in the Salvini tradition.

Perhaps the two most outstanding modern exponents of the violent Othello were Orson Welles and Frederick Valk. Both of these actors had imposing physiques and dominating stage personalities. Valk's performance was emotionally highly charged and his Moor was the least reluctant to be tempted; he seemed to embrace greedily all Iago's insinuations, so that the rapid fall was harrowing but never touching. It was the melodramatic in Welles's portrayal that struck most critics. His giantised costume, his exaggerated gestures and the insistent sexuality created an initial impression of extraordinary power, as though Welles, 'a great, lumbering, dazed bull',

[1] *The Times*, 22 January 1935.   [2] *The Times*, 20 June 1949.

were enveloped on stage in a 'dreadful fog of menace and horror'.[1] But his quiet sonorousness aroused sympathy rather than pity and one could not help 'wondering why a man who appears to be both shrewd and self-controlled should suddenly start behaving very unreasonably'.[2] Only one modern actor has attempted a synthesis of the dignity and the passion, the tenderness and the violence. Anthony Quayle's portrait possessed an assurance in both parts of the play so that the nobility and savagery were equally plain and never allowed to cancel each other out.

Three remarkable black actors have followed Ira Aldridge's pioneering appearance. Earle Hyman imposed himself on the whole play, becoming 'the storm centre... carrying the whirlwind with him and letting Iago buzz busily at the vulnerable edges';[3] and James Earle Jones was similarly strong and authoritative in the early scenes and reached heights of jealousy amounting to madness later. Paul Robeson was the outstanding black Othello and one of the most vividly remembered of all actors of the role, with some experienced theatregoers thinking that they were seeing the play for the first time. He made full use of his physical attributes and vocal endowment to give a noble plainness to the hero who was 'physically powerful with the gentleness that often accompanies great strength'.[4] Most of his admirers noted the consciousness of race in Robeson's performance, which for some gave it a seriousness of purpose that made all others seem trivial, but for others militated against the tragic sense of the original.

By far the most successful Othello of recent years has been Laurence Olivier's. The basis of his interpretation was the idea that the hero is essentially narcissistic and self-dramatising. With his careful imitation of West Indian gait and gesture, his heavily Negroid make-up and his self-regarding sensuousness and alienation, this actor produced a virtuoso solo performance of astonishing vocal inventiveness that etched a portrait of a primitive man, at odds with the sophisticated society into which he has forced himself, relapsing into barbarism as a result of hideous misjudgement.

There have been a number of distinguished modern Iagos, some building on the Victorian advances made in playing the role. For example, Richard Burton at the Old Vic in 1956 followed Kean's and Booth's lead and so embodied sincerity that 'not by the least wink or snicker does his outward action demonstrate the native act and figure of his heart';[5] and Emrys James at Stratford-upon-Avon in 1971 was a later version: 'an army lad whose high jinks can turn to calculated vice at the drop of a handkerchief'.[6]

More originally, some actors have endowed the Ensign with characteristics derived from modern clinical psychology. Jose Ferrer, Robeson's Iago, played a motiveless villain in a brilliant technical performance that was 'credible only to the extent to which we are led to fall in with his cerebral excitement, his non-moral temperament and magnetism, and his enjoyment of his own self and his own variety'.[7] Also in America, Alfred Drake played the part with a manically obsessive malice, and Mitchell

[1] *New Statesman and Nation*, 27 October 1951.
[2] *The Spectator*, 26 October 1951.
[3] *San Francisco Chronicle*, 7 July 1957.
[4] *Theatre Arts* 27 (December 1943), 701.
[5] *The Observer*, 25 February 1956.
[6] *The Guardian*, 11 September 1972.
[7] *New Republic*, 1 November 1943.

9a   Edmund Kean as Iago (1814)

9b   Jose Ferrer as Iago (1943)

9c   Sarah Siddons as Desdemona (1785)

9d   Ellen Terry as Desdemona (1881)

Ryan was an even more sick creature hinting at the Ancient's twisted mind with small half-completed gestures. Leo McKern, Quayle's Iago, was similarly psychopathic, bustling and enormously self-assured as he went about the mad business that is the Ensign's life. Some actors have attempted to give stage life to the subconscious homosexuality that certain critics have detected as his 'real' motive. Most remarkable in this regard was Olivier's Iago, when he played opposite Richardson in 1935; he was clearly in love with Othello and covered his longing with a joky malignity.

In looking back over the play's stage history to date, it would appear that the central role is not one that calls for great innovation or ingenious new approaches. It demands rather an actor who can combine apparently contradictory character traits into a wholeness which audiences find credible, who can hit upon that magical satisfying balance that in their different ways Betterton, Kean, Barry, Salvini, Robeson and Tearle all possessed for their times.

When one considers certain aspects of *Othello* – its sexual intensity, its exotic content, its powerfully expressed emotional states, its starkly contrasted moral oppositions – there can be no surprise that it should have attracted the attention of two of the greatest composers of Italian opera: Gioacchino Rossini and Giuseppe Verdi.

Rossini's *Otello* (1816), though seldom performed today, was considered a masterpiece in its time, and was revolutionary in being the first Italian opera to equip its recitatives with full orchestral accompaniment rather than that of the single keyboard. In the first two acts the librettist took great liberties with the original. In an echo of Cinthio, Iago becomes a rejected suitor of Desdemona, and Shakespeare's cowardly Roderigo is transformed into so ardent a lover that he actually fights a duel with Othello, whose heroic stature is debased in the opera to that of a rather whining and irritable tenor. The handkerchief, in conformity to the operatic conventions of the time, is replaced by a lock of hair enclosed in a love-letter of Desdemona's that is intercepted and wrongly interpreted owing to its lacking a proper address. The third act, however, follows the final scenes of the play with more fidelity and is generally considered much superior musically to the rest of the work, with an exquisite setting of the Willow Song and an interpolated final prayer by Desdemona of the highest quality.

It is, of course, Verdi's opera which has had, since its first triumphant performance at La Scala in 1887, a history of stage performances as distinguished as that of the play itself. Composed forty years after his *Macbeth* and six years before his *Falstaff*, *Otello* is rightly considered his masterpiece and one of the three or four most profound works in the whole of the operatic repertoire.

Verdi was fortunate in having as his librettist Arrigo Boito, who was not only a famous poet but also a composer in his own right.[1] His text is a remarkable feat of necessary compression, the play's 3500 lines being reduced to 800. To achieve this he drastically cut the roles of Cassio, Roderigo and Emilia, and dropped Bianca altogether. The play's Venetian scenes are omitted, so that the opera can begin with

---

[1] *Mefistofele* (first perf. 1868); *Nerone* (first perf. 1924).

the crowd in Cyprus awaiting the triumphal landing of Otello. This excision not only enabled the focus to be placed on the main conflict between the three protagonists, but allowed Boito to work some of the play's first-act material into later scenes with telling musical effect. For instance, Iago's manipulation of Roderigo (1.3) and his bitterness at Cassio's promotion (1.1) are woven into the opera after Otello's arrival; and Othello's speech, 'Keep up your bright swords' (1.2.59), makes its appearance in the opera as he quells the brawl caused by Cassio's drunken behaviour. Perhaps the most remarkable example of this kind of transposition is the love duet with which the first act ends. In Verdi's hands the long quasi-conversational musical interplay, of which he was already a master, becomes a vocal re-enactment of the love soon to be wrecked, the expression of which contains the details of its origin, that Shakespeare dramatises in 1.1–1.3 of his play.

Some of the other changes made by Boito may be mentioned briefly. Iago sows the first seeds of doubt in Otello's mind before Desdemona's pleading for Cassio's reinstatement, thus allowing for a more rapid growth of the jealousy. The handkerchief is picked up by Emilia and seized by Iago while Otello and Desdemona are present. The serenade of Desdemona by the country people is placed later so as to provide an ironical musical comment on the early stages of Iago's temptation. Iago's soliloquies are compressed into his famous aria 'Credo in un Dio che m'ha creato simile a sè' in the second act. The final act fuses several of the play's scenes and makes both cuts and additions. Emilia's prattle about infidelity (4.3) is cut out; the play's Willow Song is stripped of much of its ironical application; and Desdemona is given a remarkable *Ave Maria* to sing before the statue of the Virgin immediately before Otello's entrance.

There is no doubt that Boito sacrificed much of what makes the play rich. For example, the dense poetic texture of the dialogue, many of the most memorable lines and much of the psychological shading of the characters are largely gone. Verdi's score makes no effort to restore these aspects of the play by musical means; rather it offers us an operatic equivalent of the experience that the play contains. The thrilling orchestral evocation of the storm before the first act gives aural reality to the symbolic weight of separation and prognosticated discord that the tempest-tossed voyage to Cyprus has in the play. The celebratory music of the chorus in Act 1 and its climax in Otello's opening words, 'Esultate! l'orgoglio musulmans sepolto è in mar', serve to suggest the heroic stature that his verbal music endows him with in the play. The quartet which constitutes the handkerchief scene in the opera allows for a simultaneous unfolding of the psychological levels of interaction not possible in the play, as the mezzo-soprano and the baritone voices dispute the possession of the ocular proof, and the soprano begs forgiveness for her transgression and the tenor voices his fears about his blackness and his age.

Other musical effects result from the interplay of the solo voices and their setting against larger vocal units. The chorus supplies the backdrop of jubilation at the arrival of the embassy from Venice for the tenor–baritone duet that plots Desdemona's death. The play's overhearing scene is a brilliant trio shot through with complex ironies that inhabit the differing levels of awareness of the three singers. The people's voices in the distance sing their salute to the 'Lion of Venice' as on stage Iago flicks his foot

at the body of the unconscious Otello with the words, 'Ecco il Leone!' Perhaps most
poignant of all are the musical echoes which perform something of the same function
as the allusive imagery in the play, such as Otello's final kiss, 'Un bacio, un bacio
ancora, un altro bacio', while the orchestra recalls the motif of the first-act love duet.

As one distinguished musicologist has rightly said: '*Otello* is the only opera to
challenge a Shakespearean tragedy and emerge undimmed by the comparison.'[1]

The title role of the opera makes special demands because of the combination of
acting and vocal skill required, so that many of the greatest tenors have not been able
to count it among their triumphs. Of the older generation of singers Tamagno, the
first Otello, was the leading exponent until his death. Up to the Second World War
Zenatello and Slezak and later Martinelli were internationally acclaimed for their
performances; and, more recently, outstanding interpreters of the role have included
Vinay, del Monaco, Vickers, McCracken and Domingo. Among the sopranos who
have been successful as Desdemona are Tetrazzini, Eames, Rethberg, Caniglia,
Tebaldi, Scotto and Te Kanawa; and memorable Iagos have been sung by Maurel,
Kraus, Tibbett, Scotti, Biasini, McNeill and Milnes.

There is a third opera based upon the play – that composed by A. Machavariani
which was given its first performance in Tbilisi in 1963. The London theatre of the
1960s spawned another kind of musical version, the 'rock opera' entitled *Catch My
Soul!*, which raised two interesting questions: why anyone should want to do it; and
being done why anyone should wish to hear it.

---

[1] W. Dean, 'Verdi's *Otello*: a Shakespearian masterpiece', *S.Sur.* 21 (1968), 96.

NOTE ON THE TEXT

The text of this edition is based on a conflation of the 1622 quarto (Q1) and the First Folio of 1623 (F), which the present editor believes represent two Shakespearean versions of the play. The collations record the choices of readings made between Q1 and F, and give also the rejected readings in substantive and semi-substantive variants, lineation and punctuation when it seriously affects the sense. The origin of all emendations adopted from Q2 (1630), the later Folios (1632, 1664, 1685), and from eighteenth-century and nineteenth-century editions is always recorded; but other emendations or suggestions for emendation are only listed when they have been considered possible alternatives to the reading of the present text or when they are discussed in the Commentary or supplementary notes. The collations do not include corrections of obvious misprints, turned letters, broken type, simple expansions, or modernisations of spelling. In the format of the collations, the authority for this edition's reading follows immediately after the square bracket enclosing the quotation from the text. Other readings, if any, follow in chronological order. For a full discussion of Q1 and F and the evidence for and theories of their relationship, see the Textual Analysis, pp. 193–207 below.

Othello

LIST OF CHARACTERS

OTHELLO, 'the Moor', a general in the service of Venice
BRABANTIO, 'father to Desdemona', a Venetian Senator
CASSIO, 'an honourable lieutenant' to Othello
IAGO, 'a villain', ensign to Othello
RODERIGO, 'a gulled gentleman'
DUKE OF VENICE
SENATORS of Venice
MONTANO, 'Governor of Cyprus'
GENTLEMEN 'of Cyprus'
LODOVICO, a noble Venetian, kinsman of Brabantio
GRATIANO, a noble Venetian, brother of Brabantio
SAILORS
CLOWN, servant of Othello
DESDEMONA, 'wife to Othello' and daughter of Brabantio
EMILIA, 'wife to Iago'
BIANCA, 'a courtesan', mistress of Cassio
MESSENGER
HERALD
OFFICERS
GENTLEMEN
MUSICIANS
ATTENDANTS

Notes

This is one of the seven dramatis personae that appear at the end of plays in F, all of which seem designed to avoid having large areas of blank page. It may, therefore, have been made up in the printing-house. The descriptions of characters, here appearing in quotation marks, are those of F, which have been amplified following the practice of Rowe and later editors.

OTHELLO, the Moor It is not known where Shakespeare found the name, as the hero of Cinthio's story is called simply 'un Moro'. It is possible that the name was partly modelled on Thorello in Jonson's *Every Man in His Humour* (1598) and changed to suggest Othoman and the Ottoman Turks.

CASSIO In Cinthio's story Cassio is called 'un Capo di squadra' (= a corporal or captain).

IAGO In Cinthio's story the villain is called 'un Alfiero' (= an ensign). 'Iago' or 'Jago' is the Spanish form of 'James' and Shakespeare could have found the name in Holinshed's Catalogue of Kings in his *Chronicles* (1577).

MONTANO, Governor of Cyprus Montano is so described in 2.1 SD in Q1; but there is some confusion about his actual rank in the play. See Textual Analysis, p. 197 below.

DESDEMONA Called 'Disdemona' in Cinthio's story; reference is made in the discussion following the tale to the meaning of the name: Δνσδαίμυν (= unfortunate).

OTHELLO, THE MOOR OF VENICE

1.1 *Enter* RODERIGO *and* IAGO.

RODERIGO Tush, never tell me, I take it much unkindly
    That thou, Iago, who hast had my purse
    As if the strings were thine shouldst know of this.
IAGO 'Sblood, but you will not hear me.
    If ever I did dream of such a matter,   5
    Abhor me.
RODERIGO Thou told'st me thou didst hold him in thy hate.
IAGO Despise me if I do not: three great ones of the city,
    In personal suit to make me his lieutenant,
    Off-capped to him; and by the faith of man,   10
    I know my price, I am worth no worse a place.
    But he, as loving his own pride and purposes,
    Evades them with a bombast circumstance,
    Horribly stuffed with epithets of war,

List of characters] The Names of the Actors. F *(following the text); not in* QI. *The order of listing is that of* F, *material from which is enclosed in single quotation marks.* BRABANTIO...Senator] Brabantio, *Father to Desdemona.* F; *not in* QI LODOVICO...GRATIANO...Venetian] Lodouico, *and* Gratiano, *two Noble Venetians.* F; *not in* QI   Act I, Scene I 1.1] *Actus Primus. Scœna Prima.* F; *not in* QI   0 SD RODERIGO *and* IAGO] F; *Iago and* Roderigo QI   1 Tush,] QI; *not in* F   2 thou...hast] F; you...has QI   4–6] *Steevens;* 'Sblood...me / ...me QI; But you'll...dream / ...me F 4 'Sblood] QI; *not in* F   7] QI; Thou...me / ...hate F   8] QI; Despise me / ...city F   10 Off-capped] F; Oft capt QI

Act 1, Scene 1

1 **never tell me** A common phrase expressing disbelief; as in American slang 'You don't say.'

3 **this** Usually taken to refer to Othello's marriage; but in view of Roderigo's reproach in 7 and Iago's detailed knowledge in 156–8, it would appear rather that Iago has just told Roderigo that Othello had informed him of his planned elopement.

4 **'Sblood** i.e. by Christ's blood; a very strong oath which F omits, in keeping with its policy of censoring the profanities that are found in QI. See Textual Analysis, pp. 201–2 below.

7 **him** It is noticeable that Othello remains unnamed throughout the scene and is only identified for the first time at 33 as 'his Moorship'.

10 **Off-capped** Removed their hats as a sign of respect. Both this reading from F and QI's 'Oft-capt' are defensible, but the sense of the passage indicates that the 'great ones' made their application to Othello on Iago's behalf on only one occasion, when they were told of Cassio's appointment. See supplementary note; see also 1.2.23 n. 'unbonneted'.

13 **bombast circumstance** rhetorically inflated circumlocution. Compare Iago's other comment on Othello's manner of speech at 2.1.212–14.

14 **stuffed** 'Bombast' was literally cotton material used for lining or padding garments.

14 **epithets** terms; with some suggestion here of technical military terminology.

And in conclusion,   15
Non-suits my mediators. For 'Certes', says he,
'I have already chosen my officer.'
And what was he?
Forsooth, a great arithmetician,
One Michael Cassio, a Florentine,   20
A fellow almost damned in a fair wife,
That never set a squadron in the field,
Nor the devision of a battle knows
More than a spinster, unless the bookish theoric,
Wherein the togèd consuls can propose   25
As masterly as he. Mere prattle without practice
Is all his soldiership. But he, sir, had the election,
And I, of whom his eyes had seen the proof
At Rhodes, at Cyprus, and on other grounds
Christian and heathen, must be lee'd and calmed   30

15 And in conclusion] Q1 ; *not in* F   17–18] *Pope; one line*, F, Q1   17 chosen] Q1 ; chose F   25 togèd] Q1 ; Tongued F
29 other] Q1 ; others F   30 Christian] Q1 ; Christen'd F   30 be lee'd] *conj. Heath;* be led Q1 ; be be-leed F

15 **And in conclusion** 'Conclusion' could be used as a legal term meaning 'a totally binding decision' (*OED* sv *sb* 13), which carries on the legal flavour of 'suit' at 9 and 'Non-suits' at 16.

16 **Non-suits** Causes a withdrawal of the petition of.

16 **Certes** Assuredly; probably a monosyllable here.

19 **arithmetician** Iago's sneer is that Cassio is a theoretical soldier with no practical experience of war, a point he develops at 21–6. Compare Mercutio's similar disdain of Tybalt's swordsmanship: 'he fights by the book of arithmetic' (*Rom.* 3.1.102). The allusion may also be to Cassio's having the ballistic expertise and skills of an artillery rather than an infantry officer.

20 **a Florentine** i.e. a foreigner, not a Venetian. See Cassio's use of his own countrymen as a standard of honesty at 3.1.38, and Iago's stress on his Venetian origin at 3.3.203–5, 5.1.89–91. There may also be a reference to the Florentines' fame as bankers and accountants which is taken up at 19 and 31.

21 **almost…wife** This has occasioned a great deal of comment. Most obviously it seems a version of the Italian proverb, 'l'hai tolta bella? tuo danno', or its English equivalent, 'Who has a fair wife needs more than two eyes' (Tilley w377); but in the play Cassio is clearly not married. It is possible that at

this point in the play's composition Shakespeare intended to have Cassio married, but later decided to use Bianca for the handkerchief episode. See p. 16 above, and supplementary note.

22 **set** dispose, arrange. A technical military term: see *OED* sv *v* 70.

22 **squadron** A small unit of troops, usually twenty-five men.

23 **devision of a battle** devising or planning of the movement of an army.

24 **spinster** This did not automatically mean a woman in Jacobean English; but, in view of Iago's misogyny, it probably does here.

24 **bookish theoric** textbook theory.

25 **togèd** i.e. dressed in an official gown or toga (like ancient Roman senators). F's 'tongued' has been defended as meaning 'prattling' (so that their soldiership like Cassio's is 'mere prattle'); but it is more likely that F's reading is a compositor's misinterpretation of his manuscript copy similar to that which produced 'woolvish tongue' for 'woolvish toge' in *Cor.* 2.3.115.

25 **propose** hold forth, expound.

27 **had the election** was selected.

29–30 **At Rhodes…heathen** This is the first reference to the crusading wars which are the background of the tragedy. See p. 10 above.

30 **be lee'd** A ship is in the lee when another ship stands between it and the wind and so prevents it

By debitor and creditor; this counter-caster,
He, in good time, must his lieutenant be,
And I, God bless the mark, his Moorship's ancient.
RODERIGO By heaven, I rather would have been his hangman.
IAGO Why, there's no remedy. 'Tis the curse of service;   35
Preferment goes by letter and affection,
Not by the old gradation, where each second
Stood heir to the first. Now sir, be judge yourself
Whether I in any just term am affined
To love the Moor.
RODERIGO   I would not follow him then.   40
IAGO O sir, content you.
I follow him to serve my turn upon him.
We cannot all be masters, nor all masters
Cannot be truly followed. You shall mark
Many a duteous and knee-crooking knave,   45
That doting on his own obsequious bondage,
Wears out his time much like his master's ass
For nought but provender, and when he's old, cashiered.
Whip me such honest knaves. Others there are
Who, trimmed in forms and visages of duty,   50

---

33 God] Q1 ; *not in* F   33 Moorship's] F ; Worships Q1   35] *Rowe*; Why...remedy / ...service F, Q1   35 Why] F ;
But Q1   37 Not by the] Q1 ; And not by F   38] F ; Stood...first / ...self Q1   39 affined] F ; assign'd Q1   43 all
be] F ; be all Q1   48 nought] F ; noughe Q1   49–52] F ; Whip...knaves / ...forms / ...hearts / ...throwing / ...
lords Q1

---

from moving; which is how Iago views himself –
unable to advance owing to Cassio's intervention.
F's 'be be-leed' is possible; but the metre and Q1's
'be-led' and the use of 'calmed' rather than
'becalmed' make Malone's emendation attractive.

31 **debitor and creditor** book-keeper. See 20 n.
above.

31 **counter-caster** one who reckons with
counters or tokens, a petty accountant.

32 **in good time** Lit. 'opportunely', but used
ironically here.

33 **God...mark** A phrase of unknown origin,
meaning roughly 'God help us!'

33 **Moorship's** The quibble is with 'Worship's'
(Q1's reading). This is the first example of Iago's
obsession with Othello's race and colour.

33 **ancient** ensign (originally the army's
standard-bearer).

35 **service** the military life.

36 **Preferment** Promotion.

36 **letter and affection** personal recommen-
dation and favouritism.

37 **old gradation** Old-fashioned method of
steady advancement from rank to rank.

39 **term** way, manner.

39 **affined** bound, constrained.

41 **content you** be pacified.

44 **truly** loyally, faithfully.

44 **shall mark** cannot avoid observing.

45 **knee-crooking knave** bowing servant. Compare *Ham.* 3.2.61–2: 'crook the pregnant hinges of
the knee / Where thrift may follow fawning'.

47 **time** working life.

47–8 **much like...cashiered** Compare *JC*
4.1.21–30 where Antony describes Lepidus as a man
requiring this kind of treatment.

49 **me** Lit. 'for me'. An ethical dative.

50 **trimmed** decked out.

50 **visages** appearances.

Keep yet their hearts attending on themselves,
And throwing but shows of service on their lords,
Do well thrive by them; and when they have lined their coats,
Do themselves homage. These fellows have some soul,
And such a one do I profess myself. 55
For, sir,
It is as sure as you are Roderigo,
Were I the Moor, I would not be Iago;
In following him, I follow but myself.
Heaven is my judge, not I for love and duty, 60
But seeming so for my peculiar end.
For when my outward action doth demonstrate
The native act and figure of my heart
In complement extern, 'tis not long after
But I will wear my heart upon my sleeve 65
For daws to peck at. I am not what I am.

RODERIGO What a full fortune does the thick-lips owe,
If he can carry it thus!

IAGO   Call up her father:
Rouse him, make after him, poison his delight,
Proclaim him in the street, incense her kinsmen, 70
And though he in a fertile climate dwell,
Plague him with flies: though that his joy be joy,

53–4] *Rowe;* Do…them / …coats / …homage / …soul F, Q1   54 These] F; Those Q1   56] *Capell; part of 55* F, Q1   60–1] F; Heaven…I / …so / …end Q1   62 doth] F; does Q1   66] F; For…at / …am Q1   66 daws] F; Doues Q1   67 full] Q1; fall F   67 thick-lips] Q1; Thicks-lips F   70 street] Q1; Streets F

52 **throwing** bestowing.
52 **but shows** mere outward appearances.
53 **lined their coats** gained all they can.
54 **Do themselves homage** Turn their attentions totally to their own interests.
58 **Were I…Iago** If I were in Othello's position, I would be able to see through the kind of apparently loyal service a subordinate like me is giving him.
61 **peculiar** personal, private.
63 **native act and figure** real action and intention.
64 **complement extern** outward demonstration.
65 **upon my sleeve** This is where servants wore the badge indicating the master they served. Iago

dissociates himself from such obvious displays of allegiance, because he is not what he seems to be.
66 **daws** Jackdaws were proverbially stupid and obsessed with snapping up trifles, which seems to be Iago's point here. Q1's 'doues' has been defended, but Iago would surely be more concerned at his heart's being fathomed by a foolish creature than by a notoriously mild one.
67 **full fortune** perfect good luck.
67 **thick-lips** This is the first piece of evidence that Othello is conceived as being Negroid rather than Arab.
67 **owe** possess.
68 **carry** get away with, succeed in.
69 **him…him…his** All refer to Othello.

Yet throw such chances of vexation on't
As it may lose some colour.

RODERIGO Here is her father's house; I'll call aloud.   75

IAGO Do, with like timorous accent and dire yell,
As when, by night and negligence, the fire
Is spied in populous cities.

RODERIGO What ho, Brabantio! Signior Brabantio, ho!

IAGO Awake! What ho, Brabantio! Thieves, thieves!   80
Look to your house, your daughter, and your bags!
Thieves, thieves!

BRABANTIO [*appears*] *above at a window.*

BRABANTIO What is the reason of this terrible summons?
What is the matter there?

RODERIGO Signior, is all your family within?   85

IAGO Are your doors locked?

BRABANTIO   Why, wherefore ask you this?

IAGO Zounds, sir, you're robbed; for shame, put on your gown;
Your heart is burst; you have lost half your soul;
Even now, now, very now, an old black ram
Is tupping your white ewe. Arise, arise;   90
Awake the snorting citizens with the bell,
Or else the devil will make a grandsire of you.
Arise, I say!

BRABANTIO   What, have you lost your wits?

73 chances] F; changes Q1; charges *conj. Walker*   73 on't] F; out Q1   80] F; Awake...Brabantio / Thieves, thieves,
thieves Q1   82 SD] *Bra. Aboue.* F; Brabantio *at a window.* Q1   83] Q1; What...terrible / Summons F   86 your doors
locked] F; all doore lockts Q1   87 Zounds] Q1; *not in* F   89 now, now,] F; now, Q1   92–3 Or...say] F; *one line in*
Q1

73 **chances** Most editors follow Q1 and read
'changes' (i.e. disturbances) which could scarcely
fail to affect Othello's joy. Iago is suggesting rather
that Roderigo should take steps which will cause
'possibilities of vexation' that *may* affect Othello's
present happiness.

74 **As it may** That may cause it to.

76 **like timorous** such frightening.

77 **by night...fire** i.e. a fire caused by
negligence at night.

82 SD *window* Most Elizabethan stages appear
to have had a balcony or upper acting-area, and
some had windows towards the side of a rear
balcony over the entry doors. See the reconstruction

of the Blackfriars Playhouse in I. Smith, *Shakespeare's Blackfriars Playhouse*, 1964, p. 307.

84 **the matter** your business.

87 **Zounds** i.e. by Christ's wounds; a strong
oath.

87 **gown** An outdoor gown worn over day
clothes; although it is possible that Iago is referring
to Brabantio's senatorial robe. There may be a
quibble on 'robed/robbed'.

88 **burst** broken.

90 **tupping** covering sexually (from a northern
dialect form of the noun 'tup' meaning 'ram').

91 **snorting** snoring.

92 **devil** i.e. Othello, because he is black.

RODERIGO Most reverend signior, do you know my voice?

BRABANTIO Not I; what are you?   95

RODERIGO My name is Roderigo.

BRABANTIO   The worser welcome;
I have charged thee not to haunt about my doors;
In honest plainness thou hast heard me say
My daughter is not for thee. And now in madness,
Being full of supper and distempering draughts,   100
Upon malicious bravery dost thou come
To start my quiet.

RODERIGO Sir, sir, sir –

BRABANTIO   But thou must needs be sure
My spirit and my place have in them power
To make this bitter to thee.

RODERIGO   Patience, good sir.   105

BRABANTIO What tell'st thou me of robbing? This is Venice;
My house is not a grange.

RODERIGO   Most grave Brabantio,
In simple and pure soul I come to you.

IAGO Zounds, sir; you are one of those that will not serve God if the
devil bid you. Because we come to do you service and you think   110
we are ruffians, you'll have your daughter covered with a Barbary
horse, you'll have your nephews neigh to you, you'll have
coursers for cousins, and jennets for germans.

BRABANTIO What profane wretch art thou?

IAGO I am one, sir, that comes to tell you your daughter and the Moor   115
are now making the beast with two backs.

---

96 worser] F; worse Q1   101 bravery] Q1; knauerie F   104 spirit...them] Q1; spirits...their F
106–7 What...grange] Q1; What...robbing / ...grange F   109 Zounds] Q1; *not in* F   110 and] F; *not in* Q1
115 comes] F; come Q1   116 now] Q1; *not in* F

---

100 **distempering** exciting, disturbing.

101 **bravery** noisy, showy display. Compare
Ham. 5.2.79–80: 'the bravery of his grief did put
me / Into a towering passion'. F's 'knauery' has
been defended, though 'malicious' then becomes
superfluous. Brabantio is referring to Roderigo's
disturbing his sleep with noisy drunken behaviour,
not to the viciousness of the action.

102 **start my quiet** disturb my rest. Metrically
this line is completed by the first line of Brabantio's
next speech. Roderigo's words are an attempted
interruption and thus extrametrical.

104 **spirit and my place** character and my
position as senator.

107 **grange** house in the country (hence
isolated).

108 **simple and pure** sincere and disinterested.

111–12 **Barbary horse** i.e. the Moorish Othello
(with a pun on 'barbarian'). The north coastal
regions of Africa were famous for thoroughbred
horses.

112 **nephews** close relatives; here 'grandsons'.

112 **neigh** There is probably a pun on
'nay' = deny their title to your blood and culture.

113 **jennets** small Spanish horses.

113 **germans** close kinsmen.

114 **profane** foul-mouthed.

116 **making...backs** copulating. We learn,
however, from 2.3.10 that the marriage is not
consummated in Venice.

BRABANTIO Thou art a villain.

IAGO   You are a senator.

BRABANTIO This thou shalt answer; I know thee, Roderigo.

RODERIGO Sir, I will answer anything. But I beseech you
    If't be your pleasure and most wise consent   120
    (As partly I find it is) that your fair daughter,
    At this odd-even and dull watch o'the night,
    Transported with no worse nor better guard,
    But with a knave of common hire, a gondolier,
    To the gross clasps of a lascivious Moor: 125
    If this be known to you, and your allowance,
    We then have done you bold and saucy wrongs.
    But if you know not this, my manners tell me,
    We have your wrong rebuke. Do not believe
    That from the sense of all civility   130
    I thus would play and trifle with your reverence.
    Your daughter, if you have not given her leave,
    I say again, hath made a gross revolt,
    Tying her duty, beauty, wit, and fortunes
    In an extravagant and wheeling stranger   135
    Of here and everywhere. Straight satisfy yourself.
    If she be in her chamber or your house,
    Let loose on me the justice of the state
    For thus deluding you.

BRABANTIO   Strike on the tinder, ho!
    Give me a taper; call up all my people.   140
    This accident is not unlike my dream;

120-36 If't...yourself.] F; *not in* Q1   122 odd-even] *Malone;* odde Euen F   139 thus deluding you] F; this delusion Q1

117 **You are a senator** There are two ways of delivering this line: (1) with Iago suppressing some uncomplimentary name on the tip of his tongue and substituting 'senator'; (2) with ironical politeness, thus casting doubt on the dignity of Brabantio's position.

118 **thou** Specifically addressed to Roderigo.

118 **answer** be called to account for.

119 **answer** give a satisfactory reply to any charge.

120 **wise** knowing, fully informed.

121 **partly I find** I am half-convinced (in view of your reception of my news).

122 **odd-even** just after midnight. Compare *Mac.* 3.4.125-6: 'What is the night? / Almost at odds with morning, which is which.'

124 **knave** servant.

124 **gondolier** Pronounced 'gòndolier'.

126 **your allowance** something approved of by you.

127 **saucy** insolent.

128 **manners** knowledge of correct social behaviour.

130 **from...civility** contrary to every feeling of good conduct.

131 **your reverence** the respect due to you.

134 **wit** intelligence.

135 **extravagant and wheeling** extremely vagrant and wide-ranging.

136 **Straight satisfy** Immediately ascertain the facts for.

140 **taper** candle.

141 **accident** occurrence.

Belief of it oppresses me already.
Light, I say, light! *Exit*

IAGO Farewell, for I must leave you.
It seems not meet nor wholesome to my place
To be produced, as if I stay I shall, 145
Against the Moor. For I do know the state,
However this may gall him with some check,
Cannot with safety cast him; for he's embarked
With such loud reason to the Cyprus wars,
Which even now stands in act, that, for their souls, 150
Another of his fathom they have none
To lead their business; in which regard,
Though I do hate him as I do hell's pains,
Yet, for necessity of present life,
I must show out a flag and sign of love, 155
Which is indeed but sign. That you shall surely find him,
Lead to the Sagittary the raisèd search,
And there will I be with him. So farewell. *Exit*

Enter Brabantio in his nightgown, and SERVANTS *with torches.*

BRABANTIO It is too true an evil. Gone she is,
And what's to come of my despisèd time 160
Is nought but bitterness. Now Roderigo,
Where didst thou see her? O unhappy girl!
With the Moor, say'st thou? Who would be a father?
How didst thou know 'twas she? O she deceives me

---

143 SD] F; *not in* Q1   144 place] F; pate Q1   145 produced] Q1; producted F   147 However] How euer F, Q1; Now euer Q1 *(some copies)*   151 none] F; not Q1   153 hell's pains] Q1; hell apines F; hell-pains *Dyce* 156–7] F; Which...surely / ...search Q1   157 Sagittary] F; Sagittar Q1   158 SD] Q1; *Enter Brabantio, with Seruants and Torches.* F   164 she deceives] F; thou deceiuest Q1

144 **meet** fitting.
144 **place** position (as Othello's ensign).
145 **produced** i.e. as a witness.
147 **gall...check** irritate him with some reprimand; lit. 'slightly hurt a horse by pulling back the rein'.
148 **cast** discharge.
148–9 **embarked...to** about to be engaged in.
149 **loud reason** shouted agreement (by the Senate).
150 **stands in act** 'are in progress', or perhaps 'are about to break out'.
150 **for their souls** to save themselves.
151 **fathom** capability.
154 **life** livelihood.
155 **flag** Perhaps a quibble on his post as ensign.

157 **Sagittary** The name of a house or inn where Othello and Desdemona have taken lodgings, so called because of its sign of Sagittarius or Centaur. It is not the Venetian armoury as some editors have suggested.
158 SD *nightgown* dressing-gown.
160 **despisèd time** Either 'the rest of my life, which is now odious to me', or 'the remainder of my existence, in which people will look with scorn on me'.
164 **she deceives** Q1's 'thou deceiuest' may be defended as being a direct address to the absent Desdemona or it may be the result of the compositor or copyist carrying on the 'thou' in lines 162, 163, 164.

    Past thought! What said she to you? Get more tapers,   165
    Raise all my kindred. Are they married, think you?

RODERIGO Truly I think they are.

BRABANTIO O heaven! How got she out? O treason of the blood!
    Fathers, from hence trust not your daughters' minds
    By what you see them act. Is there not charms   170
    By which the property of youth and maidhood
    May be abused? Have you not read, Roderigo,
    Of some such thing?

RODERIGO   Yes, sir, I have indeed.

BRABANTIO Call up my brother. O that you had had her!
    Some one way, some another. Do you know   175
    Where we may apprehend her and the Moor?

RODERIGO I think I can discover him, if you please
    To get good guard and go along with me.

BRABANTIO Pray you lead on. At every house I'll call;
    I may command at most. Get weapons, ho!   180
    And raise some special officers of night:
    On, good Roderigo; I'll deserve your pains.

                                            Exeunt

1.2 *Enter* OTHELLO, IAGO *and* ATTENDANTS *with torches.*

IAGO Though in the trade of war I have slain men,
    Yet do I hold it very stuff o'the conscience
    To do no contrived murder. I lack iniquity

168] Q1; Oh...out / ...blood F   171 maidhood] F; manhood Q1   173 Yes...indeed] F; I haue sir Q1   174 that]
Q1; would F   179 you lead] F; lead me Q1   181 night] Q1; might F   **Act 1, Scene 2**   1.2] *Scena Secunda.* F; *not
in* Q1   2 stuff] F; stuft Q1   2 o' the] o' th' F; of Q1

170 **charms** spells (or perhaps love philtres).

171 **property** nature.

171 **maidhood** Q1's 'manhood' has been defended as meaning 'humanity'; but F's reading has the required implication of impressionable immaturity.

177 **discover him** reveal where he is.

180 **command at** demand help from.

181 **night** This reading from Q1 is supported by reference to a long description of the Venetian 'officers of night' found in Lewes Lewkenor's translation (1599) of Contarino's *De Magistratibus et Republica Venetorum.* F's 'might' has been half-heartedly defended on the grounds that, if officers of the night were the normal watch, there would have been no need for Brabantio to call them 'special'. See p. 10 above.

182 **deserve your pains** recompense you for your trouble.

Act 1, Scene 2

1–5 Finding Othello at the Sagittary, Iago has been giving him his own untrue version of his conversation with Roderigo, as well as a true account of Brabantio's fury.

1 **trade** actual business.

2 **very stuff** essential material (carrying on the metaphor implicit in 'trade').

3 **contrived** premeditated, planned, cold-blooded.

Sometimes to do me service. Nine or ten times
I had thought to have yerked him here, under the ribs.   5
OTHELLO 'Tis better as it is.
IAGO   Nay, but he prated,
And spoke such scurvy and provoking terms
Against your honour,
That, with the little godliness I have,
I did full hard forbear him. But I pray, sir,   10
Are you fast married? For be sure of this,
That the magnifico is much beloved,
And hath in his effect a voice potential
As double as the duke's. He will divorce you,
Or put upon you what restraint and grievance   15
The law, with all his might to enforce it on,
Will give him cable.
OTHELLO   Let him do his spite;
My services which I have done the signiory
Shall out-tongue his complaints. 'Tis yet to know –
Which, when I know that boasting is an honour,   20
I shall provulgate – I fetch my life and being
From men of royal siege, and my demerits
May speak unbonneted to as proud a fortune

---

4 Sometimes] QI; Sometime F   5] F; I...here / ...ribs QI   8–9] *Pope; one line in* F, QI   10 pray, sir,] pray sir,
QI; pray you Sir, F   11 For be sure] QI; Be assur'd F   15 and] QI; or F   16 The] F; That QI   17 Will] F;
Weele QI   20 Which...know] F; *not in* QI   21 provulgate] QI; promulgate F   22 siege] F; height QI

5 **yerked** jabbed (here, with a sword or dagger).
5 **him** i.e. Roderigo.
7 **scurvy** insulting.
10 **full...him** restrained myself with great difficulty from attacking him.
11 **fast** firmly.
12 **magnifico** i.e. Brabantio. The chief noblemen of Venice were called *Magnifici*.
13 **in his effect...potential** at his command a powerful influence.
14 **As double...duke's** This suggests that Shakespeare believed that the duke had two votes to the senator's one, a misapprehension that William Thomas in *The History of Italy* (1549) claimed was common in England. Yet there are several accurate accounts of Venetian voting procedures in Lewkenor's translation (1599) of Contarino's *De Magistratibus et Republica Venetorum*. The lines need not be specific, and may mean simply that Brabantio's opinion carried in effect the same weight as the duke's.

15 **grievance** injury, punishment.
16 **enforce it on** cause it to be applied with the utmost rigour.
17 **cable** scope (a nautical term).
17 **spite** utmost harm to me.
18 **signiory** oligarchy of Venice.
19 **out-tongue** outweigh; lit. 'cry louder than'.
19 **to know** unknown.
21 **provulgate** make known. F's 'promulgate' is possible, but it usually carried the idea of official publication.
22 **siege** literally 'seat of authority', but here 'rank' as in *Ham.* 4.7.76. QI's 'height' is possible, meaning 'high rank' as in *R2* 1.2.189.
22 **demerits** worth, merits, as in *Cor.* 1.1.272.
23 **unbonneted** with all due respect (having removed their hats), without impertinence. Nearly all modern editors take the meaning to be 'without taking off their hats', supporting this interpretation by reference to *Cor.* 2.2.27, 'bonneted', which is too ambiguous in its context to be of any help. The

As this that I have reached. For know, Iago,
But that I love the gentle Desdemona,   25
I would not my unhousèd free condition
Put into circumscription and confine
For the sea's worth. But look what lights come yond!

IAGO Those are the raisèd father and his friends;
    You were best go in.

OTHELLO   Not I; I must be found.   30
    My parts, my title, and my perfect soul
    Shall manifest me rightly. Is it they?

IAGO By Janus, I think no.

        Enter CASSIO, *with* OFFICERS *and torches.*

OTHELLO The servants of the duke and my lieutenant!
    The goodness of the night upon you, friends.   35
    What is the news?

CASSIO   The duke does greet you, general,
    And he requires your haste-post-haste appearance
    Even on the instant.

OTHELLO   What is the matter, think you?

CASSIO Something from Cyprus, as I may divine.
    It is a business of some heat. The galleys   40
    Have sent a dozen sequent messengers
    This very night at one another's heels;
    And many of the consuls, raised and met,
    Are at the duke's already. You have been hotly called for,
    When, being not at your lodging to be found,   45

28] F; For…worth / …yonder Q1   28 yond] F; yonder Q1   29 Those] F; These Q1   32 Is it] F; it is Q1
33 SD] *Enter Cassio, with Torches.* F *(after 28)*; *Enter* Cassio *with lights, Officers, and torches.* Q1 *(after* worth *in 28)*
34] Q1; The…dukes / …lieutenant F   34 duke] Q1; Dukes F   35 you] F; your Q1   41 sequent] F; frequent Q1

---

tenor of Othello's lines is that he is fully aware of
the way his marriage will be viewed by the
Venetians, but his birth and achievements in fact
enable him to claim to be the equal of Desdemona
without infringing the standards of modest and
polite behaviour. See 1.1.10 n.

  23 **proud a fortune** elevated a success.
  25 **gentle** retiring, soft-natured; with a pun on
'of noble birth'.
  26 **unhousèd** unconfined (by marriage). Contrast the mischievous version at 1.1.135–6.
  27 **confine** restriction.
  28 **sea's worth** i.e. treasures lying on the
sea bed. Compare *H5* 1.2.163–5: 'rich…as is
the…bottom of the sea / With sunken wrack and

sumless treasuries'; and Clarence's dream in *R3*
1.4.24–33.
  29 **raisèd** who has been got out of bed; with a
pun on 'angered'.
  31 **parts** natural gifts, character.
  31 **title** legal right, position as a husband.
  31 **perfect soul** fully prepared conscience.
Compare *MM* 5.1.180–2, 'when you have / A
business for yourself, pray heaven you then / Be
perfect'.
  33 **Janus** The Roman two-faced god of beginnings; ironically appropriate for Iago to swear by.
  38 **matter** business.
  39 **divine** guess.
  40 **heat** urgency.

The senate hath sent about three several quests
To search you out.

OTHELLO   'Tis well I am found by you.
I will but spend a word here in the house,
And go with you.   [*Exit*]

CASSIO   Ancient, what makes he here?

IAGO Faith, he tonight hath boarded a land carrack;   50
If it prove lawful prize, he's made for ever.

CASSIO I do not understand.

IAGO   He's married.

CASSIO   To who?

[*Enter Othello.*]

IAGO Marry, to – Come, captain, will you go?

OTHELLO   Have with you.

CASSIO Here comes another troop to seek for you.

Enter BRABANTIO, RODERIGO *and* OFFICERS *with lights and*
weapons.

IAGO It is Brabantio; general, be advised,   55
He comes to bad intent.

OTHELLO   Holla, stand there!

RODERIGO Signior, it is the Moor.

BRABANTIO   Down with him, thief!

IAGO You, Roderigo? Come, sir, I am for you.

OTHELLO Keep up your bright swords, for the dew will rust them.
Good signior, you shall more command with years   60
Than with your weapons.

46 hath] F; *not in* Q1   46 about] F; aboue Q1   48–9 I...you] F; *one line in* Q1   48 but] F; *not in* Q1   49 SD] *Rowe;*
not in F, Q1   52 SD] *Rowe; not in* F, Q1   53 Have with you] F; Ha, with who? Q1   54 SD] *Enter Brabantio, Rodorigo,*
with Officers, and Torches. F; *Enters Brabantio, Roderigo, and others with lights and weapons.* Q1   59–61] Q1; *as prose*
in F

46 **about** all over the city.
46 **several quests** separate search parties.
49 **makes he** is he doing.
50 **carrack** A large treasure ship, such as those
that carried the wealth of America to Spain. In using
this metaphor Iago is debasing Othello's marriage
by viewing it as an act of high-seas piracy.
'Boarded' has a sexual connotation.
52 **I do not understand** As Cassio knew of
Othello's wooing (see 3.3.93–5), actors such as
Edwin Booth claimed that this line should be played

with a great deal of feigned surprise; but see
pp. 16–17 above.
53 **Marry** By the Virgin Mary; a mild oath.
53 **Have** I'll go.
58 Iago takes immediate steps to protect himself
and his 'purse' should a brawl develop, by singling
out Roderigo as his opponent.
59 **dew** i.e. rather than blood. Othello's scorn is
that of the professional fighter towards civilian
brawlers.

BRABANTIO O thou foul thief! Where hast thou stowed my
        daughter?
        Damned as thou art, thou hast enchanted her,
        For I'll refer me to all things of sense,
        If she in chains of magic were not bound,   65
        Whether a maid so tender, fair, and happy,
        So opposite to marriage that she shunned
        The wealthy curlèd darlings of our nation,
        Would ever have, t'incur a general mock,
        Run from her guardage to the sooty bosom   70
        Of such a thing as thou – to fear, not to delight.
        Judge me the world, if 'tis not gross in sense
        That thou hast practised on her with foul charms,
        Abused her delicate youth with drugs or minerals
        That weakens motion. I'll have't disputed on;   75
        'Tis probable and palpable to thinking.
        I therefore apprehend and do attach thee
        For an abuser of the world, a practiser
        Of arts inhibited and out of warrant.
        Lay hold upon him. If he do resist,   80
        Subdue him at his peril.
OTHELLO   Hold your hands,
        Both you of my inclining and the rest.
        Were it my cue to fight, I should have known it
        Without a prompter. Where will you that I go
        To answer this your charge?
BRABANTIO   To prison, till fit time   85
        Of law and course of direct session
        Call thee to answer.
OTHELLO   What if I do obey?

62] Q1; O…thief / …daughter F   64 things] F; thing Q1   65] F; *not in* Q1   68 darlings] Q1; Deareling F
72–7] F; *not in* Q1   78 For] F; Such Q1   84 Where] Q1; Whether F   85 To] F; And Q1   87 I] Q1; *not in* F

62 **stowed** hidden away, lodged.
63 **enchanted** cast a spell on. See 1.1.170–3.
64 **refer me** to have recourse to as authority; as
in *WT* 3.2.115.
64 **all things of sense** all reasonable creatures.
69 **general mock** public ridicule.
70 **her guardage** her father's guardianship.
71 **fear** be frightened.
72 **gross in sense** palpably obvious; as in *AWW*
1.3.172.
74 **minerals** poisonous mineral drugs.

75 **weakens motion** dulls the normal perceptive
faculties.
75 **disputed on** contested, debated (by experts).
77 **attach** arrest.
78 **abuser of the world** corrupter of society.
79 **arts inhibited…warrant** magical practices
which are prohibited and illegal.
82 **of my inclining** on my side. Compare *Ant.*
4.6.12–13: 'did dissuade / Great Herod to incline
himself to Caesar'.
86 **course of direct session** specially convened
sitting of a court of justice.

How may the duke be therewith satisfied,
Whose messengers are here about my side
Upon some present business of the state   90
To bring me to him?

OFFICER   'Tis true, most worthy signior;
The duke's in council, and your noble self
I am sure is sent for.

BRABANTIO   How? The duke in council?
In this time of the night? Bring him away;
Mine's not an idle cause. The duke himself,   95
Or any of my brothers of the state,
Cannot but feel this wrong as 'twere their own;
For if such actions may have passage free,
Bondslaves and pagans shall our statesmen be.

                                    Exeunt

1.3 *Enter* DUKE *and* SENATORS, *set at a table with lights, and*
ATTENDANTS.

DUKE There is no composition in these news
          That gives them credit.

1 SENATOR   Indeed they are disproportioned.
          My letters say a hundred and seven galleys.

DUKE And mine, a hundred and forty.

2 SENATOR   And mine, two hundred;
          But though they jump not on a just accompt –   5
          As in these cases where the aim reports
          'Tis oft with difference – yet do they all confirm
          A Turkish fleet, and bearing up to Cyprus.

DUKE Nay, it is possible enough to judgement:
          I do not so secure me in the error,   10

91 bring] F; beare Q1   Act 1, Scene 3   1.3] *Scæna Tertia.* F; *not in* Q1   0 SD] Q1 ; *Enter Duke, Senators, and Officers.* F
1 these] Q1 ; this F   4 and] Q1 ; *not in* F   6 the aim] F; they aym'd Q1   10 in] F; to Q1

90 **present** immediate.
95 **idle cause** trifling, unimportant legal case.
96 **brothers of the state** fellow senators.
98 **have passage free** go unchecked.

Act 1, Scene 3
1 **composition** consistency, agreement.
2 **credit** credibility.

2 **disproportioned** inconsistent.
5 **jump** agree, coincide. Compare *Shr.* 1.1.190:
'Both our inventions meet and jump in one.'
5 **just accompt** exact numbering.
6 **aim** estimate.
9 **to judgement** when carefully considered.
10 **secure me in the error** feel safe because of
the inconsistency.

       But the main article I do approve
       In fearful sense.
SAILOR *(Within)*   What ho! What ho! What ho!
OFFICER A messenger from the galleys.

               Enter a SAILOR.

DUKE   Now, what's the business?
SAILOR The Turkish preparation makes for Rhodes;
       So was I bid report here to the state   15
       By Signior Angelo.
DUKE How say you by this change?
1 SENATOR   This cannot be,
       By no assay of reason. 'Tis a pageant
       To keep us in false gaze. When we consider
       The importancy of Cyprus to the Turk,   20
       And let ourselves again but understand
       That as it more concerns the Turk than Rhodes,
       So may he with more facile question bear it,
       For that it stands not in such warlike brace,
       But altogether lacks the abilities   25
       That Rhodes is dressed in. If we make thought of this,
       We must not think the Turk is so unskilful
       To leave that latest which concerns him first,
       Neglecting an attempt of ease and gain
       To wake and wage a danger profitless.   30
DUKE Nay, in all confidence he's not for Rhodes.

---

11 article] F; Articles Q1   12 SH SAILOR] F; *One* Q1   13 SH OFFICER] F; *Sailor* Q1   13 galleys] F; Galley Q1
13 what's] F; *not in* Q1   13 SD *a* SAILOR] *Saylor* F *(after 12)*; *a Messenger* Q1 *(after* sense *in 12)*   16] F; *not in* Q1
17–18 This...be, / ...pageant] F; This...reason / ...pageant Q1   24–30] F; *not in* Q1   31 Nay] F; And Q1

11 **main article** item which the reports have in common.

11–12 **approve...sense** believe as cause for alarm.

14 **preparation** fleet fitted out for battle.

16 **Signior Angelo** Presumably one of the captains of the Venetian galleys. See p. 10 above.

17 **by** about. Compare *Ado.* 5.1.302–3: 'virtuous / In any thing that I do know by her'.

18 **assay** test.

18 **pageant** pretence, show.

19 **in false gaze** looking in the wrong direction, with our attention diverted.

23 **may** can.

23 **more...bear** an easier trial of strength over power.

24 **For that** Because.

24 **warlike brace** state of military preparedness.

25 **abilities** defensive capability.

26 **dressed in** equipped with.

27 **unskilful** lacking in judgement.

29 **attempt...gain** easy and profitable undertaking.

30 **wake and wage** stir up and risk. For 'wage' compare *1H4* 4.4.19–20: 'I fear the power of Percy is too weak / To wage an instant trial with the King.'

OFFICER Here is more news.

Enter a MESSENGER.

MESSENGER The Ottomites, reverend and gracious,
   Steering with due course toward the isle of Rhodes
   Have there injointed with an after fleet.   35
I SENATOR Ay, so I thought. How many, as you guess?
MESSENGER Of thirty sail, and now they do restem
   Their backward course, bearing with frank appearance
   Their purposes toward Cyprus. Signior Montano,
   Your trusty and most valiant servitor,   40
   With his free duty recommends you thus,
   And prays you to believe him.
DUKE 'Tis certain then for Cyprus.
   Marcus Luccicos, is not he in town?
I SENATOR He's now in Florence.
DUKE   Write from us to him   45
   Post-post-haste dispatch.
I SENATOR Here comes Brabantio and the valiant Moor.

Enter BRABANTIO, OTHELLO, CASSIO, IAGO, RODERIGO *and*
       OFFICERS.

DUKE Valiant Othello we must straight employ you
   Against the general enemy Ottoman.
   [*To Brabantio*] I did not see you: welcome, gentle
     signior;   50
   We lacked your counsel and your help tonight.

---

32 SD *a* MESSENGER] F; *a* 2. *Messenger* QI 35 injointed] QI; inioynted them F 36] F; *not in* QI 37 SH MESSENGER] F; *not in* QI 37 restem] F; resterine QI 42 believe] F, QI; relieve *conj. Capell* 44 he] F; here QI 45–6 Write…dispatch] *Pope;* Write…us / …dispatch F; *one line in* QI 45–6 us…haste] vs, / To him, Post, Post-haste, F; vs, wish him post, post hast QI 47 SD CASSIO, IAGO, RODERIGO] F; Roderigo, Iago, Cassio, Desdemona QI *(after 46)* 50 SD] *Theobald; not in* F, QI 51 lacked] F; lacke QI

35 injointed…after united with a following.
37–8 restem…course steer back to their original course.
38–9 bearing…toward making openly for.
41 free duty recommends willing service informs.
42 believe The emendation 'relieve' has been popular since the eighteenth century; but Montano seems rather to be giving information of guaranteed authority in the formal language of state, as the Duke's response at 43–4 suggests.
44 Luccicos There has been a good deal of speculation about this name and the function of its introduction here. Some editors take it as a corrupt form of 'Luccicus' or 'Lucchese' (an Italian, Marco Lucchese, being resident in London as master of an ordinary in the early seventeenth century), and suggest that a knowledgeable Cypriot resident in Italy is intended. It is surely a theatrical device for indicating the urgent action forced on the duke by the news and to emphasize the singular importance of Othello.
48 straight immediately.
49 general universal (because anti-Christian).
50 gentle noble.

BRABANTIO So did I yours. Good your grace, pardon me:
　　　　　Neither my place nor aught I heard of business
　　　　　Hath raised me from my bed, nor doth the general care
　　　　　Take hold on me; for my particular grief　　　　　　　55
　　　　　Is of so flood-gate and o'erbearing nature
　　　　　That it engluts and swallows other sorrows
　　　　　And yet is still itself.

DUKE　　　　　　　　　　　Why, what's the matter?

BRABANTIO My daughter! O, my daughter!

SENATORS　　　　　　　　　　　Dead?

BRABANTIO　　　　　　　　　　　　Ay, to me.
　　　　　She is abused, stol'n from me, and corrupted　　　　60
　　　　　By spells and medicines bought of mountebanks;
　　　　　For nature so preposterously to err,
　　　　　Being not deficient, blind, or lame of sense,
　　　　　Sans witchcraft could not.

DUKE Whoe'er he be that in this foul proceeding　　　　　65
　　　　　Hath thus beguiled your daughter of herself,
　　　　　And you of her, the bloody book of law
　　　　　You shall yourself read in the bitter letter
　　　　　After your own sense, yea, though our proper son
　　　　　Stood in your action.

BRABANTIO　　　　　　　　Humbly I thank your grace.　　　70
　　　　　Here is the man: this Moor, whom now it seems
　　　　　Your special mandate for the state affairs
　　　　　Hath hither brought.

ALL　　　　　　　　　　We are very sorry for't.

DUKE [*To Othello*] What in your own part can you say to this?

---

55 Take] F; Take any QI　　55 on] F; of QI　　55 grief] F; griefes QI　　58 yet] *Rowe*; it F, QI　　59 SH SENATORS]
Sen. F; *All.* QI　　63] F; *not in* QI　　64 Sans] F; Since QI; Saunce QI *(some copies)*　　69 your] F; its QI　　69 yea]
F; *not in* QI　　74 SD] *Theobald*; *not in* F, QI

53 **place** public office.
55–7 **for my…sorrows** Proverbial: 'The
greater grief drives out the less' (Tilley G446).
55 **particular** personal.
56 **flood-gate** A sluice-gate which holds back
water; but here used to mean the torrent of water
so held back. Compare *1H4* 2.4.394: 'For tears do
stop the flood-gates of her eyes.'
56 **o'erbearing** overwhelming.
57 **engluts** devours, gulps down.
60 **abused** wronged, harmed.
61 **mountebanks** charlatans.
63 **deficient** naturally defective, simple-minded.
63 **lame of sense** of faulty sensory perception.
64 **Sans** Without (French, Latin).

66 **beguiled…herself** cunningly robbed your
daughter of her normal natural reactions.
67 **bloody** death-dealing. Witchcraft was a
capital crime.
68–9 **You…sense** Compare Tilley L111: 'To
have the law in one's own hand'.
69 **After…sense** According to your own
interpretation; i.e. presumably *au pied de la lettre*.
Some editors favour QI's 'its' over F's 'yours',
citing Venice's pride in its impartial justice.
69 **our proper** my own.
70 **Stood…action** Faced your charge.
71 For a possible staging of this scene, see
illustration 4, p. 19 above.

BRABANTIO Nothing, but this is so.   75
OTHELLO Most potent, grave, and reverend signiors,
  My very noble and approved good masters,
  That I have tane away this old man's daughter,
  It is most true; true I have married her;
  The very head and front of my offending   80
  Hath this extent, no more. Rude am I in my speech
  And little blessed with the soft phrase of peace,
  For since these arms of mine had seven years' pith
  Till now some nine moons wasted, they have used
  Their dearest action in the tented field;   85
  And little of this great world can I speak
  More than pertains to feats of broil and battle;
  And therefore little shall I grace my cause
  In speaking for myself. Yet, by your gracious patience,
  I will a round unvarnished tale deliver   90
  Of my whole course of love: what drugs, what charms,
  What conjuration and what mighty magic –
  For such proceedings I am charged withal –
  I won his daughter.
BRABANTIO   A maiden never bold;
  Of spirit so still and quiet that her motion   95
  Blushed at herself; and she, in spite of nature,
  Of years, of country, credit, everything,
  To fall in love with what she feared to look on?
  It is a judgement maimed and most imperfect
  That will confess perfection so could err   100
  Against all rules of nature, and must be driven
  To find out practices of cunning hell

---

82 soft] F; set QI **87** feats] F; feate QI **87** broil] QI; Broiles F **91**] QI; Of…love /…charms F **93** proceedings
I am] proceeding I am F; proceedings am I QI **94–5** A…bold / Of…] F; A…spirit / …motion QI **94–5** bold;
Of spirit] bold: Of Spirit F; bold of spirit, QI **99** maimed] QI; main'd F **100** could] F; would QI

77 approved esteemed.
80 head and front whole extent; lit. 'height and breadth'.
81 Rude Unrefined, unpractised.
82 soft Many editors prefer QI's 'set', taking Othello to refer to his lack of oratorical 'good set terms' (*AYLI* 2.7.17). But the point Othello is making here is that his 'rude' idiom is appropriate to a military existence, as opposed to the 'soft' language required by civilian life.
83 pith strength. Compare *H5* 3.Chor.20–1: 'grandsires, babies, and old women, / Either past or not arriv'd to pith and puissance'.

84 moons wasted months ago.
85 dearest most important.
90 round plain, blunt.
92 conjuration magical incantation.
93 withal with.
95–6 her motion…herself she was embarrassed by her own natural impulses.
97 years i.e. the difference in age between Desdemona and Othello. Compare 3.3.267–8.
97 credit reputation.
102 practices evil machinations.

Why this should be. I therefore vouch again
That with some mixtures powerful o'er the blood
Or with some dram conjured to this effect   105
He wrought upon her.

DUKE   To vouch this is no proof
Without more wider and more overt test
Than these thin habits and poor likelihoods
Of modern seeming do prefer against him.

1 SENATOR But, Othello, speak: 110
Did you by indirect and forcèd courses
Subdue and poison this young maid's affections?
Or came it by request and such fair question
As soul to soul affordeth?

OTHELLO   I do beseech you
Send for the lady to the Sagittary   115
And let her speak of me before her father.
If you do find me foul in her report,
The trust, the office I do hold of you,
Not only take away, but let your sentence
Even fall upon my life.

DUKE   Fetch Desdemona hither.   120

OTHELLO Ancient, conduct them: you best know the place.
                    [*Exit Iago with two or three Attendants*]
And till she come, as truly as to heaven
I do confess the vices of my blood,
So justly to your grave ears I'll present
How I did thrive in this fair lady's love,   125
And she in mine.

DUKE   Say it, Othello.

106 SH DUKE] QI; *not in* F   106 vouch] F; youth QI   107 wider] F; certaine QI   107 overt] QI; ouer F   108 Than
these] F; These are QI   109 seeming do] F; seemings, you QI   110 SH I SENATOR] QI; *Sen.* F   115 Sagittary] F;
Sagittar QI   118] F; *not in* QI   121] QI; Ancient...them / ...place F   121 SD] *Capell subst.; not in* F; *Exit two or
three.* QI *(after 120)*   122 till] QI; tell F   122 truly] QI; faithfull F   123] F; *not in* QI

104 **blood** sexual passion.
105 **dram** dose.
105 **conjured to this effect** magically created
for this purpose.
106 **To vouch...proof** Proverbial: 'Accusation is no proof' (Tilley S1019).
107 **wider** fuller.
107 **test** testimony, evidence.
108 **thin habits** insubstantial outward appearances.
108 **poor likelihoods** weak inferences, tenuous
indications.

109 **modern seeming** commonplace assumptions. Compare *AYLI* 2.7.156: 'wise saws and
modern instances'.
111 **indirect** underhand.
111 **forcèd courses** means used against the will
of the victim.
113 **question** conversation.
117 **foul** guilty.
123 **blood** nature.
124 **justly** truthfully, exactly.

OTHELLO Her father loved me, oft invited me,
　　　　　 Still questioned me the story of my life
　　　　　 From year to year – the battles, sieges, fortunes
　　　　　 That I have passed.　　　　　　　　　　　　　　130
　　　　　 I ran it through, even from my boyish days
　　　　　 To the very moment that he bade me tell it;
　　　　　 Wherein I spake of most disastrous chances,
　　　　　 Of moving accidents by flood and field,
　　　　　 Of hair-breadth scapes i'th'imminent deadly breach,　　135
　　　　　 Of being taken by the insolent foe
　　　　　 And sold to slavery; of my redemption thence,
　　　　　 And with it all my travels' history:
　　　　　 Wherein of antres vast and deserts idle,
　　　　　 Rough quarries, rocks, and hills whose heads touch
　　　　　　　　 heaven,　　　　　　　　　　　　　　　　140
　　　　　 It was my hint to speak – such was the process:
　　　　　 And of the cannibals that each other eat,
　　　　　 The Anthropophagi, and men whose heads
　　　　　 Do grow beneath their shoulders. This to hear
　　　　　 Would Desdemona seriously incline;　　　　　　145
　　　　　 But still the house affairs would draw her thence,
　　　　　 Which ever as she could with haste dispatch
　　　　　 She'd come again, and with a greedy ear
　　　　　 Devour up my discourse; which I observing
　　　　　 Took once a pliant hour and found good means　　150
　　　　　 To draw from her a prayer of earnest heart
　　　　　 That I would all my pilgrimage dilate *fell in ful*

---

129 battles] Q1; Battaile F　129 fortunes] Q1; Fortune F　133 spake] Q1; spoke F　134 by] F; of Q1　138 with
it all] Q1; portance in F　138 travels'] Q1; Trauellours F　139 antres] *Theobald*; Antrees Q1; Antars F　140 and]
Q1; *not in* F　140 heads] Q1; head F　141 the] Q1; my F　142 other] Q1; others F　144 Do grow] Q1; Grew F
144 This] Q1; These things F　146 thence] Q1; hence F　147 Which] F; And Q1

128 Still Continually.

134 moving accidents stirring adventures.

135 scapes escapes.

138 with it all F's 'portance in' (= conduct during) is rather out of keeping with the modesty Othello is trying to project in this self-defence.

139 antres caves (Latin *antra*).

139 idle desolate, empty. Compare *R2* 3.4.66: 'idle hours'.

140 Rough quarries Rugged precipices, jagged mountain sides.

141 hint opportunity, cue.

143 Anthropophagi Cannibals. Anthropophagi and headless men (blemmyae) were mentioned by

Pliny (7.2). Accounts of them were also to be found in Sir John Mandeville's *Travels* (1499), which was still being read in the seventeenth century, and his 'wonders' were often represented pictorially in contemporary maps. Sir Walter Ralegh reports their existence in *The Discovery of Guiana* (1595), as does Laurence Keymis in *A Relation of the Second Voyage to Guiana* (1596). Compare *Temp.* 3.3.46–7: 'there were such men / Whose heads stood in their breasts'.

150 pliant suitable, opportune.

152 dilate tell in full. Compare *Err.* 1.1.122–3: 'Do me the favour to dilate at full / What have befall'n.'

Whereof by parcels she had something heard,
But not intentively. I did consent,
And often did beguile her of her tears   155
When I did speak of some distressful stroke
That my youth suffered. My story being done,
She gave me for my pains a world of sighs:
She swore, in faith, 'twas strange, 'twas passing strange,
'Twas pitiful, 'twas wondrous pitiful;   160
She wished she had not heard it, yet she wished
That heaven had made her such a man. She thanked me,
And bade me, if I had a friend that loved her,
I should but teach him how to tell my story,
And that would woo her. Upon this hint I spake: 165
She loved me for the dangers I had passed,
And I loved her that she did pity them.
This only is the witchcraft I have used.
Here comes the lady: let her witness it.

Enter DESDEMONA, *Iago and Attendants.*

DUKE I think this tale would win my daughter too.   170
Good Brabantio, take up this mangled matter at the best:
Men do their broken weapons rather use
Than their bare hands.

BRABANTIO   I pray you hear her speak.
If she confess that she was half the wooer,
Destruction on my head if my bad blame   175
Light on the man! Come hither, gentle mistress;
Do you perceive in all this noble company
Where most you owe obedience?

DESDEMONA   My noble father,
I do perceive here a divided duty:
To you I am bound for life and education;   180

---

153 parcels] F; parcell QI   154 intentively] QI; instinctiuely F   156 distressful] F; distressed QI   158 sighs] QI; kisses F   159 in] F; I QI   165 hint] F; heate QI   169] F; Here...lady / ...it QI   169 SD *Attendants*] F; *the rest* QI   175 On my head] F; lite on me QI

153 **by parcels** piecemeal.
154 **intentively** with continuous attention.
155 **beguile her of** steal from her, coax from her. Compare *Tro.* 4.4.33–6: 'where injury of chance...rudely beguiles our lips / Of all rejoindure'; and *Wiv.* 4.5.36–8: 'the very same man that beguil'd Master Slender of his chain cozen'd him of it'. Contrast the Duke's use of the same word at 66 above.
159 **passing** exceedingly.
162 **had made her** i.e. she had been born.
171 **take...best** Compare 'Make the best of a bad bargain' (Tilley B326).
180 **education** upbringing.

My life and education both do learn me
How to respect you. You are lord of all my duty;
I am hitherto your daughter. But here's my husband;
And so much duty as my mother showed
To you, preferring you before her father,   185
So much I challenge that I may profess
Due to the Moor my lord.

BRABANTIO   God bu'y! I have done.
Please it your grace, on to the state affairs.
I had rather to adopt a child than get it.
Come hither, Moor: 190
I here do give thee that with all my heart
Which, but thou hast already, with all my heart
I would keep from thee. For your sake, jewel,
I am glad at soul I have no other child,
For thy escape would teach me tyranny   195
To hang clogs on them. I have done, my lord.

DUKE Let me speak like yourself and lay a sentence
Which as a grise or step may help these lovers
Into your favour.
When remedies are past the griefs are ended   200
By seeing the worst which late on hopes depended.
To mourn a mischief that is past and gone
Is the next way to draw new mischief on.
What cannot be preserved when fortune takes,
Patience her injury a mockery makes.   205
The robbed that smiles steals something from the thief;

182 lord of all my] Q1 ; the Lord of F   187 bu'y] Q1 ; be with you F   192] F; *not in* Q1   197] Q1 ; Let...self / ...
sentence F   199] Q1 ; *not in* F   203 new] F ; more Q1

181 **learn** teach.
182 **all my duty** all the respect that is due to you as my father.
186 **challenge** claim.
187 **bu'y** be with you.
188 **on to** let us proceed with.
189 **get** beget.
191 **with all my heart** in which my whole heart was wrapped up.
193 **For your sake** On your account.
195 **escape** elopement.
196 **clogs** shackles. Lit. blocks of wood tied to the legs of animals to prevent their straying.
197 **like yourself** on your behalf and as you would speak (if you were not in your present frame of mind).

197 **lay a sentence** apply a maxim (Latin *sententia*).
198 **grise** step. Compare *Tim.* 4.3.16–17: 'for every grize of fortune / Is smooth'd by that below'.
200 Proverbial: 'Never grieve for that you cannot help' (Tilley G453).
200 **remedies** hopes of cure.
201 **which** i.e. the griefs, worst expectations.
201 **late on hopes depended** were bolstered until recently by hopeful expectations.
202 **mischief** misfortune.
203 **next** nearest, quickest.
204–5 **What...makes** i.e. patient endurance enables one to take inevitable losses as trifles; compare 'A good heart conquers ill fortune' (Tilley H305).

He robs himself that spends a bootless grief.

BRABANTIO So let the Turk of Cyprus us beguile,
We lose it not so long as we can smile;
He bears the sentence well that nothing bears   210
But the free comfort which from thence he hears;
But he bears both the sentence and the sorrow
That to pay grief must of poor patience borrow.
These sentences, to sugar or to gall,
Being strong on both sides, are equivocal.   215
But words are words; I never yet did hear
That the bruisèd heart was piercèd through the ear.
Beseech you now, to the affairs of the state.

DUKE The Turk with a most mighty preparation makes for Cyprus.
Othello, the fortitude of the place is best known to you; and   220
though we have there a substitute of most allowed sufficiency,
yet opinion, a more sovereign mistress of effects, throws a
more safer voice on you. You must therefore be content to
slubber the gloss of your new fortunes with this more stubborn
and boisterous expedition.   225

OTHELLO The tyrant custom, most grave senators,
Hath made the flinty and steel couch of war
My thrice-driven bed of down. I do agnise

---

217 piercèd] F, Q1; pieced *Theobald*   217 ear] Q1; eares F   218 Beseech...now,] Q1; I humbly beseech you proceed F
218 the state] Q1; state F   219 a] F; *not in* Q1   222 more] F; *not in* Q1   226 grave] F; great Q1   227 couch]
Pope; Coach F; Cooch Q1

207 spends a bootless indulges in an unavailing. Compare *JC* 3.1.75: 'Doth not Brutus bootless kneel?'
210–13 He bears...borrow Brabantio's distinction is between the easy comfort of an indifferent platitude and the real cost of patience to the man whose deeper interest is violated.
211 free unmixed with sorrow.
213 poor Because patience has nothing to lend.
214 gall bitterness. Compare *Tro.* 2.2.144: 'You have the honey still, but these the gall.'
216–17 I never...ear This idea is given extended expression in *Ado* 5.1.15–32.
217 the bruised...ear the broken heart was reached (or lanced, and so cured) by words. Compare *LLL* 5.2.753: 'Honest plain words best pierce the ear of grief.' John Lyly in *Euphues* (ed. R. W. Bond), I, 212, writes of a grief being ripe enough to lance and so cure. Many editors emend 'piercèd' to 'pieced' (= mended).
220 fortitude strength of the defences.
221 substitute deputy (i.e. Montano).

221 allowed sufficiency acknowledged ability.
222 opinion public opinion.
222 more sovereign...effects more paramount arbiter of what should be done.
222–3 throws...you judges you are the more reliable.
224 slubber slobber, sully. Compare *1H4* 2.4.309–11: 'to tickle our noses with speargrass to make them bleed, and then to beslubber our garments with it'.
224 stubborn harsh, rough.
225 boisterous violent. Compare *John* 3.4.135–6: 'A sceptre snatch'd with an unruly hand / Must be as boisterously maintain'd.'
226–8 The tyrant...down Proverbial: 'Custom makes all things easy' (Tilley C933).
227 flinty and steel The allusion is to sleeping on the ground in armour.
228 thrice-driven i.e. of the softest feathers (because they have been winnowed three times).
228 agnise acknowledge, confess to.

A natural and prompt alacrity
I find in hardness, and do undertake   230
These present wars against the Ottomites.
Most humbly, therefore, bending to your state,
I crave fit disposition for my wife,
Due reference of place and exhibition
With such accommodation and besort   235
As levels with her breeding.

DUKE   If you please,
Be't at her father's.

BRABANTIO   I'll not have it so.

OTHELLO Nor I.

DESDEMONA   Nor I; I would not there reside
To put my father in impatient thoughts
By being in his eye. Most gracious duke,   240
To my unfolding lend your prosperous ear
And let me find a charter in your voice
T'assist my simpleness.

DUKE   What would you, Desdemona?

DESDEMONA That I did love the Moor to live with him,
My downright violence and storm of fortunes   245
May trumpet to the world. My heart's subdued
Even to the very quality of my lord.
I saw Othello's visage in his mind

230 do] F; would Q1   231 These] *Malone;* This F, Q1   234 reference] F; reuerence Q1   236–7 If...father's.] Q1
(one line); Why at her Fathers? F   238 Nor I; I would not] Q1; Nor would I F   241 your prosperous] F; a gracious
Q1   243 T'assist] F; And if Q1   243 you, Desdemona?] F; you – speake. Q1   244 did] Q1; *not in* F   245 storm]
F; scorne Q1   247 very quality] F; vtmost pleasure Q1

229 **alacrity** eagerness.
230 **hardness** hardship.
232 **state** authority.
234 **Due reference of place** Appropriate assigning of a residence.
234 **exhibition** financial support.
235 **besort** appropriate companions or attendants.
236 **levels with** is suitable to.
236 **breeding** social position.
241 **unfolding** disclosure, explanation.
241 **prosperous** favourable.
242 **charter** permission (with perhaps the sense of publicly conceded official support).
243 **simpleness** innocence, lack of sophistication.
245 **downright violence** absolute violation of the norm.

245 **storm of fortunes** This means either 'my taking my future by storm' or 'the upheaval created for my future life'. Shakespeare may be recalling a phrase in Lewkenor's translation (1599) of Contarino's *De Magistratibus et Republica Venetorum.* Some editors prefer Q1's 'scorne' and thus see Desdemona proving her love for Othello by asserting what she has sacrificed for him. That these two words could be confused by a compositor in reading the handwriting of the period is suggested by the crux in *Tro.* 1.1.37: 'as when the sun doth light a scorn/storm'.
247 **quality** nature.
248–50 **I saw...consecrate** This seems to echo Cinthio's introduction to the source story: 'he who wishes to form a true judgement of beauty must admire not only the body, but rather the minds and habits of those who present themselves to his view' (Bullough, VII, 240).

And to his honours and his valiant parts
Did I my soul and fortunes consecrate.   250
So that, dear lords, if I be left behind
A moth of peace, and he go to the war,
The rites for which I love him are bereft me,
And I a heavy interim shall support
By his dear absence. Let me go with him.   255
OTHELLO Let her have your voice.
Vouch with me, heaven, I therefore beg it not
To please the palate of my appetite,
Nor to comply with heat the young affects
In my distinct and proper satisfaction,   260
But to be free and bounteous to her mind.
And heaven defend your good souls that you think
I will your serious and great business scant
For she is with me. No, when light-winged toys
Of feathered Cupid seel with wanton dullness   265
My speculative and officed instruments,
That my disports corrupt and taint my business,
Let housewives make a skillet of my helm,
And all indign and base adversities

253 which] QI; why F   **256–7** Let...heaven, I] F; Your voyces Lords: beseech you let her will, / Haue a free way.
I QI   **259** the] F, QI; and *conj. Steevens*; of the *Keightley*   **260** my] F, QI; me *Upton*   **260** distinct] *Theobald*; defunct
F, QI; disjunct *Malone Var.*; defect *Upton*; defenc't *Tollet*; default *conj. Jourdain*   **261** to her] F; of her QI
263 great] F; good QI   **264** For] QI; When F   **265** Of] F; And QI   **265** seel] F; foyles QI   **266** officed] F;
actiue QI   **266** instruments] QI; Instrument F

249 valiant parts military virtues.

250 soul and fortunes whole being and future.

252 moth drone, idler.

253 rites rites of love. Compare *Rom.* 3.2.8–9: 'Lovers can see to do their amorous rites / By their own beauties.' Owing to the vagaries of Jacobean orthography F's and QI's spelling 'rites' could mean 'rights' also; and some editors have taken the word to mean Desdemona's 'privileges' in sharing Othello's military life and dangers for which she says she loves him at 248–50. Ultimately the choice of reading is determined by one's interpretation of Desdemona's character as (1) a girl so modest that she would not dream of saying in public that she desires Othello sexually, or (2) a girl who is frank and open to the point of simplicity. See pp. 27–8 above.

255 dear A possible quibble: (1) that I can least afford; (2) emotionally affecting.

256 voice consent.

259–60 to comply...satisfaction The general sense here is clear enough: Othello believes that he is too mature to be at the mercy of unbridled sexual desire, and that although he expects physical satisfaction in marriage, he also values just as highly mental sympathy with his wife. The exact meaning is more difficult to arrive at without some emendation of the text of F and QI. I follow Theobald in changing 'defunct' to 'distinct' on the grounds that such a misreading is paleographically possible and demands least dislocation of the text. See supplementary note for a full discussion.

259 comply with heat satisfy eagerly.

259 young affects newly felt emotions.

260 distinct individual.

261 free generous.

262 defend forbid.

262 think should think.

265 seel blind (from the practice in falconry of sewing up the eyelids of the young hawk).

266 speculative...instruments powers of perception which are for the purpose of my duty. See supplementary note.

267 disports sexual pleasures.

267 taint impair.

268 skillet small cooking pot.

269 indign unworthy (Latin *indignus*).

Make head against my estimation!   270
DUKE Be it as you shall privately determine,
    Either for her stay or going. Th'affair cries haste,
    And speed must answer it. You must hence tonight.
DESDEMONA Tonight, my lord?
DUKE   This night.
OTHELLO   ··   With all my heart.
DUKE At nine i'the morning, here we'll meet again.   275
    Othello, leave some officer behind
    And he shall our commission bring to you
    With such things else of quality and respect
    As doth import you.
OTHELLO   So please your grace, my ancient:
    A man he is of honesty and trust.   280
    To his conveyance I assign my wife,
    With what else needful your good grace shall think
    To be sent after me.
DUKE   Let it be so.
    Good night to everyone. [*To Brabantio*] And noble
        signior,
    If virtue no delighted beauty lack,   285
    Your son-in-law is far more fair than black.
1 SENATOR Adieu, brave Moor; use Desdemona well.
BRABANTIO Look to her, Moor, if thou hast eyes to see:
    She has deceived her father and may thee.
OTHELLO My life upon her faith!
        Exeunt [*Duke, Brabantio, Cassio, Senators and Attendants*]

270 estimation] F; reputation Q1   272 her] F; *not in* Q1   272 affair cries] F; affaires cry Q1   273 it] F; *not in* Q1
273 You...tonight.] Q1; *assigned to* / *Sen.* / *in* F   273 hence] Q1; away F   274 DESDEMONA Tonight, my lord?] Q1;
not in F   274 DUKE This night.] Q1; *not in* F   275 nine] F; ten Q1   278 With] Q1; And F   278 and] F; or Q1
279 import] F; concerne Q1   279 So] F; *not in* Q1   284 SD] *Capell*; *not in* F, Q1   288 if...eyes] F; haue a quick
eye Q1   289 and may] F; may doe Q1   290 SD] *Theobald subst.*; *Exit.* F; *Exeunt.* Q1

270 **Make head** Take up arms, mount an attack.
Compare *1H4* 3.1.63–4: 'Three times hath Henry
Bullingbrook made head / Against my power.'
270 **estimation** reputation.
272 **cries** calls for.
278 **quality and respect** importance and
relevance.
279 **import** concern.
280 **honesty** This is the first time Iago is
associated verbally with this quality which the other
people in the play believe to be most characteristic
of him.

281 **conveyance** escorting.
285–6 **If virtue...black** Proverbial: 'He is
handsome that handsome does' (Tilley D410); and
see an extended treatment of the same idea in *TN*
3.4.367–70.
285 **delighted** delightful. Compare *Cym.*
5.4.101–2: 'to make my gift / The more delay'd,
delighted'.
289 Proverbial: 'He that once deceives is ever
suspected' (Tilley D180). See 3.3.208 for Iago's use
of this.

                         Honest Iago   290
My Desdemona must I leave to thee;
I prithee, let thy wife attend on her,
And bring her after in the best advantage.
Come, Desdemona, I have but an hour
Of love, of worldly matters and direction   295
To spend with thee. We must obey the time.
                         Exeunt Othello and Desdemona

RODERIGO Iago.

IAGO What say'st thou, noble heart?

RODERIGO What will I do, think'st thou?

IAGO Why, go to bed and sleep.   300

RODERIGO I will incontinently drown myself.

IAGO If thou dost, I shall never love thee after. Why, thou silly
gentleman?

RODERIGO It is silliness to live, when to live is torment: and then we
have a prescription to die, when death is our physician.   305

IAGO O villainous! I have looked upon the world for four times seven
years, and since I could distinguish betwixt a benefit and an
injury, I never found a man that knew how to love himself. Ere
I would say I would drown myself for the love of a guinea-hen,
I would change my humanity with a baboon.   310

RODERIGO What should I do? I confess it is my shame to be so fond,
but it is not in my virtue to amend it.

IAGO Virtue? A fig! 'Tis in ourselves that we are thus or thus. Our
bodies are our gardens, to the which our wills are gardeners. So
that if we will plant nettles or sow lettuce, set hyssop and weed   315

---

293 her] Q1; them F   295 worldly matters] Q1; wordly matter F   296 SD] *Exit Moore and* Desdemona Q1; *Exit.* F
302 If] F; Well, if Q1   302 after] F; after it Q1   304 torment] F; a torment Q1   304–5 we have] Q1; haue we F
306 O villainous] F; *not in* Q1   307 betwixt] F; betweene Q1   308 a man] Q1; man F   314 our gardens] F;
gardens Q1

293 **in the best advantage** at the most favourable opportunity.

295 **direction** instructions.

296 **time** present pressing necessity.

301 **incontinently** at once.

305 **prescription** A quibble: (1) right based on long tradition; compare *3H6* 3.3.93–4: 'a silly time / To make prescription for a kingdom's worth'; (2) a doctor's order.

306 **villainous** pernicious nonsense.

309 **guinea-hen** Usually this means 'prostitute', which is how Iago views all women.

311 **fond** infatuated.

312 **virtue** nature.

313 **A fig** A derogatory term, usually accompanied by a vulgar gesture of shooting the thumb between the first and second fingers.

315–16 **if we will . . . thyme** Nettles and lettuce were considered horticultural opposites, having the complementary qualities of dryness and wetness and so believed to aid the growth of each other. The aromatic herbs, hyssop and thyme, were also believed to have the same qualities; compare John Lyly, *Euphues* (ed. R. W. Bond), 1, 187, 'good Gardeiners who in their curious knottes mixe Hisoppe wyth Time as ayders the one to the growth of the other, the one beeinge drye, the other moyste'. Thus some editors' emendation of 'thyme' to 'tine' (= tare, vetch) rather misses the point.

315 **set** plant.

up thyme, supply it with one gender of herbs or distract it
with many, either to have it sterile with idleness or manured with
industry, why the power and corrigible authority of this lies in
our wills. If the balance of our lives had not one scale of reason
to poise another of sensuality, the blood and baseness of our   320
natures would conduct us to most preposterous conclusions. But
we have reason to cool our raging motions, our carnal stings,
our unbitted lusts; whereof I take this, that you call love, to be
a sect or scion.

RODERIGO It cannot be.   325

IAGO It is merely a lust of the blood and a permission of the will. Come,
be a man. Drown thyself? Drown cats and blind puppies. I
have professed me thy friend, and I confess me knit to thy
deserving with cables of perdurable toughness. I could never
better stead thee than now. Put money in thy purse. Follow   330
thou these wars; defeat thy favour with an usurped beard. I say,
put money in thy purse. It cannot be that Desdemona should
long continue her love to the Moor – put money in thy
purse – nor he his to her. It was a violent commencement, and thou
shalt see an answerable sequestration – put but money in thy   335
purse. These Moors are changeable in their wills – fill thy purse
with money. The food that to him now is as luscious as locusts

316 thyme] Time F, Q1; tine *Walker*   319 balance] Q1; braine F; beam *Theobald*   323 our unbitted] Q1; or vnbitted F
324 sect] F, Q1; set *Johnson*   328 have] F; *not in* Q1   331 thou these] *Rowe*; thou the F; these Q1   332 be] Q1;
be long F   333 long] Q1; *not in* F   333 to] F; vnto Q1   334 his] F; *not in* Q1   334 commencement] Q1;
Commencement in her F

316 **supply** fill.

316 **gender** kind.

316–17 **distract it with** divide it among.

318 **corrigible authority** corrective power.

319 **balance** scales. Although this is the usual
Shakespearean usage, some editors follow Theobald
and emend to 'beam', of which they take F's
'braine' to be a misreading.

320 **poise** counterbalance.

320 **blood** natural passions.

321 **conclusions** experiments.

322 **motions** impulses.

322 **stings** compelling desires. Compare *MM*
1.4.59: 'wanton stings and motions of the sense'.

323 **unbitted** unbridled, unrestrained by a curb.

324 **sect or scion** branch or graft. Some editors,
wishing to make the horticultural metaphor
completely consistent, follow Johnson in emending
'sect' to 'set' (= cutting from a plant).

328–9 **thy deserving** what is due to thee.

329 **perdurable** everlasting.

330 **stead** be of use to. Compare *TGV*

2.1.113–14: 'so it stead you…I will write a
thousand times as much'.

330 **Put money in thy purse** Proverbial saying
(Tilley M1090), meaning 'provide yourself for
success'.

331 **defeat…beard** disfigure your face with a
false beard. Iago may be quibbling here at
Roderigo's expense: i.e. 'pretend you are a real
man'. Compare *TN* 5.1.250: 'my masculine
usurp'd attire'.

334–5 **It was…sequestration** Proverbial:
'Such beginning such end' (Tilley B262).

335 **answerable sequestration** correspond-
ingly violent separation.

336 **wills** sexual desires.

337 **locusts** According to Gerarde's *Herbal*
(1597), 'The carob groweth in Apulia…and other
countries eastward, where the cods are so full of
sweet juice that it is used to preserve ginger…This
is of some called St. John's bread, and thought to
be that which is translated *locusts*.' See Matt. 3.4.

shall be to him shortly as acerb as the coloquintida. She
must change for youth; when she is sated with his body she
will find the error of her choice. Therefore put money in thy   340
purse. If thou wilt needs damn thyself, do it a more delicate way
than drowning. Make all the money thou canst. If sanctimony
and a frail vow betwixt an erring barbarian and a super-subtle
Venetian be not too hard for my wits and all the tribe of hell, thou
shalt enjoy her – therefore make money. A pox of drowning   345
thyself! It is clean out of the way. Seek thou rather to be hanged
in compassing thy joy than to be drowned and go without her.

RODERIGO Wilt thou be fast to my hopes, if I depend on the issue?

IAGO Thou art sure of me. Go make money. I have told thee often, and
I retell thee again and again, I hate the Moor. My cause is   350
hearted: thine hath no less reason. Let us be conjunctive in
our revenge against him. If thou canst cuckold him, thou dost
thyself a pleasure, me a sport. There are many events in the womb
of time which will be delivered. Traverse! Go, provide thy money.
We will have more of this tomorrow. Adieu.   355

RODERIGO Where shall we meet i'the morning?

IAGO At my lodging.

RODERIGO I'll be with thee betimes.

IAGO Go to; farewell. Do you hear, Roderigo?

RODERIGO What say you?   360

IAGO No more of drowning, do you hear?

RODERIGO I am changed.

IAGO Go to; farewell. Put money enough in your purse.

RODERIGO I'll sell all my land.   *Exit*

---

338 acerb as the] QI; bitter as F   338–9 She...youth] F; *not in* QI   340 error] QI; errors F   340 choice. Therefore]
F; choyce; shee must haue change, shee must. Therefore QI   343 a super-subtle] QI; super-subtle F   345 of] F; a
QI   346 thyself] F; *not in* QI   348 if...issue] F; *not in* QI   350 retell] F; tell QI   351 hath] F; has QI
351 conjunctive] F; communicatiue QI   353 me] F; and me QI   360–3] QI; *not in* F   364] F; *not in* QI   364 SD
Exit] F; *Exit Roderigo* QI *(after 362)*

338 **acerb** bitter.

338 **coloquintida** Colocynth, a bitter apple
used as a laxative, and according to Gerarde's
Herbal (1597) found in the Sinaitic desert and the
southern coast of the Mediterranean.

339 **for youth** for a younger man.

342 **Make** Raise.

342 **sanctimony** holiness (of the marriage
bond).

343 **erring** A quibble: (1) wandering; (2) sinful
(because anti-Christian).

343 **super-subtle** exceptionally refined or delicate. Compare *Temp.* 2.1.42–3: 'of subtle, tender,
and delicate temperance'.

346 **clean out of the way** a completely
inappropriate course of action.

347 **compassing** achieving; with a pun on
'embracing'.

348 **fast to** in complete support of.

351 **hearted** deeply felt.

351 **conjunctive** allied.

354 **Traverse!** A military order for setting
troops in motion; but it is not known whether it was
for marching forward, retreating, or turning. As also
in *2H4* 3.2.272.

358 **betimes** early.

IAGO Thus do I ever make my fool my purse;   365
    For I mine own gained knowledge should profane
    If I would time expend with such a snipe
    But for my sport and profit. I hate the Moor,
    And it is thought abroad that 'twixt my sheets
    He's done my office. I know not if't be true   370
    Yet I, for mere suspicion in that kind,
    Will do as if for surety. He holds me well:
    The better shall my purpose work on him.
    Cassio's a proper man: let me see now;
    To get his place and to plume up my will   375
    In double knavery. How? How? Let's see.
    After some time, to abuse Othello's ear
    That he is too familiar with his wife;
    He hath a person and a smooth dispose
    To be suspected, framed to make women false.   380
    The Moor is of a free and open nature,
    That thinks men honest that but seem to be so,
    And will as tenderly be led by the nose
    As asses are.
    I have't. It is engendered. Hell and night   385
    Must bring this monstrous birth to the world's light.   *Exit*

2.1 *Enter* MONTANO *and two* GENTLEMEN.

MONTANO What from the cape can you discern at sea?
1 GENTLEMAN Nothing at all; it is a high-wrought flood.
    I cannot 'twixt the heaven and the main
    Descry a sail.

367 a] Q1; *not in* F   **370** He's] Ha's Q1; She ha's F   **371** Yet] Q1; But F   **375** his] F; this Q1   **375** plume] F;
make Q1   **376** In] F; A Q1   **376** Let's] F; let me Q1   **377** ear] Q1; eares F   **379** hath] F; has Q1   **381** is of] F;
not in Q1   **381** nature] F; nature too Q1   **382** seem] F; seemes Q1   **383–4**] F; *one line in* Q1   **386** SD] Q1; *not in* F
Act 2, Scene 1   **2.1**] *Actus Secundus. Scena Prima.* F; *Actus 2. Scœna 1.* Q1   **0** SD] F; *Enter* Montanio, *Gouernor of*
Cypres, *with two other Gentlemen.* Q1   **3** heaven] F; hauen Q1

366 gained knowledge practical wisdom and experience.
367 snipe A long-billed bird, used as a type of worthlessness.
371 kind regard.
372 surety certainty.
372 holds me well esteems me.
374 proper handsome.
375 plume glorify, set a plume in the cap of.
377 abuse deceive.

379 dispose manner, disposition.
383 tenderly easily, effortlessly.
383–4 be led...are Proverbial (Tilley N233, T221).

Act 2, Scene 1
    0 SD MONTANO See note to list of characters, and Textual Analysis, p. 197 below.
    2 high-wrought flood angry sea.

MONTANO Methinks the wind does speak aloud at land,   5
        A fuller blast ne'er shook our battlements.
        If it hath ruffianed so upon the sea,
        What ribs of oak, when mountains melt on them,
        Can hold the mortise? What shall we hear of this?
2 GENTLEMAN A segregation of the Turkish fleet: 10
        For do but stand upon the banning shore,
        The chidden billow seems to pelt the clouds;
        The wind-shaked surge, with high and monstrous mane,
        Seems to cast water on the burning Bear
        And quench the guards of th'ever-fixèd Pole.   15
        I never did like molestation view
        On the enchafèd flood.
MONTANO   If that the Turkish fleet
        Be not ensheltered and embayed, they are drowned:
        It is impossible they bear it out.

                Enter a third GENTLEMAN.

3 GENTLEMAN News, lads! Our wars are done: 20
        The desperate tempest hath so banged the Turks
        That their designment halts. A noble ship of Venice
        Hath seen a grievous wrack and sufferance
        On most part of their fleet.
MONTANO How? Is this true?
3 GENTLEMAN   The ship is here put in,   25

5 does speak] Q1; hath spoke F   8 mountains] F; the huge mountaine Q1   8 on them] F; *not in* Q1   11 banning]
Q1; Foaming F   12 chidden] F; chiding Q1   13 mane] *Knight*; Maine F; mayne Q1   15 fixèd] F; fired Q1
19 they] Q1; to F   19 SD *third*] Q1; *not in* F   20 lads! Our] F; Lords, your Q1   21 Turks] F; Turke Q1
22–3] F; That…seen / …sufferance Q1   22 A noble] F; Another Q1   24 their] F; the Q1   25–6 The…Cassio]
Q1; *one line in* F

   7 ruffianed raged. Compare *2H4* 3.1.22:
'ruffian billows'.
   8 mountains mountainous seas.
   9 hold the mortise keep their joints intact.
   10 segregation dispersal.
   11–12 the banning…clouds The idea is that
the shore is cursing or forbidding the encroachment
of the mountainous waves which then, so rebuked,
fall back and rise up, seeming to strike the clouds.
F's 'foaming shore' and Q1's 'chiding billows' give
a rather different and less vivid picture; hence the
editorial decision to conflate the more dramatic
elements of Q1 and F.
   13 monstrous mane mane like a wild beast.
The pun is with 'main' (= sea).

   14 Bear The constellation Ursa Minor.
   15 guards The two stars in Ursa Minor, which
were second in brightness to the Pole Star and used
with it for navigation purposes, were known as the
Guardians. See *Mac.* 4.1.53–4 for a similar
metaphor of violent disruption, and for another
allusion to the uniquely constant position of the Pole
Star, *JC* 3.1.60–2.
   16 like molestation similar upheaval.
   17 enchafèd flood enraged sea.
   18 embayed protected in a bay.
   19 bear it out weather the storm.
   22 designment halts enterprise is crippled.
   23 sufferance damage.

A Veronesa; Michael Cassio,
Lieutenant to the warlike Moor Othello,
Is come on shore; the Moor himself at sea,
And is in full commission here for Cyprus.

MONTANO I am glad on't; 'tis a worthy governor.   30

3 GENTLEMAN But this same Cassio, though he speak of comfort
Touching the Turkish loss, yet he looks sadly
And prays the Moor be safe; for they were parted
With foul and violent tempest.

MONTANO   Pray heaven he be;
For I have served him, and the man commands   35
Like a full soldier. Let's to the seaside, ho!
As well to see the vessel that's come in
As to throw out our eyes for brave Othello,
Even till we make the main and th'aerial blue
An indistinct regard.

3 GENTLEMAN   Come, let's do so;   40
For every minute is expectancy
Of more arrivance.

Enter CASSIO.

CASSIO Thanks, you the valiant of this warlike isle
That so approve the Moor. O, let the heavens
Give him defence against the elements,   45
For I have lost him on a dangerous sea.

MONTANO Is he well shipped?

CASSIO His bark is stoutly timbered, and his pilot
Of very expert and approved allowance;
Therefore my hopes, not surfeited to death,   50
Stand in bold cure.
[*A shout*] *within, 'A sail, a sail, a sail!'*

28 on shore] F; ashore QI   30] QI; I...on't / ...governor F   33 prays] QI; praye F   34 heaven] QI; Heauens F   36] F; Like...soldier / ...ho QI   39–40 Even...regard] F; *not in* QI   42 arrivance] QI; Arriuancie F   43 you] F; to QI   43 this] QI; the F   43 warlike] F; worthy QI   44 O] F; and QI   45 the] F; their QI   51 SD.1] *Within. A Saile, a Saile, a Saile.* F; *Mess. A saile, a saile, a saile.* QI

26 **Veronesa** As this is 'a noble ship of Venice', it must presumably have been fitted out or built in Verona. It has been suggested that there may lie behind F's spelling 'Verennessa' some particular type of ship, perhaps a cutter whose name was derived from the Italian nautical term *verrinare* (= to cut through).

32 **sadly** gravely, seriously. Compare *Rom.* I.I.199: 'Tell me in sadness, who is that you love.'

36 **full** perfect, complete.

39–40 **the main...regard** the sea and sky become indistinguishable.

41 **is expectancy** gives expectation.

42 **arrivance** people arriving.

44 **approve** honour.

49 **approved allowance** tested reputation.

50–1 **not surfeited...cure** not being excessively optimistic are nevertheless confident.

Enter a MESSENGER.

CASSIO What noise?

MESSENGER The town is empty; on the brow o'the sea
 Stand ranks of people and they cry, 'A sail!'

CASSIO My hopes do shape him for the governor.   55
     A shot [is heard within].

2 GENTLEMAN They do discharge their shot of courtesy;
 Our friends at least.

CASSIO   I pray you, sir, go forth,
 And give us truth who 'tis that is arrived.

2 GENTLEMAN I shall.   *Exit*

MONTANO But, good lieutenant, is your general wived? 60

CASSIO Most fortunately: he hath achieved a maid
 That paragons description and wild fame;
 One that excels the quirks of blazoning pens
 And in th'essential vesture of creation
 Does tire the ingener.

Enter Second Gentleman.

       How now? Who's put in? 65

2 GENTLEMAN 'Tis one Iago, ancient to the general.

CASSIO He's had most favourable and happy speed:
 Tempests themselves, high seas, and howling winds,
 The guttered rocks and congregated sands,
 Traitors enscarped to clog the guiltless keel, 70

---

51 SD.2 *Enter a* MESSENGER] QI; *not in* F 53 SH MESSENGER] QI; *Gent.* F 55 governor] F; guernement QI
55 SD] *not in* F; *A shot.* QI *(after least at 57)* 56, 66, 94 SH 2 GENTLEMAN] 2 *Gent.* QI; *Gent.* F 56 their] F; the QI
57 friends] F; friend QI 59 SH 2 GENTLEMAN] 2 *Gen.* QI; *Gent.* F 63 quirks of] F; *not in* QI 65 tire the ingener]
Knight; tyre the Ingeniuer F; beare all excellency QI 65 How] F; *not in* QI 67 SH CASSIO] F; *assigned to / 2 Gent. /
in* QI 68 high] F; by QI 70 enscarped to clog] QI; ensteep'd, to enclogge F

53 **brow o' the sea** cliff-edge.

55 **My...for** I hope it is.

62 **paragons...fame** equals extravagant praise
and most unrestrained report.

63–5 Compare *Ant.* 5.2.97–100: 'Nature wants
stuff / To vie strange forms with fancy; yet
t'imagine / An Antony were nature's piece 'gainst
fancy, / Condemning shadows quite.'

63 **quirks** extravagant conceits. Compare *Ado*
2.3.236–7: 'some odd quirks and remnants of wit
broken on me'.

63 **blazoning** Originally a heraldic term, this
word had come to mean 'proclaiming the praises
of'.

64 **essential...creation** absolute beauty of the
human form.

65 **tire the ingener** outstrip the artist's imagination, transcend human imagination; with a pun on
'tire' (= clothe, attire). See supplementary note.

67 **speed** Celerity and fortune are both contained
in the word here.

69 **guttered** jagged with gullies, furrowed.

70 **enscarped** drawn up into ridges. F's 'ensteep-
ed' (= submerged) is accepted by most editors; but
the tenor of Cassio's lines is that the natural features
of the sea normally behave as active antagonists to
shipping.

As having sense of beauty do omit
Their mortal natures, letting go safely by
The divine Desdemona.
MONTANO   What is she?
CASSIO She that I spake of, our great captain's captain,
Left in the conduct of the bold Iago,   75
Whose footing here anticipates our thoughts
A se'nnight's speed. Great Jove Othello guard
And swell his sail with thine own powerful breath,
That he may bless this bay with his tall ship,
Make love's quick pants in Desdemona's arms,   80
Give renewed fire to our extincted spirits,
And bring all Cyprus comfort.

Enter DESDEMONA, IAGO, EMILIA *and* RODERIGO.

                              O, behold,
The riches of the ship is come on shore!
You men of Cyprus, let her have your knees.
Hail to thee, lady! And the grace of heaven,   85
Before, behind thee, and on every hand,
Enwheel thee round.
DESDEMONA   I thank you, valiant Cassio.
What tidings can you tell me of my lord?
CASSIO He is not yet arrived; nor know I aught
But that he's well, and will be shortly here.   90
DESDEMONA O, but I fear – how lost you company?
CASSIO The great contention of the sea and skies
Parted our fellowship.
[*A shout*] *within*, '*A sail, a sail!*' [*A shot is heard.*]
                              But hark, a sail!
2 GENTLEMAN They give their greeting to the citadel:
This likewise is a friend.

72 mortal] F; common QI   74] QI; She...of / ...captain F   74 spake] F; spoke QI   80 Make...in] F; And swiftly
come to QI   81] F; Giue...fire / ...spirits QI   82 And...comfort] QI; *not in* F   82 SD] QI (*after 80*); *Enter
Desdemona, Iago, Rodorigo, and Æmilia.* F (*after 80*)   83 on shore] F; ashore QI   84 You] F; Ye QI   88 me] QI;
not in F   91] QI; O...fear / ...company F   92 the] QI; *not in* F   93 SD *A shot is heard.*] Capell subst.; *not in* F,
QI   94 their] QI; this F

71–2 **omit...natures** forbear to exercise their
deadly natural propensities. There may also be an
opposition implied between mortal and divine.
    76 **footing** landing. Compare *John* 5.1.66:
'upon the footing of our land'.
    77 **se'nnight** week.
    79 **tall** gallant.

81 **extincted** extinguished, dulled; an allusion
to the theory of humours.
    87 **Enwheel** Encircle.
    93 **Parted our fellowship** Separated our ships.
    94 **give their greeting** i.e. by firing a salvo;
compare 56 above.

CASSIO   See for the news.   95
                                    [*Exit Second Gentleman*]
Good ancient, you are welcome. [*To Emilia*] Welcome,
    mistress.
Let it not gall your patience, good Iago,
That I extend my manners. 'Tis my breeding
That gives me this bold show of courtesy.
                    [*He kisses Emilia.*]
IAGO Sir, would she give you so much of her lips   100
    As of her tongue she oft bestows on me
    You would have enough.
DESDEMONA Alas, she has no speech.
IAGO   In faith, too much:
    I find it still when I have list to sleep.
    Marry, before your ladyship, I grant   105
    She puts her tongue a little in her heart
    And chides with thinking.
EMILIA   You've little cause to say so.
IAGO Come on, come on; you are pictures out of doors, bells in
    your parlours, wild-cats in your kitchens, saints in your injuries,
    devils being offended, players in your housewifery, and   110
    housewives in your beds.
DESDEMONA O fie upon thee, slanderer!
IAGO Nay, it is true, or else I am a Turk:
    You rise to play and go to bed to work.
EMILIA You shall not write my praise.
IAGO   No, let me not.   115
DESDEMONA What wouldst thou write of me, if thou shouldst
    praise me?

---

95 See...news] F; So speakes this voyce QI   95 SD] *Capell subst.; not in* F, QI   96 SD] *Rowe; not in* F, QI   99 SD]
Johnson subst.; not in F, QI   100 Sir] F; For QI   101 oft bestows] F; has bestowed QI   103 In faith] F; I know QI
104 still] F; I QI   104 when] F; for when QI   104 list] QI; leaue F   108 of doors] of doore F; adores QI   112
SH DESDEMONA] F; *not in* QI   116] F; What...me / ...me QI   116 thou write] QI; write F

97 **gall** irritate.
98–9 **extend...courtesy** stretch my greeting,
for it is my training in polished behaviour that
guides me to this gesture of welcome.
104 **still** always.
104 **list** a desire.
105 **before your ladyship** in your ladyship's
presence.
107 **chides with thinking** keeps her shrewish
inclinations in her thoughts.
108–11 **you are...beds** Proverbial: 'Women

are in church saints, abroad angels, at home devils'
(Tilley W702).
108 **pictures** silent appearances (of virtue).
108 **bells** i.e. noisy.
109 **wild-cats** spitfires.
109 **saints in your injuries** adopt a saintly air
when you are claiming to be injured.
110 **players** deceivers, triflers.
111 **housewives** i.e. economical with your
sexual favours; or perhaps 'hard workers'.
113 **Turk** i.e. infidel (and thus my word is not
worthy of belief).

IAGO O, gentle lady, do not put me to't,
    For I am nothing if not critical.

DESDEMONA Come on, assay. There's one gone to the harbour?

IAGO Ay, madam. 120

DESDEMONA [*Aside*] I am not merry, but I do beguile
    The thing I am by seeming otherwise –
    Come, how wouldst thou praise me?

IAGO I am about it, but indeed my invention
    Comes from my pate as birdlime does from frieze – 125
    It plucks out brains and all. But my muse labours,
    And thus she is delivered:
    'If she be fair and wise, fairness and wit,
    The one's for use, the other useth it.'

DESDEMONA Well praised! How if she be black and witty? 130

IAGO 'If she be black, and thereto have a wit,
    She'll find a white that shall her blackness fit.'

DESDEMONA Worse and worse.

EMILIA   How if fair and foolish?

IAGO 'She never yet was foolish that was fair,
    For even her folly helped her to an heir.' 135

DESDEMONA These are old fond paradoxes to make fools laugh
i'th'alehouse. What miserable praise hast thou for her that's foul
and foolish?

IAGO 'There's none so foul and foolish thereunto,
    But does foul pranks which fair and wise ones do.' 140

DESDEMONA O heavy ignorance! Thou praisest the worst best. But
what praise couldst thou bestow on a deserving woman indeed? One

---

119] Q1; Come...assay / ...harbour F   121 SD] *conj. Delius; not in* F, Q1   124–6] Q1; *as prose in* F   126 brains] F; braine Q1   129 useth] F; vsing Q1   130] Q1; Well praised / ...witty F   132 fit] F; hit Q1   135 an heir] F; a haire Q1   136–8] F; These...alehouse / ...her / ...foolish Q1   136 fond] F; *not in* Q1   141 Thou praisest] F; that praises Q1

119 **assay** try, tackle it.
121–2 **beguile...I am** divert attention from my state of anxiety. Compare *Tit.* 4.1.35: 'beguile thy sorrow'.
125 **birdlime** A sticky substance spread on bushes to catch small birds; compare *3H6* 5.6.13: 'The bird that hath been limed in a bush'.
125 **frieze** A coarse woollen cloth (from which birdlime would be difficult to remove).
126 **labours** A quibble: (1) works hard; (2) tries to give birth.
127 **is delivered** A quibble: (1) produces; (2) gives birth.

130 **black** dark-haired or brown-complexioned; and thus by Jacobean standards 'ugly'.
130 **witty** quick of apprehension.
132 **white** The pun is on (1) fair lover; (2) wight (= person).
132 **fit** suit. Like Q1's 'hit' this word contains a sexual innuendo.
135 **folly** The pun is on (1) foolishness; (2) unchastity. Compare 5.2.133: 'She turned to folly, and she was a whore.'
136 **old fond paradoxes** hackneyed and foolish sayings; as 'Fair and foolish, long and lazy, little and loud' (Tilley F28).
137 **foul** ugly, sluttish.
139 **thereunto** in addition.

that in the authority of her merit did justly put on the vouch of
very malice itself?

IAGO 'She that was ever fair, and never proud,   145
    Had tongue at will, and yet was never loud;
    Never lacked gold, and yet went never gay;
    Fled from her wish, and yet said "Now I may";
    She that being angered, her revenge being nigh,
    Bade her wrong stay, and her displeasure fly;   150
    She that in wisdom never was so frail
    To change the cod's head for the salmon's tail;
    She that could think and ne'er disclose her mind,
    See suitors following and not look behind;
    She was a wight, if ever such wight were –'   155

DESDEMONA To do what?

IAGO 'To suckle fools and chronicle small beer.'

DESDEMONA O, most lame and impotent conclusion! Do not learn of
him, Emilia, though he be thy husband. How say you, Cassio, is
he not a most profane and liberal counsellor?   160

CASSIO He speaks home, madam; you may relish him more in the
soldier than in the scholar.

IAGO [*Aside*] He takes her by the palm. Ay, well said; whisper.
With as little a web as this will I ensnare as great a fly as Cassio.
Ay, smile upon her, do. I will gyve thee in thine own courtship.   165
You say true, 'tis so indeed. If such tricks as these strip you out
of your lieutenantry, it had been better you had not kissed your
three fingers so oft, which now again you are most apt to play the

143 merit] F; merrits Q1   154] F; *not in* Q1   155 such wight] Q1; *such wightes* F   157–60] F; O…conclusion / …
husband / …liberal / …counsellor Q1   161–2] F; He…him / …scholar Q1   163 SD] *Rowe; not in* F, Q1
164 With] F; *not in* Q1   164 I] F; *not in* Q1   164 fly] F; Flee Q1   165 gyve…courtship] F; catch you in youre owne
courtesies Q1   167 kissed] F; rist Q1

143–4 **put on the vouch of very** commend the
testimony of even. Compare *H8* 1.1.157–8: 'To
th'King I'll say't, and make my vouch as
strong / As shore of rock.'

147 **gay** elaborately dressed.

152 **To change…tail** The exact meaning is
obscure. On the surface it apparently means 'to
exchange something worthless for something more
valuable'; but there is clearly sexual innuendo in
'cod's head' (= penis) and 'tail' (= pudendum).

152 **change** exchange, accept.

155 **wight** person.

157 **chronicle small beer** keep petty household
accounts, be concerned with trivialities.

160 **profane** worldly; ribald (*OED* sv *a* 3).

160 **liberal** licentious. Compare *Ham.* 4.7.170:
'That liberal shepherds give a grosser name'.

161 **home** directly and to the point (a term from
fencing). Compare *Ant.* 1.2.105: 'Speak to me
home, mince not the general tongue.'

161 **relish him more in** appreciate him
better in the character of.

163 **well said** well done. Compare *Tit.* 4.3.64:
'Now, masters, draw. [*They shoot.*] O, well said,
Lucius.'

165 **gyve…courtship** fetter, shackle yourself
in your own courtly manners.

167–8 **kissed…oft** A courtly gesture of a
gentleman to a lady; compare *LLL* 4.1.145–6: 'To
see him walk before a lady… / To see him kiss his
hand'.

sir in. Very good, well kissed, an excellent courtesy! 'Tis so
indeed. Yet again your fingers to your lips? Would they were   170
clyster-pipes for your sake!

> *Trumpets within.*

The Moor! I know his trumpet.

CASSIO   'Tis truly so.

DESDEMONA Let's meet him and receive him.

CASSIO   Lo, where he comes!

> *Enter* OTHELLO *and* ATTENDANTS.

OTHELLO O, my fair warrior!

DESDEMONA   My dear Othello!

OTHELLO It gives me wonder great as my content   175
    To see you here before me. O, my soul's joy,
    If after every tempest come such calms,
    May the winds blow till they have wakened death,
    And let the labouring bark climb hills of seas,
    Olympus-high, and duck again as low   180
    As hell's from heaven. If it were now to die,
    'Twere now to be most happy; for I fear
    My soul hath her content so absolute
    That not another comfort like to this
    Succeeds in unknown fate.

DESDEMONA   The heavens forbid   185
    But that our loves and comforts should increase,
    Even as our days do grow.·

OTHELLO   Amen to that, sweet powers!
    I cannot speak enough of this content;
    It stops me here; it is too much of joy.

> *They kiss.*

    And this, and this, the greatest discords be   190

---

169 Very] F; *not in* QI   169 an] QI; and F   170 to] F; at QI   171 SD] QI; *not in* F   173 SD] F; *follows 172* trumpet *in* QI   176] QI; To...me / ...joy F   177 calms] F; calmenesse QI   186] QI; But...loves / ...increase F   187 powers] F; power QI   189 SD] QI *(after 190)*; *not in* F   190 discords] F; discord QI

169 **sir** fine gentleman.

171 **clyster-pipes** medical syringes for enemas and vaginal douches.

172 **trumpet** trumpet-call. Each commander had his own recognisable signal; compare *MV* 5.1.122: 'Your husband is at hand, I hear his trumpet.'

175 **my content** the fulfilment of my desire.

177 Proverbial (Tilley s908).

185 **Succeeds** The present tense is used for the subjunctive.

189 **stops me here** i.e. prevents me in my heart.

That e'er our hearts shall make.

IAGO [*Aside*]   O, you are well tuned now!
But I'll set down the pegs that make this music,
As honest as I am.

OTHELLO   Come, let us to the castle.
News, friends; our wars are done; the Turks are drowned.
How does my old acquaintance of this isle?   195
Honey, you shall be well desired in Cyprus;
I have found great love amongst them. O my sweet,
I prattle out of fashion and I dote
In mine own comforts. I prithee, good Iago,
Go to the bay and disembark my coffers;   200
Bring thou the master to the citadel;
He is a good one, and his worthiness
Does challenge much respect. Come, Desdemona,
Once more well met at Cyprus!

           Exeunt [*all except Iago and Roderigo*]

IAGO [*To a departing Attendant*] Do thou meet me presently at the   205
harbour. [*To Roderigo*] Come hither. If thou be'st valiant – as
they say base men being in love have then a nobility in their
natures more than is native to them – list me. The lieutenant
tonight watches on the court of guard. First, I must tell thee this:
Desdemona is directly in love with him.   210

RODERIGO With him? Why, 'tis not possible!

IAGO Lay thy finger thus, and let thy soul be instructed. Mark me
with what violence she first loved the Moor but for bragging and
telling her fantastical lies. And will she love him still for prating?

---

191 SD] *Rowe; not in* F, Q1   191–3 O...am] Q1; *prose in* F   194] Q1; News...done / ...drowned F   195 does] F;
doe Q1   195 my] F; our Q1   195 this] F; the Q1   199 own] F; one Q1   204 SD] *Cam. subst.; Exit Othello and
Desdemona.* F; *Exit.* Q1   205 SD] *Delius subst.; not in* F, Q1   206 SD] *Capell; not in* F, Q1   206 hither] Q1; thither F
209 must] F; will Q1   214 And will she] Q1; To F

192 **set down the pegs** i.e. slacken the strings
(as of a stringed instrument).
193 **As honest as I am** For all my supposed
honesty.
196 **well desired** warmly welcomed (and sought
out as a guest).
198 **out of fashion** irrelevantly.
199 **comforts** happiness.
200 **coffers** boxes and trunks.
201 **master** captain (of the ship that brought
me).
203 **challenge** claim, deserve.

205 **presently** Normally this word means
'immediately', but here it appears to have its
modern sense.
206–8 **as they...them** Compare 'Love makes
the villain courteous' (proverbial).
207 **base** lowly born.
209 **court of guard** guard-house.
210 **directly** undoubtedly.
212 **thus** i.e. on his lips. The phrase is proverbial
for 'keep quiet' (Tilley F239).
213 **but** only.
214 **still** continually.

Let not thy discreet heart think it. Her eye must be fed. And   215
what delight shall she have to look on the devil? When the blood
is made dull with the act of sport, there should be, again to
inflame it and to give satiety a fresh appetite, loveliness in
favour, sympathy in years, manners and beauties: all which the
Moor is defective in. Now for want of these required conveniences,   220
her delicate tenderness will find itself abused, begin to heave the
gorge, disrelish and abhor the Moor. Very nature will instruct
her in it, and compel her to some second choice. Now, sir, this
granted – as it is a most pregnant and unforced position – who
stands so eminent in the degree of this fortune as Cassio does? – a   225
knave very voluble; no further conscionable than in putting on
the mere form of civil and humane seeming for the better
compassing of his salt and most hidden loose affection.
Why none; why none – a slipper and subtle knave, a finder
out of occasions, that has an eye can stamp and counterfeit   230
advantages, though true advantage never present itself; a
devilish knave! Besides, the knave is handsome, young, and hath
all those requisites in him that folly and green minds look after.
A pestilent complete knave; and the woman hath found him
already.   235

RODERIGO I cannot believe that in her; she's full of most blest
condition.

IAGO Blest fig's end! The wine she drinks is made of grapes. If she

---

215 thy] F; the QI   215 it] F; so QI   217 again] QI; a game F   218 to give] F; giue QI   218 satiety] F; saciety
QI   218 loveliness] F; Loue lines QI   221 in] F; to QI   225 eminent] F; eminently QI   227 humane] F; hand-
QI   228 compassing] QI; compasse F   228 most] F; *not in* QI   228 loose] F; *not in* QI   228 affection] F; affections
QI   229 Why…none] F; *not in* QI   229 slipper and subtle] F; subtle slippery QI   230 out] QI; *not in* F
230 occasions] QI; occasion F   230 has] QI; he's F   231 advantages] F; the true aduantages QI
231 though…advantage] F; *not in* QI   231 itself] F; themselues QI   231–2 a…knave] F; *not in* QI   234 hath] F;
has QI

---

216 devil See 1.1.92 n.

217 sport coitus. Compare *Lear* 1.1.22–3: 'yet
was his mother fair, there was good sport at his
making'.

219 favour appearance.

219 sympathy agreement, correspondence.

220 required conveniences requisite conditions of sexual desire. Compare *Tro.* 3.3.6–8:
'expos'd myself / From certain and possess'd
conveniences / To doubtful fortunes'.

221 tenderness…abused sensibility will find
itself disgusted.

221–2 heave the gorge vomit.

222 Very nature Natural reactions themselves.

224 pregnant cogent.

224 position hypothesis.

225 in the degree as next in line for.

226 voluble plausible, glib.

226 conscionable conscientious.

227 humane polite.

228 salt lecherous. Compare *Ant.* 2.1.21: 'Salt
Cleopatra'.

229 slipper slippery.

230 occasions opportunities.

230 stamp coin.

233 green unripe; hence 'immature'. Compare
Ant. 1.5.74: 'when I was green in judgment'.

234 found him seen sympathetically what he is
after.

236–7 blest condition heavenly disposition.

238 fig's end See 1.3.313 n.

had been blest she would never have loved the Moor. Blest
pudding! Didst thou not see her paddle with the palm of his   240
hand? Didst not mark that?

RODERIGO Yes, that I did; but that was but courtesy.

IAGO Lechery, by this hand: an index and obscure prologue to the
history of lust and foul thoughts. They met so near with their lips
that their breaths embraced together – villainous thoughts,   245
Roderigo! When these mutualities so marshal the way, hard
at hand comes the master and main exercise, the incorporate
conclusion. Pish! But, sir, be you ruled by me. I have brought
you from Venice; watch you tonight; for the command, I'll lay't
upon you. Cassio knows you not; I'll not be far from you. Do you   250
find some occasion to anger Cassio, either by speaking too loud or
tainting his discipline, or from what other course you please,
which the time shall more favourably minister.

RODERIGO Well.

IAGO Sir, he's rash and very sudden in choler, and haply with his   255
truncheon may strike at you: provoke him that he may; for even
out of that will I cause these of Cyprus to mutiny, whose
qualification shall come into no true taste again but by the
displanting of Cassio. So shall you have a shorter journey to your
desires by the means I shall then have to prefer them, and the   260
impediment most profitably removed without the which there
were no expectation of our prosperity.

RODERIGO I will do this, if you can bring it to any opportunity.

IAGO I warrant thee. Meet me by and by at the citadel. I must fetch
his necessaries ashore. Farewell.   265

RODERIGO Adieu.   *Exit*

239-40 Blest pudding] F; *not in* QI   240-1 Didst...that] F; *not in* QI   242 that I did] F; *not in* QI   243 obscure]
F; *not in* QI   245-6 villainous...Roderigo] F; *not in* QI   246 mutualities] QI; mutabilities F   246 hard] F; hand
QI   247 master and] F; *not in* QI   248 Pish] F; *not in* QI   249 the] F; your QI   252 course] F; cause QI
255-6 with his truncheon] QI; *not in* F   258 taste] F; trust QI   258 again] F; again 't QI   261 the] F; *not in* QI
263 you] F; I QI

240 **paddle with** stroke suggestively. Compare
WT 1.2.115: 'to be paddling palms and pinching
fingers'.

243 **index...to** indicator of; lit. 'table of
contents prefacing'. Compare *R3* 2.2.149: 'As
index to the story we late talk'd of'.

246 **mutualities** reciprocal intimacies.

247 **incorporate** carnal, bodily.

252 **tainting** disparaging, sneering at. Compare
H8 3.1.55: 'To taint that honor every good tongue
blesses'.

253 **minister** provide.

255 **haply** perhaps.

256 **truncheon** baton of office.

258 **qualification...again** i.e. appeasement
shall not be reattained (lit. 'allayment shall not make
it able to be swallowed').

260 **prefer** forward, promote.

264 **warrant** assure.

264 **by and by** immediately.

265 **his** i.e. Othello's.

IAGO That Cassio loves her, I do well believe't;
    That she loves him, 'tis apt and of great credit.
    The Moor, howbeit that I endure him not,
    Is of a constant, loving, noble nature;   270
    And I dare think he'll prove to Desdemona
    A most dear husband. Now, I do love her too,
    Not out of absolute lust – though peradventure
    I stand accountant for as great a sin –
    But partly led to diet my revenge,   275
    For that I do suspect the lusty Moor
    Hath leaped into my seat, the thought whereof
    Doth like a poisonous mineral gnaw my inwards;
    And nothing can or shall content my soul
    Till I am evened with him, wife for wife;   280
    Or failing so, yet that I put the Moor
    At least into a jealousy so strong
    That judgement cannot cure. Which thing to do,
    If this poor trash of Venice, whom I trace
    For his quick hunting, stand the putting on,   285
    I'll have our Michael Cassio on the hip,
    Abuse him to the Moor in the rank garb –
    For I fear Cassio with my night-cap too –
    Make the Moor thank me, love me, and reward me,
    For making him egregiously an ass,   290
    And practising upon his peace and quiet
    Even to madness. 'Tis here, but yet confused;
    Knavery's plain face is never seen till used.   *Exit*

270 loving, noble] F; noble, louing Q1   276 lusty] F; lustfull Q1   279 or] F; nor Q1   280 evened] F; euen Q1
284 trace] F; crush Q1; trash *Steevens²*; leash *conj. Bailey*   287 rank] Q1; right F   288 cap] Q1; Cape F

268 **apt…credit** likely and most believable.

272–4 **Now, I do…sin** In Cinthio's source story, 'the wicked Ensign…fell ardently in love with Disdemona' (Bullough, VII, 243–4).

274 **accountant** accountable.

275 **diet** feed.

277 **leaped…seat** For a similar sexual connotation in an equestrian metaphor, see Cleopatra's exclamation in *Ant.* 1.5.21: 'O happy horse, to bear the weight of Antony!'.

278 **mineral** drug.

284–5 **trace…hunting** follow after because of his lively sexual pursuit (of Desdemona). For a discussion of the many suggested emendations, see supplementary note.

285 **stand the putting on** persist in doing what I incite him to. Compare *Cor.* 2.3.251–2: 'Say you ne'er had done't…but by our putting on.'

286 **on the hip** at my mercy. Proverbial (Tilley H474).

287 **Abuse** Slander.

287 **rank garb** lascivious manner.

291 **practising upon** plotting against.

2.2 *Enter Othello's* HERALD *with a proclamation.*

HERALD It is Othello's pleasure, our noble and valiant general, that
upon certain tidings now arrived importing the mere perdition
of the Turkish fleet, every man put himself into triumph: some
to dance, some to make bonfires, each man to what sport and revels
his addiction leads him; for besides these beneficial news, it is   5
the celebration of his nuptial. So much was his pleasure should
be proclaimed. All offices are open, and there is full liberty of
feasting from this present hour of five till the bell have told
eleven. Heaven bless the isle of Cyprus and our noble general
Othello!   *Exit* 10

[**2.3**] *Enter* OTHELLO, DESDEMONA, CASSIO *and* ATTENDANTS.

OTHELLO Good Michael, look you to the guard tonight.
       Let's teach ourselves that honourable stop,
       Not to out-sport discretion.
CASSIO Iago hath direction what to do;
       But notwithstanding with my personal eye   5
       Will I look to't.
OTHELLO   Iago is most honest.
       Michael, good night; tomorrow with your earliest
       Let me have speech with you – Come, my dear love,
       The purchase made, the fruits are to ensue;

Act 2, Scene 2 2.2] *Scena Secunda.* F; *not in* QI   0 SD *Othello's* HERALD *with*] F; *a Gentleman reading* QI   I SH
HERALD] F; *not in* QI   3 every] F; *that euery* QI   4 to make] F; *make* QI   5 addiction] Q2; *addition* F; *minde* QI
6 nuptial] F; *Nuptialls* QI   7–8 of feasting] F; *not in* QI   8 have] F; *hath* QI   9 Heaven] QI; *not in* F   10 SD] F;
not in QI   Act 2, Scene 3 2.3] *not in* F, QI   0 SD DESDEMONA...ATTENDANTS] F; *Cassio and* Desdemona QI
2 that] F; *the* QI   4 direction] F; *directed* QI

Act 2, Scene 2
2 **upon certain** because of reliable.
2 **mere perdition** total loss. Compare *Tro.*
1.3.110–11: 'what discord follows. Each thing
meets / In mere oppugnancy'; and *H5* 3.6.98–9:
'The perdition of th'athversary hath been very
great.'
3 **triumph** public festivity.
5 **addiction** inclination. Compare *H5* 1.1.54:
'Since his addiction was to courses vain'. QI's
'mind' is possible, but seems a rather plain word
for the inflated style of the proclamation.

7 **offices** e.g. kitchens, cellars, butteries (for the
distribution of food and drink). Compare *Mac.*
2.1.13: 'Sent forth great largess to your offices'.
8 **told** struck, counted.

Act 2, Scene 3
2 **stop** restraint.
3 **out-sport discretion** celebrate to excess.
7 **with your earliest** at your earliest
convenience.
9–10 **The purchase...you** i.e. our marriage
has yet to be consummated.

That profit's yet to come 'tween me and you.   10
Good night.

Exeunt Othello, Desdemona [and Attendants]

Enter IAGO.

CASSIO Welcome, Iago; we must to the watch.

IAGO Not this hour, lieutenant; 'tis not yet ten o'th'clock. Our general cast us thus early for the love of his Desdemona; who let us not therefore blame: he hath not yet made wanton the night with   15 her, and she is sport for Jove.

CASSIO She's a most exquisite lady.

IAGO And I'll warrant her full of game.

CASSIO Indeed she is a most fresh and delicate creature.

IAGO What an eye she has! Methinks it sounds a parley to   20 provocation.

CASSIO An inviting eye, and yet methinks right modest.

IAGO And when she speaks, is it not an alarum to love?

CASSIO She is indeed perfection.

IAGO Well, happiness to their sheets! Come, lieutenant, I have a stoup   25 of wine, and here without are a brace of Cyprus gallants, that would fain have a measure to the health of the black Othello.

CASSIO Not tonight, good Iago; I have very poor and unhappy brains for drinking. I could well wish courtesy would invent some other custom of entertainment.   30

IAGO O, they are our friends – but one cup; I'll drink for you.

CASSIO I have drunk but one cup tonight, and that was craftily qualified too; and behold what innovation it makes here. I am unfortunate in the infirmity and dare not task my weakness with any more.   35

---

10 That] F; The Q1   10 'tween] F; twixt Q1   11 SD] *Exit* Othello and Desdemona. Q1; *Exit.* F   13 o'th'] F; a Q1
20 to] F; of Q1   22] Q1; An...eye / ...modest F   23] Q1; And...speaks / ...love F   23 is it not] F; tis Q1
23 alarum] F; alarme Q1   24 She] F; It Q1   27 of the] Q1; of F   34 unfortunate] Q1; infortunate F

13 **Not this hour** Not for an hour yet.
14 **cast** dismissed.
16 **sport** See 2.1.217 n.
18 **full of game** sexually active. Compare *Per.* 4.6.74–5: 'Were you a gamester at five, or at seven?'
20–1 **sounds a parley to provocation** Lit. 'summons sexual desire to a meeting'.
23 **alarum** call to arms. Compare *2H6* 2.3.92: 'Sound, trumpets, alarum to the combatants.'

25 **stoup** A tankard of two quarts.
27 **fain have a measure** gladly drink a toast.
28 **unhappy** i.e. productive of an unfortunate outcome.
31 **for you** in your place.
33 **qualified** diluted.
33 **innovation** disturbance. Compare *1H4* 5.1.78: 'hurly-burly innovation'.
33 **here** i.e. in my head.

IAGO What, man! 'Tis a night of revels; the gallants desire it.

CASSIO Where are they?

IAGO Here at the door; I pray you call them in.

CASSIO I'll do't, but it dislikes me.   *Exit*

IAGO If I can fasten but one cup upon him,   40
  With that which he hath drunk tonight already,
  He'll be as full of quarrel and offence
  As my young mistress' dog. Now my sick fool Roderigo,
  Whom love hath turned almost the wrong side out,
  To Desdemona hath tonight caroused   45
  Potations pottle-deep, and he's to watch.
  Three lads of Cyprus, noble swelling spirits,
  That hold their honours in a wary distance,
  The very elements of this warlike isle,
  Have I tonight flustered with flowing cups;   50
  And they watch too. Now, 'mongst this flock of
   drunkards,
  Am I to put our Cassio in some action
  That may offend the isle. But here they come.

   Enter Cassio, MONTANO *and* GENTLEMEN.

  If consequence do but approve my dream,
  My boat sails freely, both with wind and stream.   55

CASSIO 'Fore God, they have given me a rouse already.

MONTANO Good faith, a little one; not past a pint, as I am a soldier.

IAGO Some wine, ho!

43] QI; As...dog / ...Roderigo F 44 hath] F; has QI 44 out] F; outward QI 47 lads] QI; else F 48 honours]
F; honour QI 51] QI; And...too / ...drunkards F 51 they] F; the QI 52 Am I to put] Am I put to F; I am
to put QI 53] F; That...isle / ...come QI 53 SD] F; *Enter* Montano, Cassio, *and others.* QI 56 God] QI; heauen F
57] F; Good...pint / ...soldier QI

39 **dislikes** displeases.

42 **offence** readiness to take umbrage.

43 **my young mistress' dog** i.e. a spoilt pet (proverbial).

43 **sick** love-sick.

46 **pottle-deep** to the bottom of the tankard.

47 **lads** F's 'else' has been defended as meaning 'others'; but the supporting passages in *Ham.* 1.4.33 and *John* 2.1.276 are not convincing. Some editors have suggested the error in F was due to a misreading of 'Ls' or 'Lds', common manuscript abbreviations for 'lords'; but QI's 'lads' precludes the necessity for further textual speculation.

47 **swelling** arrogant.

48 **hold...distance** are quick to take offence at anything resembling an insult to their honour.

49 **very elements** characteristic types.

50 **flustered** excited, befuddled.

51 **watch** are awake.

52 **put** incite.

54 **consequence** what happens, future events. Compare *Rom.* 1.4.107: 'Some consequence yet hanging in the stars'.

54 **approve** substantiate. Compare *MV* 3.2.79: 'approve it with a text'.

56 **rouse** large bumper of drink.

[*Sings*]
And let me the cannikin clink, clink,
And let me the cannikin clink;   60
    A soldier's a man,
    O, man's life's but a span,
Why then, let a soldier drink.
  Some wine, boys!

CASSIO 'Fore God, an excellent song.   65

IAGO I learned it in England, where indeed they are most potent in
potting. Your Dane, your German, and your swag-bellied
Hollander – drink, ho! – are nothing to your English.

CASSIO Is your Englishman so exquisite in his drinking?

IAGO Why, he drinks you with facility your Dane dead drunk; he sweats   70
not to overthrow your Almain; he gives your Hollander a vomit
ere the next pottle can be filled.

CASSIO To the health of our general!

MONTANO I am for it, lieutenant, and I'll do you justice.

IAGO O sweet England!   75

  [*Sings*]
King Stephen was and a worthy peer,
    His breeches cost him but a crown;
He held them sixpence all too dear,
    With that he called the tailor lown.

He was a wight of high renown,   80
    And thou art but of low degree;
'Tis pride that pulls the country down;
    Then take thine auld cloak about thee.
  Some wine, ho!

59, 76 SD] *Rowe; not in* F, QI   60 clink] F; clinke, clinke QI   61–2] *Capell; one line in* F, QI   62 O, man's] F; a QI   63] F; *one line in* QI   65 God] QI; Heauen F   69 Englishman] QI; Englishmen F   69 exquisite] F; expert QI   75–6] F; *one line in* QI   76 and] F; *not in* QI   83 Then] QI; *And* F   83 thine] QI; *thy* F   83 auld] Q2; *awl'd* F; *owd* QI

59–63 See supplementary note.
59 cannikin small drinking-can.
62 man's life's but a span An allusion to the version of Ps. 39.6 in the Book of Common Prayer: 'thou hast made my days as it were a span long'; compare Tilley L251. 'Span' = short time.
66–7 potent in potting heavy drinkers. On the continent the English had a reputation for being drunkards from the early sixteenth century; but some Elizabethan social commentators tended to date the nation's alcoholic addiction from the bad habits brought back by soldiers returning from the wars in the Netherlands.

67 swag-bellied pendulously paunched.
69 exquisite accomplished.
71 Almain German.
74 do you justice match your pledge.
76–83 See supplementary note.
76 and Introduced as an extra syllable for metrical reasons, as in 'When that I was and a little tine boy' (*TN* 5.1.389).
79 lown rascal, rogue.
82 pride ostentation, extravagance.

CASSIO 'Fore God, this is a more exquisite song than the other.   85
IAGO Will you hear't again?
CASSIO No, for I hold him to be unworthy of his place that does those
    things. Well, God's above all, and there be souls must be
    saved, and there be souls must not be saved.
IAGO It's true, good lieutenant.   90
CASSIO For mine own part – no offence to the general, nor any man of
    quality – I hope to be saved.
IAGO And so do I too, lieutenant.
CASSIO Ay, but by your leave, not before me; the lieutenant is to be
    saved before the ancient. Let's have no more of this; let's to our   95
    affairs. God forgive us our sins! Gentlemen, let's look to our
    business. Do not think, gentlemen, I am drunk; this is my ancient,
    this is my right hand, and this is my left hand. I am not drunk
    now, I can stand well enough, and I speak well enough.
ALL Excellent well.   100
CASSIO Why, very well then; you must not think then that I am
    drunk.   *Exit*
MONTANO To the platform, masters. Come, let's set the watch.
IAGO You see this fellow that is gone before,
                He is a soldier fit to stand by Caesar   105
            And give direction. And do but see his vice –
            'Tis to his virtue a just equinox,
            The one as long as th'other. 'Tis pity of him.
            I fear the trust Othello puts him in,
            On some odd time of his infirmity,   110
            Will shake this island.
MONTANO   But is he often thus?
IAGO 'Tis evermore the prologue to his sleep:
            He'll watch the horologe a double set,
            If drink rock not his cradle.
MONTANO   It were well

---

85 'Fore God] QI; Why F   87 to be] F; *not in* QI   88 God's] QI; heau'ns F   88 must] F; that must QI   89 and
there...saved] F; *not in* QI   93 too] F; *not in* QI   96 God] QI; *not in* F   98 hand] QI; *not in* F   99 I] F; *not in*
QI   100 SH ALL] QI; *Gent.* F   101 Why] F; *not in* QI   101 think then] F; thinke QI   109 puts] F; put QI
112 the] QI; his F   114–15 It...it] F; *one line in* QI

88 **God's above all** Proverbial phrase (Tilley   107 **just equinox** exact equivalent; i.e. the
H348).   darkness of his vice counterbalances exactly the
    92 **quality** rank.   light of his virtue.
    103 **platform** gun ramparts.   110 **odd time** chance moment.
    103 **set the watch** mount the guard.   113 **watch...set** stay awake for two revolutions
    105 **stand by** 'be lieutenant to', or perhaps 'be of the clock.
the equal of'.

The general were put in mind of it.   115
Perhaps he sees it not, or his good nature
Prizes the virtue that appears in Cassio
And looks not on his evils: is not this true?

Enter RODERIGO.

IAGO [*Aside to Roderigo*] How now, Roderigo?
 I pray you after the lieutenant, go.   120

          Exit Roderigo

MONTANO And 'tis great pity that the noble Moor
 Should hazard such a place as his own second
 With one of an ingraft infirmity;
 It were an honest action to say so
 To the Moor.

IAGO   Not I, for this fair island: 125
 I do love Cassio well, and would do much
 To cure him of this evil.
    [*A cry of*] '*Help, help!*' *within*.
      But hark! what noise?

Enter Cassio, pursuing Roderigo.

CASSIO Zounds, you rogue, you rascal!
MONTANO What's the matter, lieutenant?
CASSIO A knave teach me my duty! I'll beat the knave into a   130
 twiggen bottle.
RODERIGO Beat me?
CASSIO Dost thou prate, rogue?
    [*He strikes Roderigo.*]
MONTANO Nay, good lieutenant, I pray you, sir, hold your hand.
CASSIO Let me go, sir; or I'll knock you o'er the mazzard.   135
MONTANO Come, come, you're drunk.

117 Prizes] F; Praises Q1   117 virtue] F; vertues Q1   118 looks] F; looke Q1   119 SD] *Capell; not in* F, Q1
120 SD] Q1; *not in* F   124–5 It...Moor] F; *one line in* Q1   125 Not] F; Nor Q1   127 SD.1] *Helpe, helpe, within* Q1;
not in F   127 SD.2 *pursuing*] F; *driuing in* Q1   128 Zounds] Q1; *not in* F   130 I'll] F; but I'le Q1   131 twiggen] F;
wicker Q1   133 SD] *Capell subst.; not in* F, Q1   134] Q1; Nay...lieutenant / ...hand F   134 Nay] F; *not in* Q1
134 I pray you] F; pray Q1   135] Q1; Let...sir / ...mazzard F

122–3 hazard...With risk giving the position
of lieutenant to.
 123 ingraft deep-rooted. Compare *Lear*
1.1.297: 'the imperfections of long-ingraff'd
condition'.
 131 twiggen covered with wicker-work. Cassio
may mean he will so pattern Roderigo's hide with
his sword, or that he will chase him through the
holes in the wicker-work.
 135 mazzard head, skull. Compare *Ham.*
5.1.89–90: 'knock'd about the mazzard with a
sexton's spade'.

CASSIO Drunk?

They fight.

IAGO [*Aside to Roderigo*] Away I say, go out and cry a mutiny.

[*Exit Roderigo*]

    Nay, good lieutenant; God's will, gentlemen!
    Help ho! Lieutenant, sir! Montano, sir!   140
    Help, masters, here's a goodly watch indeed!

A bell rings.

    Who's that which rings the bell? Diabolo, ho!
    The town will rise. God's will, lieutenant, hold!
    You will be shamed forever.

Enter Othello, and GENTLEMEN *with weapons.*

OTHELLO What is the matter here?

MONTANO   Zounds, I bleed still.   145
    I am hurt to th'death.

OTHELLO   Hold for your lives!

IAGO Hold ho, lieutenant, sir; Montano, gentlemen,
    Have you forgot all place of sense and duty?
    Hold! the general speaks to you; hold, for shame!

OTHELLO Why, how now, ho! From whence ariseth this?   150
    Are we turned Turks, and to ourselves do that
    Which heaven hath forbid the Ottomites?
    For Christian shame, put by this barbarous brawl.

---

137 SD] Q1; *not in* F   138 SD.1 *Aside to Roderigo*] Capell; *not in* F, Q1   138 SD.2 *Exit Roderigo*] Q2; *not in* F, Q1
139 God's will] Q1; *Alas* F   140 Montano, sir] Q1; *Montano* F   141 SD] *A bell rung:* Q1 *(after 138); not in* F
142 which] F; *that* Q1   143 God's...hold!] Q1; *Fie, fie Lieutenant,* F   144 You will be shamed] Q1; *You'le be asham'd* F
144 SD GENTLEMEN *with weapons*] Q1; *Attendants* F   145-6 Zounds...death] *one line in* Q1; I bleed still, I am
hurt to th' death. He dies. F   145 Zounds] Q1; *not in* F   147 ho] F; *hold* Q1   148 place of sense] F, Q1; *sense of
place* Hanmer   149 hold] F; *hold, hold* Q1   150 ariseth] F; *arises* Q1   152 hath] F; *has* Q1

138 **mutiny** riot. Compare *Rom.* 1.5.80: 'You'll make a mutiny among my guests.'
142 **bell** warning-bell.
142 **Diabolo** Devil (Spanish).
143 **rise** grow riotous.
146 After 'death' F adds 'He dies' which is, if taken as a misplaced stage direction, obviously an error, since Montano speaks again at 178–88 and 199–201. It has been suggested that the words may be a desperate threat against Cassio as Montano attempts to lunge at him, or possibly an interjection of horror by Iago or another bystander with the speech heading having been dropped by F's compositor. Q2 attempts to correct F by substituting 'He faints', which some editors adopt.

148 **place** of dignity derived from. Hanmer's emendation 'sense of place and duty' is attractive as it recognises a type of inversion error common in the dramatic texts of the period, though not adopted here because the text makes sense as it stands.
151 **turned Turks** Proverbial (Tilley T609), but especially apt here.
151–2 **to ourselves...Ottomites** i.e. slaughter our own soldiers, which God has prevented the Turks from doing (by sending the storm that destroyed their fleet).
152 **forbid** prevented. Compare *Tro.* 1.3.302: 'Now heavens forbid such scarcity of youth' (F text).

He that stirs next to carve for his own rage
Holds his soul light: he dies upon his motion.   155
Silence that dreadful bell: it frights the isle
From her propriety. What is the matter, masters?
Honest Iago, that looks dead with grieving,
Speak. Who began this? On thy love, I charge thee.

IAGO I do not know. Friends all but now, even now,   160
In quarter and in terms like bride and groom,
Divesting them for bed; and then but now –
As if some planet had unwitted men –
Swords out and tilting one at other's breasts
In opposition bloody. I cannot speak   165
Any beginning to this peevish odds:
And would in action glorious I had lost
Those legs that brought me to a part of it.

OTHELLO How comes it, Michael, you are thus forgot?

CASSIO I pray you pardon me, I cannot speak.   170

OTHELLO Worthy Montano, you were wont be civil:
The gravity and stillness of your youth
The world hath noted; and your name is great
In mouths of wisest censure. What's the matter
That you unlace your reputation thus,   175
And spend your rich opinion for the name
Of a night-brawler? Give me answer to it.

MONTANO Worthy Othello, I am hurt to danger;
Your officer Iago can inform you –
While I spare speech, which something now offends me –   180
Of all that I do know; nor know I aught

154 for] F; forth QI   162 for] F; to QI   164 breasts] F; breast QI   168 Those] F; These QI   169 comes...are]
F; came...were QI   171 be] QI; to be F   174 mouths] F; men QI

154 **carve for his own rage** strike with his
sword as his fury prompts him.
155 **Holds his soul light** Values his life at little
worth.
157 **From her propriety** Out of its natural state
(of peace). Compare *TN* 5.1.146–7: 'it is the
baseness of thy fear / That makes thee strangle thy
propriety'.
161 **quarter** conduct.
161 **in terms** standing in relation to each other.
Compare *Lear* 1.2.156: 'Parted you in good terms?'
162 **Divesting** Undressing.
163 **As if...men** It was believed in astrology
that errant planets drawing too close to the
earth could 'unwit' or turn men mad. Compare

Tilley P389: 'To be planet-struck'; and see
5.2.110–12.
165 **speak** explain.
166 **peevish odds** senseless quarrel.
168 **to** i.e. to be.
172 **stillness** sober behaviour, staidness.
174 **censure** judgement. Compare *Ham.* 1.3.69:
'Take each man's censure, but reserve thy
judgment.'
175–6 **That you...opinion** The image here
appears to be of Montano 'undoing the strings of
his purse of reputation and squandering the high
opinion people have of him'.
180 **something...offends** somewhat now
hurts.

By me that's said or done amiss this night,
Unless self-charity be sometimes a vice,
And to defend ourselves it be a sin
When violence assails us.

OTHELLO   Now by heaven   185
My blood begins my safer guides to rule,
And passion having my best judgement collied,
Assays to lead the way. Zounds, if I stir,
Or do but lift this arm, the best of you
Shall sink in my rebuke. Give me to know   190
How this foul rout began, who set it on,
And he that is approved in this offence,
Though he had twinned with me, both at a birth,
Shall lose me. What, in a town of war,
Yet wild, the people's hearts brimful of fear,   195
To manage private and domestic quarrel,
In night, and on the court and guard of safety?
'Tis monstrous. Iago, who began't?

MONTANO If partially affined or leagued in office,
Thou dost deliver more or less than truth,   200
Thou art no soldier.

IAGO   Touch me not so near.
I had rather have this tongue cut from my mouth
Than it should do offence to Michael Cassio.
Yet, I persuade myself, to speak the truth
Shall nothing wrong him. This it is, general: 205
Montano and myself being in speech,
There comes a fellow crying out for help,
And Cassio following him with determined sword

---

183 sometimes] F; sometime QI   187 collied] F; coold QI   188 Zounds, if I] QI; If I once F   196 quarrel] F; quarrels QI   197 court...safety] F, QI; court of guard and safety *Theobald*   198 began 't] F; began QI   199 partially] F; partiality QI   199 leagued] *Pope*; league F, QI   202 cut] F; out QI   205 This] F; Thus QI

186 **blood** anger.

187 **collied** darkened, blackened. Compare *MND* 1.1.145: 'Brief as the lightning in the collied night'.

191 **rout** brawl, uproar.

192 **approved** in found guilty of. Compare *Ado* 4.1.301–3: 'Is 'a not approv'd in the height a villain, that hath slander'd, scorn'd, dishonor'd my kinswoman?'

194 **town of** town garrisoned for. Compare *H5* 2.4.7–8: 'To line and new repair our towns of war / With men of courage'.

196 **manage** carry on, conduct; as in *Rom.* 3.1.143: 'the unlucky manage of this fatal brawl'.

197 **on the court...safety** at the headquarters of the guard and on sentry duty. Theobald's emendation 'on the court of guard and safety' is attractive and has been adopted by many editors; but the text makes good sense.

199 Neither F nor QI is clear. By accepting Pope's emendation of 'leagued' for F's and QI's 'league', the meaning appears to be: 'If because you are bound by partiality or are confederate as soldiers in the same unit'.

To execute upon him. Sir, this gentleman
Steps in to Cassio and entreats his pause;   210
Myself the crying fellow did pursue,
Lest by his clamour – as it so fell out –
The town might fall in fright. He, swift of foot,
Outran my purpose and I returned the rather
For that I heard the clink and fall of swords   215
And Cassio high in oath, which till tonight
I ne'er might say before. When I came back –
For this was brief – I found them close together
At blow and thrust, even as again they were
When you yourself did part them.   220
More of this matter can I not report;
But men are men; the best sometimes forget.
Though Cassio did some little wrong to him,
As men in rage strike those that wish them best,
Yet surely Cassio, I believe, received   225
From him that fled some strange indignity
Which patience could not pass.

OTHELLO   I know, Iago,
Thy honesty and love doth mince this matter,
Making it light to Cassio. Cassio, I love thee,
But never more be officer of mine.   230

Enter Desdemona attended.

Look if my gentle love be not raised up!
I'll make thee an example.

DESDEMONA   What's the matter, dear?
OTHELLO All's well now, sweeting; come away to bed.
Sir, for your hurts myself will be your surgeon.

[Montano is led off]

214 the] Q1; then F   216 oath] F; oaths Q1   217 say] F; see Q1   221 can I not] Q1; cannot I F   230 SD *attended*] F; *with others* Q1   232 dear] F; *not in* Q1   233 now] Q1; *not in* F   233–4] *Pope*; All's...sweeting / ...hurts / ... surgeon F, Q1   234 SD] *conj. Malone; Lead him off* F, Q1 (*as part of Othello's speech*)

209 **this gentleman** i.e. Montano.
210 **his pause** him to stop.
214 **the rather** all the sooner.
222 **forget** i.e. themselves.
223 **him** i.e. Montano.
227 **patience could not pass** self-control could not overlook.
228 **mince this matter** Proverbial (Tilley M755).

234 **be your surgeon** pay for your medical treatment.
234 SD Both F and Q1 have 'Lead him off' as a part of Othello's speech. Malone was right in seeing this as a stage direction which had crept into the text. As White notes 'off' (= off stage) is a theatrical term and not a word that could be used with any verisimilitude by a character who is supposedly standing on the ramparts of a city.

Iago, look with care about the town,   235
And silence those whom this vile brawl distracted.
Come, Desdemona, 'tis the soldier's life
To have their balmy slumbers waked with strife.

                        Exeunt [all but Iago and Cassio]

IAGO What, are you hurt, lieutenant?

CASSIO Ay, past all surgery.   240

IAGO Marry, God forbid!

CASSIO Reputation, reputation, reputation! O, I have lost my
reputation! I have lost the immortal part of myself, and what
remains is bestial. My reputation, Iago, my reputation!

IAGO As I am an honest man, I thought you had received some bodily   245
wound: there is more of sense in that than in reputation.
Reputation is an idle and most false imposition, oft got without
merit and lost without deserving. You have lost no reputation at
all, unless you repute yourself such a loser. What, man! There
are ways to recover the general again. You are but now cast   250
in his mood, a punishment more in policy than in malice, even
so as one would beat his offenceless dog to affright an imperious
lion. Sue to him again, and he's yours.

CASSIO I will rather sue to be despised than to deceive so good a
commander with so light, so drunken, and so indiscreet an   255
officer. Drunk! And speak parrot! And squabble! Swagger!
Swear! And discourse fustian with one's own shadow! O thou

---

238 SD] *Cam. subst.; Exit* F; *Exit Moore,* Desdemona, *and attendants.* QI *(after 239)*   241 God] QI; Heauen F
242–4] F; Reputation...reputation / ...self / ...reputation / ...reputation QI   242 reputation,] F; *not in* QI
242 O] F; *not in* QI   243 part of] F; part sir of QI   245 I thought] QI; I had thought F   246 of sense] *conj. Cam.;*
sence F; offence QI   250 ways] QI; more wayes F   255 light] QI; slight F   255 so indiscreet] F; indiscreete QI
256–7 Drunk...shadow] F; *not in* QI

---

246 **of sense** of physical feeling, of sensibility.
QI's 'offence' (= hurt) makes for a banal sentence;
and F's 'sense' (= reason or physical feeling) is vague.
Iago's standard for judging all human ideals is the
purely physical, and here he is contrasting the
reality of physical pain with the imagined existence
of the abstraction 'reputation', in much the same
way as he has earlier reduced 'love' to a 'carnal
sting' (1.3.313–24). I take QI's reading to be a
mis-setting of the manuscript's 'of fence'.

247–9 **Reputation...loser** Contrast Iago's
voicing exactly the opposite view at 3.3.156–62.

247 **imposition** that which is laid on a person
by other people.

248–9 **You have...loser** Compare 'A man is
weal or woe as he thinks himself so' (Tilley M254).

250 **recover** win back (to your side).

250–1 **cast in his mood** dismissed in a
temporary state of anger.

251 **in policy** i.e. to demonstrate publicly his
control of affairs.

252–3 **would beat...lion** i.e. would punish an
innocent unimportant man in order to deter a
powerful and dangerous one. Compare Tilley D443:
'Beat the dog before the lion.'

255 **light** irresponsible. F's 'slight' implies
'worthless', which is not the quality Cassio is
stressing here.

256 **parrot** nonsense.

257 **fustian** bombastic nonsense; such as the
'fustian rascal' Pistol speaks in *2H4* 2.4.110–200.

invisible spirit of wine, if thou hast no name to be known by, let
us call thee devil!

IAGO What was he that you followed with your sword? What had he   260
done to you?

CASSIO I know not.

IAGO Is't possible?

CASSIO I remember a mass of things, but nothing distinctly: a quarrel,
but nothing wherefore. O God, that men should put an enemy   265
in their mouths to steal away their brains! That we should with joy,
pleasance, revel and applause transform ourselves into beasts!

IAGO Why, but you are now well enough. How came you thus
recovered?

CASSIO It hath pleased the devil drunkenness to give place to the devil   270
wrath; one unperfectness shows me another, to make me frankly
despise myself.

IAGO Come, you are too severe a moraler. As the time, the place, and
the condition of this country stands, I could heartily wish this had
not befallen; but since it is as it is, mend it for your own good.   275

CASSIO I will ask him for my place again; he shall tell me I am a
drunkard. Had I as many mouths as Hydra, such an answer would
stop them all. To be now a sensible man, by and by a fool, and
presently a beast! O strange! Every inordinate cup is unblessed,
and the ingredience is a devil.   280

IAGO Come, come, good wine is a good familiar creature, if it be well
used; exclaim no more against it. And, good lieutenant, I think you
think I love you.

CASSIO I have well approved it, sir. I drunk!

IAGO You or any man living may be drunk at a time, man. I'll   285
tell you what you shall do. Our general's wife is now the general.
I may say so in this respect, for that he hath devoted and given
up himself to the contemplation, mark, and denotement of her

---

265 God] Q1; *not in* F   267 pleasance, revel] F; Reuell, pleasure Q1   272 and] F; *not in* Q1   275 not] F; not so Q1
279 O strange] F; *not in* Q1   279 inordinate] F; vnordinate Q1   280 ingredience] Q1; Ingredient F   285 a] F; some
Q1   285 man] F; *not in* Q1   285 I'll] Q1; I F   287 hath] F; has Q1   288 denotement] Q2; deuotement F, Q1

---

267 **applause** 'desire for approval', or perhaps
'celebration of some event'.

273 **moraler** moraliser.

277 **Hydra** The multi-headed serpent in Greek
mythology which was killed by Hercules. Whenever
one of its heads was cut off, two more grew in its
place. Compare Tilley H278.

280 **ingredience** contents.

281 **familiar** friendly; with perhaps a quibble
on 'familiar' (= a witch's personal devil).

285 **at a time** sometime.

287 **in...that** in the light of the fact that.

288 **denotement** F's and Q1's 'deuotement'
(= adoration) is possible, although it is used nowhere
else in Shakespeare's works. However, it seems out
of keeping with 'contemplation' and 'mark'. I take
the error to be the result of either the compositors'
misreading minims in the manuscript or a
turned-letter mistake.

parts and graces. Confess yourself freely to her, importune her
help to put you in your place again. She is of so free, so kind,   290
so apt, so blest a disposition, that she holds it a vice in her
goodness not to do more than she is requested. This broken
joint between you and her husband entreat her to splinter; and
my fortunes against any lay worth naming, this crack of your love
shall grow stronger than it was before.   295

CASSIO You advise me well.

IAGO I protest, in the sincerity of love and honest kindness.

CASSIO I think it freely; and betimes in the morning I will beseech
the virtuous Desdemona to undertake for me. I am desperate of
my fortunes if they check me here.   300

IAGO You are in the right. Good night, lieutenant, I must to the watch.

CASSIO Good night, honest Iago.   *Exit*

IAGO And what's he then that says I play the villain,
    When this advice is free I give, and honest,
    Probal to thinking, and indeed the course   305
    To win the Moor again? For 'tis most easy
    Th'inclining Desdemona to subdue
    In any honest suit. She's framed as fruitful
    As the free elements; and then for her
    To win the Moor, were't to renounce his baptism,   310
    All seals and symbols of redeemèd sin,
    His soul is so enfettered to her love,
    That she may make, unmake, do what she list,
    Even as her appetite shall play the god
    With his weak function. How am I then a villain   315

290 help] F; shee'll helpe Q1   290 of] F; *not in* Q1   291 that] Q1; *not in* F   292–3 broken joint] F; braule Q1
298 I will] F; will I Q1   300 here] Q1; *not in* F   301 F; You...right / ...watch Q1   302 SD] Q1; *Exit Cassio.* F
303] Q1; And...then / ...villain F   306] Q1; To...again / ...easy F   310 were 't] Q1; were F

289 **parts** accomplishments, qualities.
290 **free** generous.
292–5 **This broken...before** Proverbial: 'A
broken bone is the stronger when it is well set'
(Tilley B515).
292–3 **broken joint** Ridley has attempted a
defence of Q1's 'Braule' (= conflict) on the grounds
that it is typical of Shakespeare's later metaphorical
style, but 'splinting a brawl' hardly qualifies as
being a metaphor at all.
293 **splinter** set in splints. Compare *R3* 2.2.118:
'splinter'd, knit, and join'd together'.
294 **lay** wager.
298 **freely** unreservedly.

299 **undertake** take up the matter.
300 **check** repulse.
304 **free** Perhaps a quibble on (1) generous, (2)
innocent.
305 **Probal** Probable (or perhaps 'reasonable').
307 **inclining** compliant.
308 **framed as fruitful** created as generous.
309 **free elements** unrestrained natural forces.
Compare *Temp.* 5.1.318–19: 'Then to the
elements / Be free.'
314 **her appetite** i.e. his sexual desire for her.
315 **weak** Because unable to resist.
315 **function** powers of operation.

To counsel Cassio to this parallel course
Directly to his good? Divinity of hell!
When devils will the blackest sins put on,
They do suggest at first with heavenly shows
As I do now. For whiles this honest fool   320
Plies Desdemona to repair his fortunes,
And she for him pleads strongly to the Moor,
I'll pour this pestilence into his ear:
That she repeals him for her body's lust;
And by how much she strives to do him good,   325
She shall undo her credit with the Moor.
So will I turn her virtue into pitch,
And out of her own goodness make the net
That shall enmesh them all.

Enter Roderigo.

How now, Roderigo?

RODERIGO I do follow here in the chase, not like a hound that hunts,   330
but one that fills up the cry. My money is almost spent; I have
been tonight exceedingly well cudgelled; and I think the issue will
be, I shall have so much experience for my pains; and so, with
no money at all, and a little more wit, return again to Venice.

IAGO How poor are they that have no patience!   335
What wound did ever heal but by degrees?
Thou know'st we work by wit and not by witchcraft,
And wit depends on dilatory time.
Does't not go well? Cassio hath beaten thee,

---

318 the] F; there Q1   320 whiles] F; while Q1   321 fortunes] Q1; Fortune F   329 enmesh] Q1; en-mash F
332 and] F; *not in* Q1   333 and so, with] F; as that comes to, and Q1   334 a little more] F; with that Q1   334 again]
F; *not in* Q1   339 hath] F; has Q1

316 **parallel** i.e. to Iago's design.

317 **Directly to** In complete accord with.

317 **Divinity of hell** Theology of the Devil.
The allusion is to Satan's citation of scripture in the
temptation of Christ in Matt. 4.6. Compare Tilley
D230.

318–19 **When devils...shows** Proverbial:
'The devil can transform himself into an angel of
light' (Tilley D231).

318 **put on** incite. Compare *MM* 4.2.115–17:
'Lord Angelo (belike) thinking me remiss in mine
office, awakens me with this unwonted putting-
on.'

319 **suggest** tempt, seduce. Compare *R2*

3.4.75–6: 'What Eve, what serpent, hath suggested
thee / To make a second fall.'

321 **Plies** Solicits.

324 **repeals** tries to procure Cassio's
reinstatement.

327 **pitch** Three possible layers of meaning: (1)
blackness, (2) something odious, (3) that which has
the power to ensnare.

331 **fills up the cry** merely makes one of the
pack. Compare *Cor.* 3.3.120: 'You common cry of
curs'.

334 **wit** intelligence.

335 Proverbial: 'He that has no patience has
nothing' (Tilley P103).

And thou by that small hurt hath cashiered Cassio.   340
Though other things grow fair against the sun,
Yet fruits that blossom first will first be ripe.
Content thyself awhile. By th'mass, 'tis morning:
Pleasure and action make the hours seem short.
Retire thee, go where thou art billeted.   345
Away, I say, thou shalt know more hereafter –
Nay, get thee gone.

                                                        Exit Roderigo
                        Two things are to be done.
My wife must move for Cassio to her mistress –
I'll set her on.
Myself the while to draw the Moor apart,   350
And bring him jump when he may Cassio find
Soliciting his wife. Ay, that's the way:
Dull not device by coldness and delay.   *Exit*

3.1 *Enter* CASSIO, MUSICIANS *and* CLOWN.

CASSIO Masters, play here; I will content your pains.
        Something that's brief, and bid 'Good morrow, general.'
                        [*They play.*]
CLOWN Why, masters, have your instruments been in Naples, that
        they speak i'th'nose thus?
1 MUSICIAN How, sir, how?
CLOWN Are these, I pray you, wind instruments?   5
1 MUSICIAN Ay, marry are they, sir.

340 hath] F; hast Q1   342 Yet] F; But Q1   343 By th'mass] Q1; Introth F   347 SD] F; *not in* Q1   347 Two] Q1;
Some Q1   349–50] Q1; *one line in* F   350 the while] *Theobald*; a while F, Q1   353 SD] F; *Exeunt.* Q1   Act 3, Scene 1
3.1] *Actus Tertius. Scena Prima.* F; *not in* Q1   0 SD MUSICIANS...CLOWN] F; *with Musitians and the Clowne* Q1
2 SD] Q2; *not in* F, Q1   3 in] F; at Q1   5 SH 1 MUSICIAN] *Mus.* F; *Boy.* Q1   6 you] F; cald Q1

341–2 **Though other...ripe** Although our
long-term plans for the seduction of Desdemona are
blossoming slowly, yet our preliminary plan against
Cassio has already borne fruit.
  348 **move** plead.
  351 **jump** exactly at the moment. Compare
Ham. 1.1.65: 'jump at this dead hour'.
  353 **device** plan, plot.
  353 **coldness** lack of energy.

Act 3, Scene 1
  1 It was a custom to wake newlyweds with music
on the morning after their first night together.
  1 **content your pains** pay for your efforts.
  3–4 The Clown may mean that the music has an
ugly nasal twang like the Neapolitan accent, but
there is probably also a reference to venereal
disease, which attacked the nose. Compare *Tro.*
2.3.18–19: 'the Neapolitan bone-ache'; and *MV*
4.1.49, where the bagpipes are said to 'sing
i'th'nose'.

CLOWN O, thereby hangs a tail.

1 MUSICIAN Whereby hangs a tale, sir?

CLOWN Marry, sir, by many a wind instrument that I know. But,   10
masters, here's money for you; and the general so likes your music
that he desires you, for love's sake, to make no more noise with
it.

1 MUSICIAN Well sir, we will not.

CLOWN If you have any music that may not be heard, to't again; but,   15
as they say, to hear music the general does not greatly care.

1 MUSICIAN We have none such, sir.

CLOWN Then put up your pipes in your bag, for I'll away. Go,
vanish into air, away!

Exeunt Musicians

CASSIO Dost thou hear, mine honest friend?   20

CLOWN No, I hear not your honest friend; I hear you.

CASSIO Prithee keep up thy quillets – there's a poor piece of gold for
thee. If the gentlewoman that attends the general's wife be
stirring, tell her there's one Cassio entreats her a little favour of
speech. Wilt thou do this?   25

CLOWN She is stirring, sir; if she will stir hither, I shall seem to notify
unto her.

CASSIO Do, good my friend.

Exit Clown

Enter IAGO.

In happy time, Iago.

IAGO You have not been abed then?

CASSIO Why, no; the day had broke before we parted.   30
I have made bold, Iago,

---

8 tail] tayle QI; tale F   9 tale] tale F; tayle QI   12 for love's sake] F; of all loues QI   18 up] F; *not in* QI
19 into air] F; *not in* QI   19 SD] *Exit Mu.* F; *not in* QI   20 hear, mine] *Theobald*; heare my QI; heare me, mine F
23 general's wife] QI; Generall F   28 Do...friend.] QI; *not in* F   28 SD.1 *Exit Clown*] F *(after 27)*; *not in* QI
31–3] *Capell*; I...wife / ...Desdemona F; I...her / ...Desdemona QI

---

8 Proverbial phrase (Tilley T48).

8 **tail** Slang term for 'penis'.

10 **wind instrument** i.e. anus.

12 **for love's sake** for the sake of any affection
you may have for him; with a pun on 'for the sake
of his erotic concentration'.

12 **noise** Pun on (1) music, (2) nose.

15 **may not** cannot.

16 **as they say** The point of this phrase is not
clear, as one would expect it to introduce some kind
of popular saying about the 'general' (= common
public) not liking music very much; but none is
known.

18 **Then...bag** Proverbial phrase (Tilley
P345); with a possible sexual joke.

18 **I'll away** This is either a misprint for 'You'll
away', or is a phrase or title of an old song now lost.

22 **quillets** verbal quibbles. Compare *1H6*
2.4.17: 'these nice sharp quillets of the law'.

26 **seem** arrange. Compare *MND* 3.1.17–18:
'let the prologue seem to say'.

28 **In happy time** You are come at an
opportune moment.

        To send in to your wife. My suit to her
        Is that she will to virtuous Desdemona
        Procure me some access.

IAGO   I'll send her to you presently;
        And I'll devise a mean to draw the Moor   35
        Out of the way, that your converse and business
        May be more free.

CASSIO   I humbly thank you for't.

                              Exit [*Iago*]
        I never knew a Florentine more kind and honest.

                Enter EMILIA.

EMILIA Good morrow, good lieutenant; I am sorry
        For your displeasure; but all will sure be well.   40
        The general and his wife are talking of it,
        And she speaks for you stoutly. The Moor replies
        That he you hurt is of great fame in Cyprus
        And great affinity, and that in wholesome wisdom
        He might not but refuse you; but he protests he loves you,   45
        And needs no other suitor but his likings
        To take the safest occasion by the front
        To bring you in again.

CASSIO   Yet I beseech you,
        If you think fit, or that it may be done,
        Give me advantage of some brief discourse   50
        With Desdemon alone.

EMILIA   Pray you, come in;
        I will bestow you where you shall have time
        To speak your bosom freely.

CASSIO   I am much bound to you.

                              Exeunt

37–8 I…honest] Capell; I…knew / …honest F, QI   37 SD] F, QI *(after* free*)*   40 sure] F; soone QI   47] QI; *not in* F   53 CASSIO…you.] F; *not in* QI   53 SD] QI; *not in* F

38 **a Florentine** i.e. even one of my own countrymen; see 1.1.20.

40 **displeasure** being out of favour. Compare *H8* 3.2.392: 'your displeasure with the King' (about Wolsey's disgrace).

44 **great affinity** related to important people.

44 **wholesome** prudent.

47 **To take…front** Compare 'Take occasion by the forelock' (Tilley T311).

47 **occasion** opportunity.

47 **front** forehead.

53 **bosom** private thoughts and feelings. Compare *H8* 1.1.112–13: 'Bosom up my counsel. / You'll find it wholesome.'

3.2 *Enter* OTHELLO, IAGO *and* GENTLEMEN.

OTHELLO These letters give, Iago, to the pilot,
    And by him do my duties to the senate.
    That done, I will be walking on the works;
    Repair there to me.
IAGO   Well, my good lord, I'll do't.   *[Exit]*
OTHELLO This fortification, gentlemen, shall we see't?   5
GENTLEMEN We'll wait upon your lordship.

                                    Exeunt

3.3 *Enter* DESDEMONA, CASSIO *and* EMILIA.

DESDEMONA Be thou assured, good Cassio, I will do
    All my abilities in thy behalf.
EMILIA Good madam, do; I warrant it grieves my husband
    As if the case were his.
DESDEMONA O, that's an honest fellow. Do not doubt, Cassio,   5
    But I will have my lord and you again
    As friendly as you were.
CASSIO   Bounteous madam,
    Whatever shall become of Michael Cassio,
    He's never anything but your true servant.
DESDEMONA I know't; I thank you. You do love my lord,   10
    You have known him long, and be you well assured
    He shall in strangeness stand no farther off
    Than in a politic distance.
CASSIO   Ay, but, lady,
    That policy may either last so long
    Or feed upon such nice and waterish diet,   15
    Or breed itself so out of circumstance,

Act 3, Scene 2 3.2] *Scæna Secunda.* F; *not in* Q1 0 SD *and*] F; *and other* Q1 2 senate] F; State Q1 4 SD] *Walker;* *not in* F, Q1 6 We'll] Well F; We Q1 Act 3, Scene 3 3.3] *Scæna Tertia.* F; *not in* Q1 3] Q1; Good...do / ... husband F 3 warrant] F; know Q1 4 case] Q1; cause F 10 I know't] F; O sir Q1 12 strangeness] F; strangest Q1 14 That] F; The Q1 16 circumstance] Q1; Circumstances F

Act 3, Scene 2
  2 do my duties pay my respects.
  3 works fortifications.
  4 Repair Return.
  6 wait upon attend.

Act 3, Scene 3
  12 strangeness estrangement.
  13 in a politic distance is expedient politically.
  15 nice thin, sparse.
  16 Either 'Or reproduce so few opportunities for my reinstatement', or 'engender excuses for my non-recall out of chance occurrences'.

That I being absent and my place supplied,
My general will forget my love and service.
DESDEMONA Do not doubt that. Before Emilia here,
I give thee warrant of thy place. Assure thee   20
If I do vow a friendship, I'll perform it
To the last article. My lord shall never rest,
I'll watch him tame and talk him out of patience;
His bed shall seem a school, his board a shrift;
I'll intermingle every thing he does   25
With Cassio's suit. Therefore be merry, Cassio;
Thy solicitor shall rather die
Than give thy cause away.

Enter OTHELLO *and* IAGO.

EMILIA Madam, here comes my lord.
CASSIO Madam, I'll take my leave.   30
DESDEMONA Why, stay and hear me speak.
CASSIO Madam, not now: I am very ill at ease,
        Unfit for mine own purposes.
DESDEMONA Well, do your discretion.

                                                    Exit Cassio

IAGO Ha! I like not that.
OTHELLO   What dost thou say?   35
IAGO Nothing, my lord; or if – I know not what.
OTHELLO Was not that Cassio parted from my wife?
IAGO Cassio, my lord? No, sure I cannot think it
        That he would steal away so guilty-like,
        Seeing you coming.
OTHELLO   I do believe 'twas he.   40

---

28 thy cause] F; thee cause: Q1   **28** SD *and* IAGO] F; Iago, *and Gentlemen* Q1   **33** purposes] F; purpose Q1
39 steal] F; sneake Q1   **40** you] Q1; your F

17–18 That I being...service Compare Tilley
F596: 'Long absent soon forgotten'.
  17 supplied filled (by someone else). Compare
1H4 3.2.32–3: 'Thy place in Council thou hast
rudely lost, / Which by thy younger brother is
supplied.'
  19 doubt fear. Compare *Wiv.* 1.4.41–2: 'I doubt
he be not well, that he comes not home.'
  20 warrant guarantee.
  22 article A legal term meaning 'clause in a
contract'.
  23 watch him tame prevent him from sleeping

until he is tractable. This was one of the means by
which young hawks were trained in falconry.
Compare *Tro.* 3.2.43–4: 'You must be watch'd ere
you be made tame'; also *Shr.* 4.1.195.
  24 board a shrift table (shall seem) a confes-
sional. With the idea that Othello shall do penance.
  27 Thy solicitor Your advocate. Compare *LLL*
2.1.28–9: 'we single you / As our best-moving fair
solicitor'.
  28 give thy cause away abandon your case.
  34 do your discretion do what you think is
discreet.

DESDEMONA How now, my lord?
    I have been talking with a suitor here,
    A man that languishes in your displeasure.
OTHELLO Who is't you mean?
DESDEMONA Why, your lieutenant, Cassio. Good my lord,   45
    If I have any grace or power to move you,
    His present reconciliation take.
    For if he be not one that truly loves you,
    That errs in ignorance, and not in cunning,
    I have no judgement in an honest face.   50
    I prithee call him back.
OTHELLO   Went he hence now?
DESDEMONA Ay, sooth; so humbled
    That he hath left part of his grief with me
    To suffer with him. Good love, call him back.
OTHELLO Not now, sweet Desdemon; some other time.   55
DESDEMONA But shall't be shortly?
OTHELLO   The sooner, sweet, for you.
DESDEMONA Shall't be tonight at supper?
OTHELLO   No, not tonight.
DESDEMONA Tomorrow dinner then?
OTHELLO   I shall not dine at home.
    I meet the captains at the citadel.
DESDEMONA Why, then, tomorrow night, or Tuesday morn,   60
    On Tuesday noon, or night; on Wednesday morn.
    I prithee name the time, but let it not
    Exceed three days. In faith, he's penitent;
    And yet his trespass, in our common reason –
    Save that, they say, the wars must make example   65
    Out of their best – is not almost a fault
    T'incur a private check. When shall he come?

---

52 Ay, sooth;] F; Yes faith, Q1   53 hath] F; has Q1   53 grief] F; griefes Q1   54 To] F; I Q1   60 or] Q1; on F
61 noon] F; morne Q1   61 on] F; or Q1   65 example] F; examples Q1   66 their] *Rowe*; her F, Q1

46 grace favour in your eyes.

47 present...take restore him immediately to favour. Onions suggests 'submission with a view to being restored to favour', but if this is the meaning then 'present' does not make much sense in the context.

49 in cunning knowingly, with complete mental awareness.

58 dinner i.e. the modern 'luncheon'.

64–7 yet his trespass...check Compare Cinthio's source story: 'He has not committed so serious an offence as to deserve such hostility' (Bullough VII, 245).

66 best i.e. the highest-ranking officers.

66 not almost hardly, barely. Compare *Err.* 5.1.181: 'I have not breath'd almost since I did see it.'

67 check reprimand.

Tell me, Othello. I wonder in my soul
What you would ask me that I should deny,
Or stand so mammering on. What! Michael Cassio,   70
That came a-wooing with you, and so many a time
When I have spoke of you dispraisingly
Hath tane your part, to have so much to do
To bring him in? By'r Lady, I could do much –
OTHELLO Prithee no more. Let him come when he will;   75
   I will deny thee nothing.
DESDEMONA   Why, this is not a boon;
   'Tis as I should entreat you wear your gloves,
   Or feed on nourishing dishes, or keep you warm,
   Or sue to you to do a peculiar profit
   To your own person. Nay, when I have a suit   80
   Wherein I mean to touch your love indeed,
   It shall be full of poise and difficult weight,
   And fearful to be granted.
OTHELLO   I will deny thee nothing.
   Whereon, I do beseech thee, grant me this,
   To leave me but a little to myself.   85
DESDEMONA Shall I deny you? No; farewell, my lord.
OTHELLO Farewell, my Desdemona, I'll come to thee straight.
DESDEMONA Emilia, come. Be as your fancies teach you;
   Whate'er you be, I am obedient.
                          Exeunt Desdemona and Emilia
OTHELLO Excellent wretch! Perdition catch my soul   90
   But I do love thee; and when I love thee not,
   Chaos is come again.
IAGO   My noble lord –

69 would] F; could Q1   70 mammering] F; muttering Q1   74 By'r Lady] Q1; Trust me F   82 difficult weight] F;
difficulty Q1   88 Be as] F; be it as Q1   89 SD] *Exit* Desd. *and* Em. Q1; *Exit.* F

70 **mammering on** hesitating.
70–3 **What...part** See above, pp. 15–16.
74 **in** i.e. into favour.
79–80 **a peculiar...person** something of special
personal advantage to yourself.
81 **touch** test, make trial of.
82 **poise** weight, importance. Compare *Lear*
2.1.120: 'Occasions, noble Gloucester, of some
poise' (Q1 text).
82 **difficult weight** momentous, hard to decide
on.
84 **Whereon** In return for which.
87 **straight** at once.

88 **fancies** inclinations.
90 **wretch** A term of endearment (as in *Rom.*
1.3.44).
91 **But I do** If I do not.
91–2 **when I...again** The allusion is to the
classical legend that Love was the first of the gods
to spring out of original chaos. Compare Ben
Jonson's *Love Freed from Ignorance and Folly*, 26–7:
'*Love.* Cruel Sphinx...without me / All again
would Chaos be'; and *The Masque of Beauty*, 282–5,
326–8.
91 **when I love thee not** if ever I were not to
love you.

OTHELLO What dost thou say, Iago?

IAGO   Did Michael Cassio,
    When you wooed my lady, know of your love?

OTHELLO He did from first to last. Why dost thou ask?   95

IAGO But for a satisfaction of my thought;
    No further harm.

OTHELLO   Why of thy thought, Iago?

IAGO I did not think he had been acquainted with her.

OTHELLO O yes, and went between us very oft.

IAGO Indeed?   100

OTHELLO Indeed? Ay, indeed. Discern'st thou aught in that?
    Is he not honest?

IAGO Honest, my lord?

OTHELLO Honest? Ay, honest.

IAGO My lord, for aught I know.

OTHELLO   What dost thou think?   105

IAGO Think, my lord?

OTHELLO Think, my lord! By heaven, he echoes me,
    As if there were some monster in his thought
    Too hideous to be shown. Thou dost mean something.
    I heard thee say even now thou lik'st not that,   110
    When Cassio left my wife. What didst not like?
    And when I told thee he was of my counsel
    In my whole course of wooing, thou cried'st 'Indeed?'
    And didst contract and purse thy brow together,
    As if thou then hadst shut up in thy brain   115
    Some horrible conceit. If thou dost love me,
    Show me thy thought.

IAGO My lord, you know I love you.

OTHELLO   I think thou dost;
    And for I know thou'rt full of love and honesty,
    And weigh'st thy words before thou giv'st them breath,   120
    Therefore these stops of thine fright me the more;

93–4 Did...love?] F; Did...lady / ...love QI   94 you] QI; he F   95] QI; He...last / ...ask F   96 thought] F;
thoughts QI   99 oft] F; often QI   101 Ay] F; *not in* QI   107 By heaven, he echoes] QI; Alas, thou ecchos't F
108 his] QI; thy F   109 dost] F; didst QI   110 even] F; but QI   113 In] QI; Of F   116 conceit] F; counsell QI
121 fright] F; affright QI

108 monster Compare 167–9 below.
114 purse knit, draw together.
116 conceit idea, conception. Compare *R3*
3.4.49–50: 'There's some conceit or other likes him
well, / When that he bids good morrow with such
spirit.'

118 you know I love you A diabolic echo of
Peter's words to the risen Christ in John 21.15: 'Yea
Lord, thou knowest that I love thee.'
121 stops breakings off, sudden pauses.

                    For such things in a false disloyal knave
                    Are tricks of custom; but in a man that's just,
                    They're close dilations, working from the heart,
                    That passion cannot rule.

IAGO   For Michael Cassio,   125
                    I dare be sworn I think that he is honest.

OTHELLO I think so too.

IAGO   Men should be what they seem;
                    Or those that be not, would they might seem none!

OTHELLO Certain, men should be what they seem.

IAGO Why then, I think Cassio's an honest man.   130

OTHELLO Nay, yet there's more in this.
                    I prithee speak to me as to thy thinkings,
                    As thou dost ruminate, and give thy worst of thoughts
                    The worst of words.

IAGO   Good my lord, pardon me;
                    Though I am bound to every act of duty,   135
                    I am not bound to that all slaves are free to.
                    Utter my thoughts! Why, say they are vile and false?
                    As where's that palace, whereinto foul things
                    Sometimes intrude not? Who has a breast so pure,
                    But some uncleanly apprehensions   140
                    Keep leets and law-days, and in session sit
                    With meditations lawful?

OTHELLO Thou dost conspire against thy friend, Iago,

---

124 dilations] F; denotements Q1; delations *conj. Johnson, Steevens*   126 be sworn] F; presume Q1   127 what] F; that Q1   132 as] F; *not in* Q1   133 thy] F; the Q1   133 thoughts] F; thought Q1   134 words] F; word Q1   136 that] Q1; that: F   136 free to] Q1; free F   139 a] Q1; that F   140 But some] Q1; Wherein F   141 session] Q1; Sessions F

---

123 **of custom** customary.

124 **close dilations** There is no agreement among editors about the exact meaning of this phrase. The two most favoured interpretations of this F reading are: (1) involuntary delays; and (2) half-hidden expressions. If one adopts Q1's 'denotements', the meaning becomes 'indications of something shut up and secret'. For a full discussion of possible emendations, see supplementary note.

125 **That passion cannot rule** Either (1) that cannot control its passions; or (2) that cannot be controlled by emotion. See supplementary note.

127–8 **Men should...none** Compare 'Be what thou would seem to be' (Tilley s214).

128 **none** Either (1) not to be men; or (2) not seem to be honest men.

136 **that all slaves are free to** i.e. the right that even slaves have to think what they wish. Compare 'Thought is free' (Tilley T244).

140 **apprehensions** ideas. As in *Tim.* 1.1.208: 'a lascivious apprehension'.

141 **leets** Courts of record, which some lords of the manor were empowered to hold yearly or half-yearly in their localities; hence 'days on which such courts were held'.

143 **conspire** This was used to describe actions by a single person as well as by a group; compare *Sonnets* 10.6: 'That 'gainst thyself thou stick'st not to conspire'.

If thou but think'st him wronged, and mak'st his ear
A stranger to thy thoughts.

IAGO   I do beseech you,   145
Though I perchance am vicious in my guess –
As I confess it is my nature's plague
To spy into abuses, and oft my jealousy
Shapes faults that are not – that your wisdom then,
From one that so imperfectly conceits,   150
Would take no notice, nor build yourself a trouble
Out of his scattering and unsure observance.
It were not for your quiet, nor your good,
Nor for my manhood, honesty, and wisdom,
To let you know my thoughts.

OTHELLO   What dost thou mean?   155

IAGO Good name in man and woman, dear my lord,
Is the immediate jewel of their souls.
Who steals my purse, steals trash; 'tis something,
            nothing,
'Twas mine, 'tis his, and has been slave to thousands:
But he that filches from me my good name   160
Robs me of that which not enriches him
And makes me poor indeed.

OTHELLO By heaven, I'll know thy thoughts.

IAGO You cannot, if my heart were in your hand,
Nor shall not, while 'tis in my custody.   165

OTHELLO Ha!

IAGO O beware, my lord, of jealousy:

---

148 oft] QI; of F   149 that your wisdom] F; I intreate you QI   149 then] QI; *not in* F   150 conceits] F; coniects
QI   151 Would] F; You'd QI   152 his] F; my QI   154 and] F; or QI   155 What...mean?] F; Zouns. QI
156 woman, dear] woman (deere F; woman's deere QI   157 their] F; our QI   158] QI; Who...trash / ...nothing F
163 By heaven] QI; *not in* F   163 thoughts] F; thought QI   166 OTHELLO Ha!] F; *not in* QI   167 my lord, of] F;
not in QI

---

148 jealousy suspicious vigilance. Compare *TN*
3.3.8–9: 'But jealousy what might befall your
travel, / Being skilless in these parts'.

150 conceits imagines, conjectures. QI's 'coniects' is possible, as the two words could easily be
confused in the Secretary hand.

152 scattering random.

156–62 Good name...indeed Hunter compares Thomas Wilson's *Art of Rhetoric* (1553): 'a
slanderer is worse than any thief, because a good
name is better than all the goods in the world...and
a thief may restore that again which he hath taken

away, but a slanderer cannot give a man his good
name which he hath taken from him'. Compare also
'A good name is better than riches' (Tilley N22);
and contrast Iago's lines giving the opposite view
at 2.3.247–9.

157 immediate directly touching, most
important.

158 trash A scornful term for money; compare
JC 4.3.72–4: 'I had rather coin my heart...than to
wring / From the hard hands of peasants their vile
trash.'

It is the green-eyed monster which doth mock
The meat it feeds on. That cuckold lives in bliss
Who certain of his fate loves not his wronger;   170
But O, what damnèd minutes tells he o'er
Who dotes, yet doubts, suspects, yet fondly loves?

OTHELLO O misery!

IAGO Poor and content is rich, and rich enough;
But riches fineless is as poor as winter   175
To him that ever fears he shall be poor.
Good God, the souls of all my tribe defend
From jealousy.

OTHELLO   Why, why is this?
Think'st thou I'd make a life of jealousy,
To follow still the changes of the moon   180
With fresh suspicions? No, to be once in doubt
Is once to be resolved. Exchange me for a goat
When I shall turn the business of my soul
To such exsufflicate and blown surmises
Matching thy inference. 'Tis not to make me jealous   185
To say my wife is fair, feeds well, loves company,
Is free of speech, sings, plays, and dances well:
Where virtue is, these are more virtuous.

---

168 mock] F, QI; make *conj. Theobald, Hanmer*   169 The] F; That QI   172 fondly] *Knight;* soundly F; strongly QI
177 God] QI; Heauen F   182 once] QI; *not in* F   184 blown] QI; blow'd F   187 well] QI; *not in* F

168–9 mock…feeds on i.e. torments its victim, the jealous man himself. See supplementary note.

170 his wronger the wife betraying him.

171 tells counts.

172 fondly foolishly. Knight's emendation of F's 'soundly' and QI's 'strongly' is demanded by the preceding pairing 'dotes/doubts'.

174 Proverbial: 'The greatest wealth is content-ment with a little' (Tilley W194).

175 fineless boundless, endless. Compare *Ham.* 5.1.106: 'Is this the fine [= end] of his fines?'

180–1 follow still…suspicions be ever drawn into new suspicions with each waxing and waning of the moon (as a madman is).

182 once once and for all.

182 resolved convinced, free from all doubt.

182 goat A type of animal lust.

183–5 When I…inference The moment I bring my mind to concentrate on such inflated and rumoured suspicions as you describe.

184 exsufflicate This is the only occurrence of

this word in the language and presumably means 'puffed up, inflated', although some editors take it to mean 'spat out'.

184 blown Usually taken in one of two senses: (1) flyblown (as in *WT* 4.4.791); (2) swollen, inflated (as in *Lear* 4.4.27). However, the meaning is surely 'bandied about, rumoured' as in *2H4* Induction 15–16, where it is used in conjuction with precisely the same vocabulary as Othello is using here: 'Rumour is a pipe / Blown by surmises, jealousies, conjectures.'

185 inference Onions and editors gloss this as 'allegation', but Othello is surely referring to the cuckold's state of mind as it is described by Iago, and therefore means 'demonstration, depiction', in the sense of 'infer' in *John* 3.1.213.

185–8 'Tis not to make…virtuous The introduction to Cinthio's source story comments on women who 'with beauty of body and under a semblance of virtue, for instance in singing, playing, dancing lightly and speaking sweetly, hide an ugly and abominable soul' (Bullough, VII, 240).

Nor from mine own weak merits will I draw
The smallest fear or doubt of her revolt,   190
For she had eyes and chose me. No, Iago,
I'll see before I doubt; when I doubt, prove;
And on the proof, there is no more but this:
Away at once with love or jealousy!

IAGO I am glad of this; for now I shall have reason   195
To show the love and duty that I bear you
With franker spirit. Therefore, as I am bound,
Receive it from me. I speak not yet of proof.
Look to your wife, observe her well with Cassio;
Wear your eyes thus: not jealous, nor secure.   200
I would not have your free and noble nature,
Out of self-bounty, be abused. Look to't.
I know our country disposition well:
In Venice they do let God see the pranks
They dare not show their husbands. Their best
     conscience   205
Is not to leave't undone, but keep't unknown.

OTHELLO Dost thou say so?

IAGO She did deceive her father, marrying you;
And when she seemed to shake and fear your looks
She loved them most.

OTHELLO   And so she did.

IAGO   Why, go to then!   210
She that so young could give out such a seeming
To seel her father's eyes up close as oak
He thought 'twas witchcraft – but I am much to blame,

---

195 this] F; it QI   200 eyes] F; eie QI   204 God] QI; Heauen F   205] QI; They...husbands / ...conscience F
205 not] F; *not in* QI   206 leave't] F; leaue QI   206 keep't] kept F; keepe QI   213] QI; He...witchcraft / ...blame F

---

189 **weak merits** i.e. lack of attractive (physical) qualities.

190 **doubt** suspicion.

190 **revolt** unfaithfulness (or revulsion leading to it). Compare *TN* 2.4.97–9: 'their love may be call'd appetite... / That suffer surfeit, cloyment, and revolt'.

200 **secure** free from suspicion. Compare *Wiv.* 2.1.233–4: 'Though Page be a secure fool, and stands so firmly on his wive's frailty'.

202 **self-bounty** innate generosity. Compare

Tim. 2.2.232–3: 'That thought is bounty's foe; / Being free itself, it thinks all others so.'

204–6 **In Venice...unknown** Proverbial: 'Live charily if not chastely' (Tilley L381).

205 **best conscience** highest idea of morality.

208 Iago echoes Brabantio's lines at 1.3.288–9.

210 **go to** there you are (colloquial).

212 **seel** See 1.3.265 n.

212 **close as oak** A proverbial saying (Tilley O1), presumably referring to the close grain of the wood.

I humbly do beseech you of your pardon
For too much loving you.

OTHELLO   I am bound to thee for ever.   215

IAGO I see this hath a little dashed your spirits.

OTHELLO Not a jot, not a jot.

IAGO   I'faith, I fear it has.
I hope you will consider what is spoke
Comes from my love. But I do see you're moved.
I am to pray you not to strain my speech   220
To grosser issues nor to larger reach
Than to suspicion.

OTHELLO I will not.

IAGO   Should you do so, my lord,
My speech should fall into such vile success
As my thoughts aimed not at. Cassio's my worthy
    friend –   225
My lord, I see you're moved.

OTHELLO   No, not much moved.
I do not think but Desdemona's honest.

IAGO Long live she so, and long live you to think so!

OTHELLO And yet how nature erring from itself –

IAGO Ay, there's the point: as, to be bold with you,   230
Not to affect many proposèd matches
Of her own clime, complexion, and degree,
Whereto we see in all things nature tends –
Foh! one may smell, in such, a will most rank,
Foul disproportion, thoughts unnatural.   235
But pardon me: I do not in position
Distinctly speak of her; though I may fear

217 I' faith] Q1; Trust me F   219] Q1; Comes…love / …moved F   219 my] Q1; your F   225] Q1; Which…
not / …friend F   225 As] Q1; Which F   225 aimed] F; aime Q1   225 at] Q1; not in F   225 worthy] F; trusty Q1
228] Q1; Long…so / …so F   230] Q1; Ay…point / …you F   234 Foh! one] F; Fie we Q1   235 disproportion]
Q1; disproportions F

215 **bound** indebted.
220 **strain** enlarge the meaning of.
221 **grosser issues** A quibble: (1) more substantial conclusions; (2) more lewd conclusions. Compare *Ham.* 4.7.169–70: 'long purples / That liberal shepherds give a grosser name'.
221 **larger** A quibble: (1) wider; (2) more licentious; as in *Ado* 4.1.52: 'I never tempted her with word too large.'
224 **success** result (as in *Tro.* 2.2.117).
227 **honest** chaste, virtuous.

231–3 **Not to affect…tends** Iago is again echoing Brabantio at 1.3.96–7.
231 **affect** look favourably on, like. Compare *TN* 2.5.23–4: 'Maria once told me she did affect me.'
234 **will** A quibble: (1) sexual desire; (2) purpose.
234 **rank** A quibble: (1) corrupt; (2) lascivious.
236–7 **in position Distinctly** in applying a deliberate proposition specifically.

Her will, recoiling to her better judgement,
May fall to match you with her country forms,
And happily repent.

OTHELLO   Farewell, farewell.   240
   If more thou dost perceive, let me know more;
   Set on thy wife to observe. Leave me, Iago.

IAGO [*Going.*] My lord, I take my leave.

OTHELLO Why did I marry? This honest creature doubtless
   Sees and knows more, much more, than he unfolds.   245

IAGO [*Returning.*] My lord, I would I might entreat your honour
   To scan this thing no farther. Leave it to time.
   Although 'tis fit that Cassio have his place –
   For sure he fills it up with great ability –
   Yet if you please to hold him off awhile,   250
   You shall by that perceive him and his means.
   Note if your lady strain his entertainment
   With any strong or vehement importunity –
   Much will be seen in that. In the mean time,
   Let me be thought too busy in my fears –   255
   As worthy cause I have to fear I am –
   And hold her free, I do beseech your honour.

OTHELLO Fear not my government.

IAGO I once more take my leave.   *Exit*

OTHELLO This fellow's of exceeding honesty   260
   And knows all qualities, with a learnèd spirit,
   Of human dealings. If I do prove her haggard,
   Though that her jesses were my dear heart-strings,

240–2] *Rowe;* Farewell, farewell / ...more / ...observe / ...Iago F; Farewell, if more / ...on / ...Iago QI
240 farewell] F; *not in* QI   243 SD] *Rowe; not in* F, QI   244] QI; Why...marry / ...doubtless F   246 SH IAGO] F;
not in QI   246 SD] *Capell; not in* F, QI   248 Although 'tis] F; Tho it be QI   250 hold] QI; *not in* F   252 his] F;
her QI   259 SD] F, QI; *not in some copies of* QI   261 qualities] QI; Quantities F   262 dealings] F; dealing QI

239 May fall...forms May begin to compare you with the style of good looks typical of her own countrymen.

240 happily haply, perhaps. As in *Shr.* 4.4.54 and *2H6* 3.1.306.

247 scan scrutinise.

251 his means the methods he uses (to recover his position).

252 strain his entertainment urge that he be received again into employment. Compare *Cor.* 4.3.43–5: 'the centurions and their charges, distinctly billeted, already i'th'entertainment'.

255 busy interfering. Compare *Ham.* 3.4.31–3:

'Thou wretched, rash intruding fool... / Thou find'st to be too busy is some danger.'

257 free innocent.

258 my government my control over my behaviour. As in *1H4* 3.1.182.

261 qualities natures, characters of people.

262 Of In regard to.

262 haggard intractable, wild (as an untrained hawk). Compare *TN* 3.1.64–5: 'like the haggard, check at every feather / That comes before his eye'.

263 jesses 'Narrow strips of soft leather, silk or other material, fastened round the legs of a trained hawk, with silver rings through which passed the line that held it to the falconer's wrist' (NS).

I'd whistle her off and let her down the wind
To prey at fortune. Haply for I am black,   265
And have not those soft parts of conversation
That chamberers have, or for I am declined
Into the vale of years – yet that's not much –
She's gone, I am abused, and my relief
Must be to loathe her. O curse of marriage,   270
That we can call these delicate creatures ours
And not their appetites! I had rather be a toad
And live upon the vapour of a dungeon
Than keep a corner in the thing I love
For others' uses. Yet 'tis the plague of great ones,   275
Prerogatived are they less than the base;
'Tis destiny unshunnable, like death:
Even then this forkèd plague is fated to us
When we do quicken. Look where she comes.

Enter Desdemona and Emilia.

If she be false, O then heaven mocks itself;   280
I'll not believe it.
DESDEMONA   How now, my dear Othello?
Your dinner and the generous islanders,
By you invited, do attend your presence.
OTHELLO I am to blame.
DESDEMONA   Why do you speak so faintly?

---

265 Haply] F; Happily Q1   268 vale] F; valt Q1   273 of] F; in Q1   274 keep] F, Q1; leepe Q1 *(some copies)*
274 the] F; a Q1   275 of] Q1; to F   279 Look where she] F; *Desdemona* Q1   279 SD] F; *after 281 in* Q1   280 O
then heaven mocks] Q1; Heauen mock'd F   282 islanders] F; Ilander Q1   284–5 Why...well] F; *one line in* Q1
284 do...faintly] F; is your speech so faint Q1

264 **whistle her off** A term used to describe the setting free of an untrainable hawk.

264 **let...wind** The way a hawk was released in order to lose it. Compare 'To go down the wind [= to ruin]' (Tilley W432).

265 **prey at fortune** fend for herself, hunt at random.

265 **Haply for** Perhaps because.

266 **soft...conversation** pleasant arts of social behaviour.

267 **chamberers** frequenters of ladies' chambers, courtly gallants; with the overtone of 'seducers' as in 'chambering' (*OED* sv *vbl sb* 2).

269 **abused** deceived, disgraced.

276 Most editors take this to mean that 'important people are less free from this curse than

men of low birth'; but I think there is also included the idea that 'the peccadilloes of the great are more likely to be widely known than those of their social inferiors'.

277 **'Tis...unshunnable** Compare 'Marriage is destiny' (Tilley M682), and 'Cuckolds come by destiny' (Tilley C889).

278 **forkèd plague** The curse of the cuckold's horns.

279 **do quicken** are conceived, are born. Compare *MM* 5.1.495.

280 **heaven mocks itself** i.e. by creating something which only appears so perfect.

282 **generous** noble. As in *MM* 4.6.13.

283 **attend** wait.

Are you not well?   285

OTHELLO I have a pain upon my forehead here.

DESDEMONA Faith, that's with watching; 'twill away again.
Let me but bind it hard, within this hour
It will be well.

OTHELLO   Your napkin is too little.
[*He puts the handkerchief from him, and she drops it.*]
Let it alone. Come, I'll go in with you.   290

DESDEMONA I am very sorry that you are not well.

                              Exeunt Othello and Desdemona

EMILIA I am glad I have found this napkin:
This was her first remembrance from the Moor.
My wayward husband hath a hundred times
Wooed me to steal it; but she so loves the token,   295
For he conjured her she should ever keep it,
That she reserves it evermore about her
To kiss and talk to. I'll have the work tane out
And give't Iago.
What he will do with it, heaven knows, not I: 300
I nothing but to please his fantasy.

                              Enter Iago.

IAGO How now? What do you here alone?

EMILIA Do not you chide; I have a thing for you.

IAGO You have a thing for me? It is a common thing –

EMILIA Ha!   305

IAGO To have a foolish wife.

EMILIA O, is that all? What will you give me now
For that same handkerchief?

---

287 Faith] Q1; Why F   288 it hard] F; your head Q1   289 well] F; well againe Q1   289 SD] Capell subst.; not in
F, Q1   291 SD] Ex. Oth. and Desd. Q1 (after 292); Exit. F (after 290)   299–300] Johnson; And…it / …not I F, Q1
301 but to please] F; know, but for Q1   301 SD] F; after 300 in Q1   304] Q1; You…me / …thing F   304 You have]
F; not in Q1   306 wife] F; thing Q1

286 upon my forehead i.e. where his cuckold's
horns grow.
287 watching lack of sleep. Compare 3.3.23
and n.
292 napkin handkerchief.
294–5 See the discussion of the play's time-
scheme, pp. 14–17 above.
294 wayward capricious, unaccountable.
296 conjured her made her swear, solemnly
commanded her.

298 work tane out embroidery copied.
301 his fantasy some capricious idea he has.
304 thing female sexual organ (as in *1H4*
3.3.117).
304 common open to everyone.
305 Ha! Emilia obviously thinks Iago is going to
raise the subject of her supposed infidelity which,
we learn from 4.2.144–6, has been a subject of
quarrel between them in the past.

IAGO   What handkerchief?

EMILIA What handkerchief!
       Why, that the Moor first gave to Desdemona,   310
       That which so often you did bid me steal.

IAGO Hast stolen it from her?

EMILIA No, faith; she let it drop by negligence,
       And to th'advantage I being here took't up.
       Look, here it is.

IAGO   A good wench! Give it me.   315

EMILIA What will you do with't, that you have been so earnest
       To have me filch it?

IAGO [*Snatching it.*]   Why, what's that to you?

EMILIA If it be not for some purpose of import,
       Give't me again. Poor lady, she'll run mad
       When she shall lack it.

IAGO   Be not acknown on't: 320
       I have use for it. Go, leave me.

                                Exit Emilia

       I will in Cassio's lodging lose this napkin
       And let him find it. Trifles light as air
       Are to the jealous confirmations strong
       As proofs of holy writ. This may do something.   325
       The Moor already changes with my poison:
       Dangerous conceits are in their natures poisons,
       Which at the first are scarce found to distaste
       But, with a little act upon the blood,
       Burn like the mines of sulphur. I did say so.   330

---

312 stolen] stolne F; stole Q1   313 No, faith;] No faith, Q1; No: but F   316–17 What…it] *Theobald;* What…been /
…it F, Q1   317 SD] *Rowe; not in* F, Q1   319 Give 't me] F; Giue mee 't Q1   320–1 Be…me] F; *one line in* Q1
320 acknown] F; you knowne Q1   326] F; *not in* Q1   329 act] F; art, Q1   330 mines] F; mindes Q1   330 SD] F;
after 329 in Q1

314 **to th'advantage** opportunely, fortunately.
318 **import** importance.
320 **lack** miss.
320 **Be not acknown on** Do not admit to any
knowledge of, feign ignorance about.
322 **I will…napkin** Compare Cinthio's source
story: 'The wicked Ensign, seizing a suitable
opportunity, went to the Corporal's room, and with
cunning malice left the handkerchief at the head of
his bed' (Bullough, VII, 247).
327 **conceits** conceptions, ideas.

328 **distaste** be distasteful.
329 **act** action. Some editors unnecessarily place
a comma after 'little', interpreting it: 'but, after a
short time, act upon the blood'.
330 **mines of sulphur** These were popularly
associated with the Aeolian Islands and Sicily.
Compare Pliny, 35: 'Sulphur…is engendered
within the Islands Aeolia, which lie between Italy
and Sicily…which do always burn by reason
thereof.'

Enter Othello.

Look where he comes! Not poppy nor mandragora,
Nor all the drowsy syrups of the world,
Shall ever medicine thee to that sweet sleep
Which thou owed'st yesterday.

OTHELLO   Ha, ha, false to me!
IAGO Why, how now, general! No more of that.   335
OTHELLO Avaunt, be gone! Thou hast set me on the rack.
I swear 'tis better to be much abused
Than but to know't a little.
IAGO   How now, my lord!
OTHELLO What sense had I of her stolen hours of lust?
I saw't not, thought it not, it harmed not me.   340
I slept the next night well, fed well, was free and merry;
I found not Cassio's kisses on her lips.
He that is robbed, not wanting what is stolen,
Let him not know't and he's not robbed at all.
IAGO I am sorry to hear this.   345
OTHELLO I had been happy if the general camp,
Pioners and all, had tasted her sweet body
So I had nothing known. O, now for ever
Farewell the tranquil mind! Farewell content!
Farewell the plumèd troops, and the big wars   350
That makes ambition virtue – O farewell!
Farewell the neighing steed and the shrill trump,
The spirit-stirring drum, th'ear-piercing fife,
The royal banner, and all quality,
Pride, pomp, and circumstance of glorious war!   355

334 me!] F; me, to me? Q1   338 know 't] F; know Q1   339 of] Q1; in F   341 fed well] F; *not in* Q1   350 troops] F; troope Q1

331 **poppy** opium.

331 **mandragora** The mandrake plant, yielding a soporific drug; compare *Ant.* 1.5.4–5: 'Give me to drink mandragora... / That I might sleep out this great gap of time'; also Tilley J101.

334 **owed'st** possessed.

339 **sense** awareness.

341 **free** untroubled.

343–4 Proverbial: 'He that is not sensible of his loss has lost nothing' (Tilley L461).

343 **wanting** missing.

347 **Pioners** i.e. pioneers; considered at this time the lowest type of soldier. Fighting men were sometimes disciplined by being sentenced to serve as pioneers. Hart quotes Davies, *Art of War* (1619), on the subject of a soldier who, on being convicted of losing his weapons, is sentenced to be 'dismissed with punishment or to be made some abject pioner'.

348 **So** If only.

350–1 **the big...virtue** Compare G. Chapman, *Revenge for Honour* (ed. T. M. Parrott) 1.1.290–3: 'glorious war / Which makes ambition (by base men termed sin) / A big and gallant virtue'.

354 **quality** essential nature.

355 **Pride** Proud display.

355 **circumstance** ceremony, pageantry.

And, O you mortal engines, whose rude throats
Th'immortal Jove's dread clamours counterfeit,
Farewell! Othello's occupation's gone.

IAGO Is't possible, my lord?

OTHELLO Villain, be sure thou prove my love a whore;   360
Be sure of it. Give me the ocular proof,
Or by the worth of mine eternal soul,
Thou hadst been better have been born a dog
Than answer my waked wrath!

IAGO   Is't come to this?

OTHELLO Make me to see't; or, at the least, so prove it   365
That the probation bear no hinge nor loop
To hang a doubt on – or woe upon thy life!

IAGO My noble lord –

OTHELLO If thou dost slander her and torture me,
Never pray more; abandon all remorse;   370
On horror's head horrors accumulate;
Do deeds to make heaven weep, all earth amazed:
For nothing canst thou to damnation add
Greater than that.

IAGO   O grace! O heaven forgive me!
Are you a man? Have you a soul? Or sense?   375
God bu'y you; take mine office. O wretched fool,
That lov'st to make thine honesty a vice!
O monstrous world! Take note, take note, O world!
To be direct and honest is not safe.
I thank you for this profit, and from hence   380
I'll love no friend, sith love breeds such offence.

OTHELLO Nay, stay: thou shouldst be honest.

356 you] F; ye QI   356 rude] F; wide QI   357 dread] F; great QI   357 clamours] F; clamor QI   360 thou] F, QI;
you QI *(some copies)*   362 mine] F; mans QI   373–4 For…that] F; *one line in* QI   374 forgive] F; defend QI
376 mine] F, QI; thine QI *(some copies)*   377 lov'st] F; liuest QI   377 thine] F, QI; mine QI *(some copies)*
381 sith] F; since QI

356 **mortal engines** deadly cannons.

357 **Jove's dread clamours** i.e. thunder.

360–70 **Villain…remorse** Compare Cinthio's
source story: 'Then the Moor, in the utmost
anguish, said, "If you do not make me see with my
own eyes what you have told me, be assured, I shall
make you realise that it would have been better for
you had you been born dumb"' (Bullough, VII,
246).

366 **probation** proof.

366 **hinge nor loop** pivot nor holding-string.

372 **amazed** paralysed with horror.

376 **bu'y** be with.

377 **vice** failing (by carrying it to excess).
Compare *Tro.* 5.3.37–8: 'Brother, you have a vice
of mercy in you, / Which better fits a lion than a
man.'

380 **profit** profitable lesson.

381 **sith** since.

381 **offence** injury (to the one who loves).

IAGO I should be wise; for honesty's a fool
    And loses that it works for.

OTHELLO   By the world,
    I think my wife be honest, and think she is not;   385
    I think that thou art just, and think thou art not.
    I'll have some proof. Her name, that was as fresh
    As Dian's visage, is now begrimed and black
    As mine own face. If there be cords or knives,
    Poison or fire or suffocating streams,   390
    I'll not endure it. Would I were satisfied!

IAGO I see, sir, you are eaten up with passion.
    I do repent me that I put it to you.
    You would be satisfied?

OTHELLO   Would? Nay, I will.

IAGO And may. But how? How satisfied, my lord?   395
    Would you, the supervisor, grossly gape on?
    Behold her topped?

OTHELLO   ,   Death and damnation! O!

IAGO It were a tedious difficulty, I think,
    To bring them to that prospect. Damn them then,
    If ever mortal eyes do see them bolster   400
    More than their own. What then? How then?
    What shall I say? Where's satisfaction?
    It is impossible you should see this,
    Were they as prime as goats, as hot as monkeys,
    As salt as wolves in pride, and fools as gross   405
    As Ignorance made drunk. But yet, I say,

384–91 OTHELLO By...satisfied!] F; *not in* Q1   387 Her] Q2; My F   392 SH IAGO] F; *not in* Q1   392 sir] Q1; *not in* F   394 satisfied?] F; satisfied. Q1   394 I] Q1; and I F   396 you, the supervisor,] you, the superuisor Q1; you the super-vision F   400 do] F; did Q1

383 **should** ought (with a quibble on 'shouldst' at 382).

388 **Dian** Diana, goddess of chastity and the moon.

389–91 **If there...endure it** Othello's first reaction to the state of hideous uncertainty is to think of methods of committing suicide.

396 **supervisor** looker-on.

397 **topped** See 1.1.90 n.

398 **tedious** hard to arrange, laborious.

400 **bolster** bed together (lit. 'sharing the same pillow'); with perhaps a sexual pun on the meaning 'support each other'.

401 **More** Other.

404 **prime** lecherous. This is the sole use of the word in this sense in Shakespeare. Compare 'As lecherous as a goat' (Tilley G167).

404 **hot** sexually excited. Compare *Tro.* 3.1.129–30: 'hot blood begets hot thoughts, and hot thoughts beget hot deeds, and hot deeds is love'.

405 **salt** lustful. Compare *Tim.* 4.3.83–6: 'Be a whore still... / Make use of thy salt hours.'

405 **pride** lust. Compare *Lucrece* 437–9: 'His hand... / Smoking with pride, march'd on, to make his stand / On her bare breast.'

406–9 **But yet...have't** Compare Cinthio's source story: 'Yet I do not lose hope of being able to show you what you do not wish to believe' (Bullough, VII, 246).

>If imputation and strong circumstances,
>Which lead directly to the door of truth,
>Will give you satisfaction, you might have't.

OTHELLO Give me a living reason she's disloyal.   410
IAGO I do not like the office;

>But sith I am entered in this cause so far –
>Pricked to't by foolish honesty and love –
>I will go on. I lay with Cassio lately,
>And being troubled with a raging tooth   415
>I could not sleep.
>There are a kind of men so loose of soul
>That in their sleeps will mutter their affairs.
>One of this kind is Cassio.
>In sleep I heard him say, 'Sweet Desdemona,   420
>Let us be wary, let us hide our loves.'
>And then, sir, he would gripe and wring my hand,
>Cry, 'O sweet creature!' and then kiss me hard,
>As if he plucked up kisses by the roots
>That grew upon my lips; then laid his leg   425
>Over my thigh, and sighed, and kissed, and then
>Cried, 'Cursèd fate that gave thee to the Moor.'

OTHELLO O monstrous, monstrous!
IAGO   Nay, this was but his dream.
OTHELLO But this denoted a foregone conclusion.
IAGO 'Tis a shrewd doubt, though it be but a dream;   430

>And this may help to thicken other proofs
>That do demonstrate thinly.

OTHELLO   I'll tear her all to pieces!
IAGO Nay, yet be wise; yet we see nothing done,

>She may be honest yet. Tell me but this:

409 might have't] F; may ha 't Q1   410 she's] F; that shee's Q1   412 in] F; into Q1   415–19] *Pope;* And...tooth / ...
men / ...mutter / ...Cassio F; And...sleep / ...soul / ...affairs / ...Cassio Q1   421 wary] F; merry Q1   423 O]
F; out Q1   423 and] Q1; *not in* F   425–7] Q1; That...thigh / ...fate / ...Moor F   425 then] Q1; *not in* F
426 sighed] Q1; sigh F   426 kissed] Q1; kisse F   427 Cried] Q1; cry F   429 denoted] F; deuoted Q1   430] Q1;
assigned to Othello in F   433 yet be] F; but be Q1

407 imputation...circumstances 'opinion
founded on strong circumstantial evidence'
(Schmidt).

413 Pricked Spurred (as in *Mac.* 1.7.25–6).

417 loose of soul i.e. loose-tongued about their
innermost thoughts.

422 gripe seize.

429 foregone conclusion previous consum-
mation.

430 'Tis a shrewd doubt It gives rise to

grievous suspicion. Compare *MV* 3.2.243: 'There
are some shrowd contents in yond same paper.' See
supplementary note.

431 thicken substantiate.

434–7 Tell me...gift Compare Cinthio's
source story: 'she sometimes carried with her a
handkerchief embroidered most delicately in the
Moorish fashion, which the Moor had given her and
which was treasured by the Lady and her husband
too' (Bullough, VII, 246).

Have you not sometimes seen a handkerchief 435
Spotted with strawberries in your wife's hand?

OTHELLO I gave her such a one; 'twas my first gift.

IAGO I know not that; but such a handkerchief –
I am sure it was your wife's – did I today
See Cassio wipe his beard with.

OTHELLO   If it be that – 440

IAGO If it be that, or any that was hers,
It speaks against her with the other proofs.

OTHELLO O that the slave had forty thousand lives!
One is too poor, too weak, for my revenge.
Now do I see 'tis true. Look here, Iago, 445
All my fond love thus do I blow to heaven;
'Tis gone.
Arise, black vengeance, from thy hollow cell!
Yield up, O love, thy crown and hearted throne
To tyrannous hate! Swell, bosom, with thy fraught, 450
For 'tis of aspics' tongues.

                    He kneels.

IAGO   Yet be content.

OTHELLO O, blood, blood, blood!

IAGO Patience, I say; your mind perhaps may change.

OTHELLO Never, Iago. Like to the Pontic Sea,
Whose icy current and compulsive course 455
Ne'er feels retiring ebb but keeps due on
To the Propontic and the Hellespont,

---

441 any that] *Malone;* any, it F, Q1   445 true] F; time Q1   446–7] *Pope; one line in* F, Q1   448 thy] Q1; the F
448 cell] Q1; hell F   451 SD] Q1 *(after* content*); not in* F   451 Yet] F; Pray Q1   452 blood, blood!] F; *Iago,* blood.
Q1   453 perhaps] Q1; *not in* F   454–61 Iago...heaven] F; *not in* Q1   456 feels] Q2; keepes F

436 **Spotted with strawberries** Embroidered with a strawberry pattern. M. C. Linthicum, *Costume in the Drama of Shakespeare and his Contemporaries*, 1936, p. 270, notes that handkerchiefs were highly prized and expensive accessories among the fashionable.

443 **slave** i.e. Cassio.

446 **fond** foolish (because given to Desdemona, but by its nature 'heavenly').

448 **thy hollow cell** Compare *Tit.* 3.1.270: 'Revenge's cave'. As the allusion is to Ate who dwelt in the infernal regions, F's 'the hollow hell' may be correct; compare *JC* 3.1.270–1: 'And Caesar's spirit ranging for revenge, / With Ate by his side come hot from hell'. But the vocative seems to demand the more specific location that Q1 supplies.

449 **hearted** located in the heart.

450 **fraught** burden, freight.

451 **aspics'** asps', venomous serpents'.

451 **content** patient, calm.

454–7 **Like to...Hellespont** This is probably a recollection of two passages in Pliny: 'And the sea Pontus evermore floweth and runneth out into Propontis, but the sea never retireth back again within Pontus' (2.97); 'Out of Pontus the sea always floweth, and never ebbeth again' (4.13). In the context of the latter passage are also found the words 'icy', 'wide' and 'compulsive course'.

454 **Pontic Sea** Black Sea.

455 **compulsive** driving onward, irresistible.

457 **Propontic** Sea of Marmora, located between the Black Sea and the Aegean.

457 **Hellespont** Dardanelles Straits, which join the Sea of Marmora and the Aegean.

Even so my bloody thoughts with violent pace
Shall ne'er look back, ne'er ebb to humble love,
Till that a capable and wide revenge   460
Swallow them up. Now by yond marble heaven,
In the due reverence of a sacred vow
I here engage my words.

IAGO   Do not rise yet.

He kneels.

Witness you ever-burning lights above,
You elements that clip us round about,   465
Witness that here Iago doth give up
The execution of his wit, hands, heart,
To wronged Othello's service. Let him command,
And to obey shall be in me remorse,
What bloody business ever.

                        [*They rise.*]

OTHELLO   I greet thy love,   470
Not with vain thanks, but with acceptance bounteous;
And will upon the instant put thee to't.
Within these three days let me hear thee say
That Cassio's not alive.

IAGO   My friend is dead;
'Tis done at your request. But let her live.   475

OTHELLO Damn her, lewd minx! O, damn her, damn her!
Come, go with me apart. I will withdraw
To furnish me with some swift means of death
For the fair devil. Now art thou my lieutenant.

IAGO I am your own for ever.   480

                                        Exeunt

---

463 SD] Iago *kneeles.* Q1 *(after 465); not in* F   **467** execution] F; excellency Q1   **467** hands] F; hand Q1   **469** in me] F; *not in* Q1; without *Dover Wilson*   **470** business] F; worke so Q1   **470** SD] *Capell subst.; not in* F, Q1   **475**] Q1; 'Tis…request / …live F   **475** at your] F; as you Q1   **476**] Q1; Damn…minx / …her F   **476** damn her, damn her] F; dam her, Q1   **479**] Q1; For…devil / …lieutenant F

460 capable ample, capacious.
461 marble Presumably the meaning is 'shining' or 'grained like marble' (as in *Tim.* 4.3.191 and *Cym.* 5.4.120), but it may also have here the sense of 'hard, unfeeling'.
465 clip encompass. Compare *Ant.* 5.2.359–60: 'No grave upon the earth shall clip in it / A pair so famous.'

467 execution operation, activities.
467 wit intelligence.
469–70 to obey…ever i.e. whatever bloody deed I am called upon to perform shall be done because of the pity I feel for Othello. See supplementary note.
472 to't to the proof (as in *AWW* 2.2.48).
476 minx wanton.

3.4 *Enter* DESDEMONA, EMILIA *and* CLOWN.

DESDEMONA Do you know, sirrah, where Lieutenant Cassio lies?

CLOWN I dare not say he lies anywhere.

DESDEMONA Why, man?

CLOWN He's a soldier, and for one to say a soldier lies is
stabbing.   5

DESDEMONA Go to. Where lodges he?

CLOWN To tell you where he lodges is to tell you where I lie.

DESDEMONA Can anything be made of this?

CLOWN I know not where he lodges, and for me to devise a lodging,
and say he lies here, or he lies there, were to lie in mine own   10
throat.

DESDEMONA Can you enquire him out, and be edified by report?

CLOWN I will catechise the world for him: that is, make questions,
and by them answer.

DESDEMONA Seek him; bid him come hither; tell him I have moved   15
my lord on his behalf and hope all will be well.

CLOWN To do this is within the compass of man's wit, and therefore
I will attempt the doing of it.   *Exit*

DESDEMONA Where should I lose that handkerchief, Emilia?

EMILIA I know not, madam.   20

DESDEMONA Believe me, I had rather lose my purse
             Full of crusadoes; and but my noble Moor
             Is true of mind and made of no such baseness
             As jealous creatures are, it were enough
             To put him to ill thinking.

EMILIA   Is he not jealous?   25

Act 3, Scene 4   3.4] *Scæna Quarta.* F; *not in* QI   0 SD CLOWN] F; *the Clowne* QI   1 Lieutenant] F; the Leiutenant
QI   4 SH CLOWN] F; *not in* QI   4 one] QI; me F   4 is] QI; 'tis F   7–8 CLOWN To...this?] F; *not in* QI
10 he lies here, or] F; *not in* QI   10 mine own] F; my QI   16 on] F; in QI   17 man's wit] F; a man QI   18 of]
QI; *not in* F   18 SD] QI; *Exit Clo.* F   19 that] QI; the F   21 lose] loose QI; haue lost F

Act 3, Scene 4

1 **sirrah** A term of address to an inferior.

1 **lies** lodges.

2 **lies** tells an untruth.

4–5 **for one...stabbing** Hart compares
Thomas Dekker, *Seven Deadly Sins*: 'He that gives
a soldier the lie looks to receive the stab.'

7 **lie** deceive.

10–11 **were to lie...throat** were to lie foully;
with a pun on 'were/where' at 10.

13–14 **I will...answer** The Clown is exploiting
the educational implications in 'edify', and alluding
to the instructional method used in the Catechism.

13 **make questions** 'ask questions'; but also
'express doubts'.

17 **compass** range, reach; with a quibble on
'moved'.

22 **crusadoes** Gold coins of Portugese origin, so
called because they bore the figure of Christ's cross.

DESDEMONA Who, he? I think the sun where he was born
    Drew all such humours from him.

Enter OTHELLO.

EMILIA   Look where he comes.

DESDEMONA I will not leave him now; let Cassio
    Be called to him. – How is't with you, my lord?

OTHELLO Well, my good lady. [*Aside*] O hardness to dissemble!   30
    How do you, Desdemona?

DESDEMONA   Well, my good lord.

OTHELLO Give me your hand. This hand is moist, my lady.

DESDEMONA It yet hath felt no age, nor known no sorrow.

OTHELLO This argues fruitfulness and liberal heart.
    Hot, hot, and moist. This hand of yours requires   35
    A sequester from liberty, fasting and prayer,
    Much castigation, exercise devout;
    For here's a young and sweating devil here
    That commonly rebels. 'Tis a good hand,
    A frank one.

DESDEMONA   You may indeed say so,   40
    For 'twas that hand that gave away my heart.

OTHELLO A liberal hand! The hearts of old gave hands;
    But our new heraldry is hands, not hearts.

DESDEMONA I cannot speak of this. Come now, your promise.

---

27 SD] Q1; *after* comes *in* F   28–9] *Steevens*³; I...be / ...lord F; I...now / ...lord Q1   28 let] Q1 *(some copies)*; till F; 'Tis Q1 *(some copies)*   30 SD] *Hanmer; not in* F, Q1   32] Q1; Give...hand / ...lady F   33 yet hath] hath F; yet has Q1   35 Hot] F; Not Q1   36 prayer] F; praying Q1   44] Q1; I...this / ...promise F   44 now] F; come Q1

27 humours Bodily fluids, the proportions of which were believed to determine a person's temperament. The reference here is to black bile, believed to cause jealousy.

28 let This reading found in some copies of Q1 is obviously correct in view of 46 below.

32 moist A moist palm was believed to indicate youthfulness and amorousness. Compare *Venus and Adonis* 25–6: 'his sweating palm, / The president of pith and livelihood'; and Tilley H86: 'A moist palm argues an amorous nature.'

34 argues is proof of.

34 fruitfulness Three layers of meaning: (1) generosity; (2) amorousness; (3) fertility. Compare *Ant.* 1.2.52–3: 'Nay, if an oily palm be not a fruitful prognostication'.

34 liberal A quibble: (1) free; (2) licentious.

36 sequester A legal term for 'restraint, imprisonment'.

37 castigation corrective discipline.

37 exercise devout religious observances.

38 sweating devil spirit of sexual desire.

39 rebels i.e. against virtuous self-control.

40 frank Two layers of meaning: (1) liberal; (2) undisguised.

42–3 The hearts...hearts Warburton detected a topical allusion to the baronetage, the new titled order – ranking below peers and above knights – instituted by James I in 1611, which bears the red hand of Ulster as its badge; but this would mean that the lines were inserted some eight years after the play was written. The heraldic idea grows quite naturally out of 'liberal' (= befitting a gentleman), and William Cornwallis clarifies the reference: 'people used to give their hands and their hearts together, but we think it a finer grace to look asquint, our hand looking one way, and our heart another' (*Essays*, 1600–1).

OTHELLO What promise, chuck?　　　　　　　　　　　　　45

DESDEMONA I have sent to bid Cassio come speak with you.

OTHELLO I have a salt and sorry rheum offends me;
　　　　Lend me thy handkerchief.

DESDEMONA　　　　　　　　　　　Here, my lord.

OTHELLO That which I gave you.

DESDEMONA　　　　　　　　　　I have it not about me.

OTHELLO Not?　　　　　　　　　　　　　　　　　　　50

DESDEMONA No, faith, my lord.

OTHELLO　　　　　　　　　　That's a fault. That handkerchief
　　　　Did an Egyptian to my mother give:
　　　　She was a charmer and could almost read
　　　　The thoughts of people. She told her, while she kept it,
　　　　'Twould make her amiable and subdue my father　　　55
　　　　Entirely to her love; but if she lost it
　　　　Or made a gift of it, my father's eye
　　　　Should hold her loathèd and his spirits should hunt
　　　　After new fancies. She dying gave it me,
　　　　And bid me when my fate would have me wive,　　　60
　　　　To give it her. I did so, and take heed on't:
　　　　Make it a darling, like your precious eye.
　　　　To lose't or give't away were such perdition
　　　　As nothing else could match.

DESDEMONA　　　　　　　　　　　Is't possible?

OTHELLO 'Tis true. There's magic in the web of it:　　　65
　　　　A sibyl, that had numbered in the world
　　　　The sun to course two hundred compasses,
　　　　In her prophetic fury sewed the work;
　　　　The worms were hallowed that did breed the silk,

---

47 sorry] F; sullen Q1　　51 faith] Q1; indeed F　　58 loathèd] F; lothely Q1　　60 wive] Q1; Wiu'd F　　63 lose 't] F; loose Q1　　67 course] F; make Q1

47 salt and sorry rheum a wretched running cold; with quibbles on 'salt' (= lustful) and 'rheum' (= humour).

53 charmer witch, enchantress.

55 amiable desirable, beloved. Compare *John* 3.4.25: 'O amiable lovely death'.

59 fancies loves.

65–8 There's magic...work The source for this was probably a passage in Ariosto's *Orlando Furioso*, 46, 64–5, in which is described Cassandra's weaving a magical tent for her brother Hector.

65 web weaving.

66 sibyl prophetess. The longevity was probably suggested by the Sibyl of Cumae as depicted in Virgil's *Aeneid*. Compare *1H6* 1.2.55–6: 'The spirit of deep prophecy she hath, / Exceeding the nine sibyls of old Rome.'

67 compasses yearly circuits.

68 prophetic fury frenzy of inspiration. Compare *LLL* 4.3.225: 'What zeal, what fury, hath inspir'd thee now?' The phrase is based on Ariosto's 'il furor profetico'.

68 work embroidered pattern.

And it was dyed in mummy, which the skilful   70
Conserved of maidens' hearts.

DESDEMONA   I'faith, is't true?

OTHELLO Most veritable; therefore look to't well.

DESDEMONA Then would to God that I had never seen't!

OTHELLO Ha? Wherefore?

DESDEMONA Why do you speak so startingly and rash?   75

OTHELLO Is't lost? Is't gone? Speak; is't out of th'way?

DESDEMONA Heaven bless us!

OTHELLO Say you?

DESDEMONA It is not lost, but what and if it were?

OTHELLO How?   80

DESDEMONA I say it is not lost.

OTHELLO   Fetch't, let me see't.

DESDEMONA Why so I can, sir; but I will not now.
This is a trick to put me from my suit.
Pray you let Cassio be received again.

OTHELLO Fetch me the handkerchief. My mind misgives.   85

DESDEMONA Come, come;
You'll never meet a more sufficient man.

OTHELLO The handkerchief!

DESDEMONA   I pray, talk me of Cassio.

OTHELLO The handkerchief!

DESDEMONA   A man that all his time
Hath founded his good fortunes on your love,   90
Shared dangers with you –

OTHELLO The handkerchief!

DESDEMONA   I'faith, you are to blame.

OTHELLO Zounds!   *Exit*

EMILIA Is not this man jealous?

DESDEMONA   I ne'er saw this before.
Sure there's some wonder in this handkerchief;   95

70 which] F; with Q1   71 Conserved] F; Conserues Q1   71 I'faith,] Q1 (I faith); Indeed? F   73 God] Q1; Heauen F
75 rash] F; rashly Q1   77 Heaven] Q1; *not in* F   80 How] F; Ha Q1   82 sir] Q1; *not in* F   84 Pray you] F;
I pray Q1   85] Q1; Fetch...handkerchief / ...misgives F   85 the] F; that Q1   86–7] Q1; *as prose in* F
88–9 DESDEMONA I pray...handkerchief!] Q1; *not in* F   92 I' faith] Q1; Insooth F   93 Zounds] Q1; Away F

70 **mummy** Concoction supposed to be derived from embalmed bodies and used for magical or medicinal purposes.

71 **Conserved of** Prepared as a drug from.

75 **startingly** disjointedly. Compare *TN* 2.2.21: 'For she did speak in starts distractedly.'

75 **rash** excitedly.

76 **out of th'way** misplaced, gone astray.

87 **sufficient** able.

94 **saw this** i.e. perceived this trait.

95 **wonder** magical quality.

I am most unhappy in the loss of it.

EMILIA 'Tis not a year or two shows us a man.

They are all but stomachs, and we all but food;
They eat us hungerly, and when they are full,
They belch us.

Enter IAGO *and* CASSIO.

Look you, Cassio and my husband.   100

IAGO There is no other way: 'tis she must do't.

And lo, the happiness! Go, and importune her.

DESDEMONA How now, good Cassio! What's the news with you?

CASSIO Madam, my former suit. I do beseech you

That, by your virtuous means, I may again   105
Exist and be a member of his love,
Whom I, with all the office of my heart,
Entirely honour. I would not be delayed.
If my offence be of such mortal kind
That nor my service past nor present sorrows,   110
Nor purposed merit in futurity,
Can ransom me into his love again,
But to know so must be my benefit:
So shall I clothe me in a forced content,
And shut myself up in some other course   115
To fortune's alms.

DESDEMONA   Alas, thrice-gentle Cassio,

My advocation is not now in tune:
My lord is not my lord; nor should I know him,
Were he in favour as in humour altered.
So help me every spirit sanctified,   120
As I have spoken for you all my best,

---

96 the] F, QI; this QI *(some copies)*   96 of it] F; *not in* QI   100] QI; They...us / ...husband F   100 SD] F; *after*
96 *in* QI   107 office] F; duty QI   110 nor my] F; neither QI   115 shut] F; shoote QI

---

98 but stomachs only appetites. Emilia characteristically sees sexual desire in terms of eating.

102 happiness good luck, fortunate occurrence.

105 virtuous efficacious.

107 office devoted service. Compare *Ant.* 1.1.5: 'office and devotion of their view'.

113 But Merely.

113 benefit i.e. because he will know the worst.

115 shut myself up in confine myself to.

116 To fortune's alms i.e. accepting whatever fortune can spare.

118–19 My lord...altered Compare Cinthio's source story: 'I do not know what to make of the Moor. He used to be all love towards me, but in the last few days he has become quite another man' (Bullough, VII, 248).

119 favour external appearance. Compare *AYLI* 5.4.26–7: 'I do remember in this shepherd boy / Some lively touches of my daughter's favour.'

And stood within the blank of his displeasure
For my free speech! You must awhile be patient.
What I can do, I will; and more I will
Than for myself I dare. Let that suffice you.   125

IAGO Is my lord angry?

EMILIA   He went hence but now
And certainly in strange unquietness.

IAGO Can he be angry? I have seen the cannon
When it hath blown his ranks into the air,
And like the devil from his very arm   130
Puffed his own brother – and is he angry?
Something of moment then. I will go meet him.
There's matter in't indeed if he be angry.

DESDEMONA I prithee do so.

                                          Exit Iago

                              Something sure of state,
Either from Venice, or some unhatched practice   135
Made demonstrable here in Cyprus to him,
Hath puddled his clear spirit; and in such cases
Men's natures wrangle with inferior things,
Though great ones are their object. 'Tis even so;
For let our finger ache, and it endues   140
Our other healthful members even to a sense
Of pain. Nay, we must think men are not gods,
Nor of them look for such observancy
As fits the bridal. Beshrew me much, Emilia,
I was – unhandsome warrior as I am –   145
Arraigning his unkindness with my soul;
But now I find I had suborned the witness

---

131 is he] F; can he be Q1   134 SD] *Exit.* F *(after 133); not in* Q1   139–42] F; Though…object / …ache / …
members / …think / …gods Q1   139 their] F; the Q1   141 a] F; that Q1   143 observancy] F; obseruances Q1

122 **within the blank of** as the centre of the target for. Compare *Ham.* 4.1.42: 'As level as the cannon to his blank'.

132 **moment** immediate importance.

134 **of state** to do with state affairs.

135 **unhatched practice** previously undisclosed conspiracy.

137 **puddled** muddied, sullied the purity of.

139 **object** real point of concern.

140 **endues** brings, leads.

142 **Nay, we…gods** Proverbial: 'We are but men, not gods' (Tilley M593).

143 **observancy** tender attention. Compare *AYLI* 5.2.94–6: '[Love] is… / All adoration, duty, and observance'.

145 **unhandsome** unskilful (with perhaps also the meaning of 'unjust').

145 **warrior** Desdemona is recalling Othello's greeting at 2.1.174.

147 **suborned the witness** influenced the witness to give false evidence.

          And he's indicted falsely.
EMILIA Pray heaven it be state matters, as you think,
          And no conception nor no jealous toy   150
          Concerning you.
DESDEMONA Alas the day, I never gave him cause.
EMILIA But jealous souls will not be answered so.
          They are not ever jealous for the cause,
          But jealous for they're jealous. 'Tis a monster   155
          Begot upon itself, born on itself.
DESDEMONA Heaven keep that monster from Othello's mind.
EMILIA Lady, amen!
DESDEMONA I will go seek him. Cassio, walk here about.
          If I do find him fit, I'll move your suit   160
          And seek to effect it to my uttermost.
CASSIO I humbly thank your ladyship.

                              Exeunt Desdemona and Emilia

                    Enter BIANCA.

BIANCA 'Save you, friend Cassio.
CASSIO   What make you from home?
          How is it with you, my most fair Bianca?
          I'faith, sweet love, I was coming to your house.   165
BIANCA And I was going to your lodging, Cassio.
          What! Keep a week away? Seven days and nights?
          Eight score eight hours? And lovers' absent hours
          More tedious than the dial eight score times!
          O weary reckoning!
CASSIO   Pardon me, Bianca.   170
          I have this while with leaden thoughts been pressed;
          But I shall in a more continuate time

149–51] Q1; Pray...be / ...conception / ...you F   155 'Tis] Q1; It is F   157 that] Q1; the F
162 SD.1 *Exeunt...Emilia*] Q1 *(after 162); Exit.* F *(after 160)*   162 SD.2 *Enter* BIANCA] F; *after* Cassio *in 163 in* Q1
164 is it] Q1; is't F   165 I' faith] Q1; Indeed F   170 O] F; No Q1   171 leaden] F; laden Q1   172 continuate] F;
conuenient Q1

---

150 **conception** fantasy, false supposition.
150 **toy** fancy, whim.
155–6 **'Tis a monster...itself** Compare
Iago's definition at 3.3.167–9.
160 **fit** receptive.
163 **'Save** i.e. God save.
167–70 **What...reckoning** See pp. 15–16
above.

168 **Eight score eight** i.e. one hundred and
sixty plus eight (= seven days and nights).
169 **the dial** the whole round of the clock.
171 The image here is based on the torture of
being pressed to death.
172 **continuate** uninterrupted. Q1's 'conuenient' is possible, but not probable.

Strike off this score of absence. Sweet Bianca,
Take me this work out.

BIANCA   O Cassio, whence came this?
This is some token from a newer friend.   175
To the felt absence now I feel a cause.
Is't come to this? Well, well.

CASSIO   Go to, woman!
Throw your vile guesses in the devil's teeth
From whence you have them. You are jealous now
That this is from some mistress, some remembrance.   180
No, by my faith, Bianca.

BIANCA   Why, whose is it?

CASSIO I know not neither; I found it in my chamber.
I like the work well. Ere it be demanded –
As like enough it will – I'd have it copied.
Take it and do't, and leave me for this time.   185

BIANCA Leave you? Wherefore?

CASSIO I do attend here on the general;
And think it no addition, nor my wish,
To have him see me womaned.

BIANCA   Why, I pray you?

CASSIO Not that I love you not.

BIANCA   But that you do not love me.   190
I pray you, bring me on the way a little,
And say if I shall see you soon at night.

CASSIO 'Tis but a little way that I can bring you,
For I attend here; but I'll see you soon.

BIANCA 'Tis very good; I must be circumstanced.   195

                                                    Exeunt

177 Well, well] F; *not in* QI   181 by my faith] QI; *in good troth* F   182] QI; I...neither / ...chamber F
182 neither] F; *sweete* QI   184 I'd] QI; *I would* F   189–90 BIANCA Why...not.] F; *not in* QI   195 SD] QI; *Exeunt*
omnes. F

173 **Strike...score** Pay off this debt. Cassio
takes up the idea in Bianca's 'reckoning' and
quibbles on 'score'. Compare *AWW* 5.3.56–7:
'That thou didst love her, strike some scores
away / From the great compt.'
174 **Take...out** Copy this embroidered pattern
for me.
175 **friend** mistress.
177 **Well, well** Compare Tilley w269: 'Well,
well is a word of malice.'
182 **I found...chamber** See 3.3.322–3.

183 **demanded** enquired for.
188 **addition** In Shakespeare this usually means
'title' (as at 4.1.102), but here the sense seems to
be 'credit to me', which it may also have in *Ham.*
1.4.19–20: 'with swinish phrase / Soil our
addition'.
189 **womaned** accompanied by a woman.
191 **bring** accompany.
195 **be circumstanced** accept conditions as
they are.

4.1 *Enter* OTHELLO *and* IAGO.

IAGO Will you think so?

OTHELLO   Think so, Iago?

IAGO   What,
       To kiss in private?

OTHELLO   An unauthorised kiss!

IAGO Or to be naked with her friend in bed
       An hour or more, not meaning any harm?

OTHELLO Naked in bed, Iago, and not mean harm?   5
       It is hypocrisy against the devil.
       They that mean virtuously and yet do so,
       The devil their virtue tempts, and they tempt heaven.

IAGO So they do nothing, 'tis a venial slip;
       But if I give my wife a handkerchief –   10

OTHELLO What then?

IAGO Why, then 'tis hers, my lord; and being hers,
       She may, I think, bestow't on any man.

OTHELLO She is protectress of her honour too.
       May she give that?   15

IAGO Her honour is an essence that's not seen:
       They have it very oft that have it not.
       But for the handkerchief –

OTHELLO By heaven, I would most gladly have forgot it.
       Thou said'st – O it comes o'er my memory,   20
       As doth the raven o'er the infected house,
       Boding to all! – he had my handkerchief.

IAGO Ay, what of that?

OTHELLO   That's not so good now.

IAGO   What

Act 4, Scene 1   4.1] *Actus Quartus. Scena Prima.* F; *Actus.* 4 Q1   0 SD] F; *Enter* Iago *and* Othello. Q1
1–2 What...private] *one line in* F, Q1   3, 5 in bed] F; abed Q1   9 So] Q1; If F   21 infected] Q1; infectious F
23–4 What...wrong] *Dyce; one line in* F, Q1

Act 4, Scene 1

6 hypocrisy...devil As hypocrisy against God
entails a pretence of good to conceal evil, so evil
actions pretending to virtue are the opposite:
'hypocrisy against the devil'.

9 So If, as long as.

17 i.e. those women who have actually lost their
honour are often credited with still having it.

21 As doth...house The raven was proverbially
a bird of ill-omen (Tilley R33). It was also thought

to be connected with the spreading of infections;
compare Christopher Marlowe, *The Jew of Malta*
(ed. L. Kirschbaum) 2.1.1–4: 'like the sad presaging
raven that tolls / The sick man's passport in her
hollow beak / And in the shadow of the silent
night / Doth shake contagion from her sable
wings'. For a more symbolic use of the same image,
see *Mac.* 1.5.38–40.

21 infected plague-stricken.

If I had said I had seen him do you wrong?
Or heard him say – as knaves be such abroad,   25
Who having by their own importunate suit
Or voluntary dotage of some mistress
Convincèd or supplied them, cannot choose
But they must blab –

OTHELLO   Hath he said anything?

IAGO He hath, my lord; but be you well assured   30
No more than he'll unswear.

OTHELLO   What hath he said?

IAGO Faith, that he did – I know not what he did.

OTHELLO What, what?

IAGO Lie –

OTHELLO   With her?

IAGO   With her, on her, what you will.

OTHELLO Lie with her? Lie on her? We say lie on her when they belie   35
her. Lie with her! Zounds, that's fulsome! Handkerchief –
confessions – handkerchief! To confess and be hanged for his
labour. First to be hanged and then to confess. I tremble at it.
Nature would not invest herself in such shadowing passion without
some instruction. It is not words that shakes me thus. Pish! Noses,   40
ears, and lips. Is't possible? – Confess? Handkerchief? O devil!

                    [*He*] *falls in a trance.*

IAGO Work on,
My medicine, work! Thus credulous fools are caught;
And many worthy and chaste dames even thus,
All guiltless, meet reproach. What ho, my lord!   45
My lord, I say! Othello!

---

27 Or] F; Or by the Q1   28 Convincèd] F, Q1; Coniured Q1 *(some copies)*   32 Faith] Q1; Why F   33 What,] F;
But Q1   36 Zounds] Q1; *not in* F   36 Handkerchief] F; handkerchers Q1   37 confessions] F; Confession Q1
37 handkerchief] F; hankerchers Q1   37–41 To...devil] F; *not in* Q1   41 SD] *Falls in a Traunce.* F; *He fals downe.*
Q1; *not in some copies of* Q1   42–6] F; *as prose in* Q1   43 work] Q1; workes F

27 **voluntary dotage** willing infatuation.

28 **Convincèd** Overcome, overpowered. Compare *Mac.* 1.7.63–4: 'his two chamberlains / Will
I with wine and wassail so convince'.

28 **supplied** satisfied sexually. Compare *MM*
5.1.210–12: 'this is the body / That took away the
match from Isabel, / And did supply thee at thy
garden-house'.

35 **belie** vilify, slander.

36 **fulsome** rank, foul. Compare *MV* 1.3.80–6:
'the ewes being rank... / And in the doing of the
deed of kind, / He stuck them up before the
fulsome ewes'.

37 **confess and be hanged** Proverbial (Tilley
c587).

38 **First to...confess** Presumably Othello
conceives of Cassio's being executed with no
shriving-time allowed.

39–40 **Nature...instruction** i.e. my natural
faculties would not become obliterated by strong
emotion unless there were some basis of fact in what
I have heard.

45 **reproach** shame, disgrace (as in *R3* 3.7.231).

Enter CASSIO.

How now, Cassio!

CASSIO What's the matter?

IAGO My lord is fallen into an epilepsy.
This is his second fit; he had one yesterday.

CASSIO Rub him about the temples.

IAGO   No, forbear.   50
The lethargy must have his quiet course.
If not, he foams at mouth and by and by
Breaks out to savage madness. Look, he stirs.
Do you withdraw yourself a little while;
He will recover straight. When he is gone,   55
I would on great occasion speak with you.

                                             [*Exit Cassio*]

How is it, general? Have you not hurt your head?

OTHELLO Dost thou mock me?

IAGO   I mock you? No, by heaven!
Would you would bear your fortune like a man!

OTHELLO A hornèd man's a monster and a beast.   60

IAGO There's many a beast then in a populous city,
And many a civil monster.

OTHELLO Did he confess it?

IAGO   Good sir, be a man:
Think every bearded fellow that's but yoked
May draw with you. There's millions now alive   65
That nightly lie in those unproper beds
Which they dare swear peculiar. Your case is better.
O, 'tis the spite of hell, the fiend's arch-mock,
To lip a wanton in a secure couch

---

46 SD] F; *after* Cassio *in* Q1   50 No, forbear] Q1; *not in* F   56 SD] *Rowe*, Q2 *(after* me *at 58); not in* F, Q1
58 you? No] Q1; you not F   59 fortune] F; fortunes Q1   63 it] F; *not in* Q1   63 Good] F, Q1; God Q1 *(some copies)*
66 lie] F; lyes Q1   69 couch] F; Coach Q1

51 **lethargy** coma, unconsciousness (as in *Cor.* 4.5.224).

56 **great occasion** an important matter.

58 **Dost thou mock me?** Othello refers to the cuckold's horns.

60 **hornèd man** cuckold.

62 **civil** civilised (as in *Rom.* Prologue 4).

64 **yoked** A quibble: (1) married; (2) burdened (with wrongs).

65 **draw** A quibble: (1) pull (like yoked oxen); (2) join.

66 **unproper** not (solely) their own (because shared by their wives' lovers). Leontes in his jealous fit has a similar vision; see *WT* 1.2.191–6.

67 **peculiar** their own.

69 **lip** kiss.

69 **secure** free from care, free from suspicion. Compare *Wiv.* 2.2.300–1: 'Page is an ass, a secure ass; he will trust his wife.'

And to suppose her chaste! No, let me know;   70
And knowing what I am, I know what she shall be.
OTHELLO O, thou art wise; 'tis certain.
IAGO   Stand you awhile apart,
Confine yourself but in a patient list.
Whilst you were here, o'erwhelmèd with your grief –
A passion most unsuiting such a man –   75
Cassio came hither. I shifted him away
And laid good scuse upon your ecstasy;
Bade him anon return and here speak with me,
The which he promised. Do but encave yourself,
And mark the fleers, the gibes, and notable scorns   80
That dwell in every region of his face;
For I will make him tell the tale anew,
Where, how, how oft, how long ago, and when
He hath and is again to cope your wife.
I say but mark his gesture. Marry, patience,   85
Or I shall say you're all in all in spleen
And nothing of a man.
OTHELLO   Dost thou hear, Iago?
I will be found most cunning in my patience,
But – dost thou hear – most bloody.
IAGO   That's not amiss.
But yet keep time in all. Will you withdraw?   90
      [*Othello withdraws.*]
Now will I question Cassio of Bianca,
A housewife that by selling her desires

74 o'erwhelmèd] F; ere while, mad Q1   75 unsuiting] Q1; resulting F; unfitting Q1 (*some copies*)   77 scuse] Q1; scuses F
78 Bade] F; Bid Q1   78 return] F; retire Q1   79 Do] F; *not in* Q1   80 fleers] F; Ieeres Q1; geeres Q1 (*some copies*)
80 gibes] F; Iibes Q1; gibes Q1 (*some copies*)   84 hath] F; has Q1   90 SD] *Rowe; not in* F, Q1

71 **what I am** i.e. a cuckold.
71 **she shall be** will happen to her.
73 **in a patient list** within the bounds of
self-control.
76 **shifted him away** got rid of him by a
stratagem.
77 **ecstasy** fit, trance; an extension of the usual
Shakespearean usage of being outside oneself.
79 **encave** conceal.
80 **fleers** sneers. Compare *Rom.* 1.5.57: 'To fleer
and scorn at our solemnity'.
80 **notable** observable, obvious.
84 **cope** A quibble: (1) meet; (2) copulate with.
85 **gesture** bearing, demeanour (as in *AYLI*
5.2.62).

86 **all in...spleen** totally governed by passion.
90 **keep time** be controlled (a musical term).
91–101 **Now will...wrong** Compare Cinthio's
source story: 'Accordingly he spoke to the Corporal
one day while the Moor was standing where he
could see them as they talked; and chatting of quite
other matters than the Lady, he laughed heartily
and, displaying great surprise, he moved his head
about and gestured with his hands, acting as if he
were listening to marvels' (Bullough, VII, 247).
92 **housewife** hussy (pronounced 'huzif' at the
time). The word could mean 'prostitute', and
clearly this is the sense in which Iago is using it here.
But Bianca appears not to be a professional
courtesan exactly (see 5.1.121–3).

Buys herself bread and clothes. It is a creature
That dotes on Cassio; as 'tis the strumpet's plague
To beguile many and be beguiled by one.   95
He, when he hears of her, cannot refrain
From the excess of laughter. Here he comes.

Enter Cassio.

As he shall smile, Othello shall go mad;
And his unbookish jealousy must construe
Poor Cassio's smiles, gestures, and light behaviours   100
Quite in the wrong. How do you now, lieutenant?

CASSIO The worser that you give me the addition
Whose want even kills me.

IAGO Ply Desdemona well and you are sure on't.
Now if this suit lay in Bianca's power,   105
How quickly should you speed!

CASSIO   Alas, poor caitiff!

OTHELLO [*Aside*] Look how he laughs already!

IAGO I never knew a woman love man so.

CASSIO Alas, poor rogue! I think, i'faith, she loves me.

OTHELLO [*Aside*] Now he denies it faintly, and laughs it out. 110

IAGO Do you hear, Cassio?

OTHELLO [*Aside*]   Now he importunes him
To tell it o'er. Go to, well said, well said!

IAGO She gives it out that you shall marry her.
Do you intend it?

CASSIO Ha, ha, ha!   115

OTHELLO [*Aside*] Do you triumph, Roman? Do you triumph?

CASSIO I marry her? What! A customer! I prithee, bear some

---

93 clothes] Q1; Cloath F   96 refrain] Q1; restraine F   97 SD] F; *after 95 in* Q1   99 construe] conster Q1; conserue F   100 behaviours] F; behauiour Q1   101 now] Q1; *not in* F   105 power] Q1; dowre F   107, 110, 111, 116, 119, 123, 126, 131, 136, 151 SD *Aside*] Theobald; *not in* F, Q1   108 a] Q1; *not in* F   109 i' faith] Q1; indeed F   110–12] F; Now...on / ...said Q1   112 o'er] F; on Q1   112 well said,] F; *not in* Q1   116 you triumph,] Q1; ye triumph, F   117–18] Q2; I...bear / ...it / ...ha F; I...wit / ...ha Q1   117 her] Q1; *not in* F   117 What! a customer!] F; *not in* Q1   117 I prithee] Q1; prythee F

94–5 'tis the...one Compare 'He that beguiles another is oft beguiled himself' (Tilley D179).

99 unbookish ignorant (of the ways of the world); as opposed to Iago's 'wisdom' (72 above).

99 construe The idea of Othello as an ignorant schoolboy is an extension of 'unbookish'.

100 light cheerful, merry (as in *TGV* 1.2.81).

102 addition title, rank.

106 speed prosper, succeed.

106 caitiff wretch.

110 faintly without seriously intending it. Compare *R2* 5.3.103: 'He prays but faintly, and would be denied.'

112 said i.e. done.

116 Roman conqueror. Presumably the association is with Roman triumphs.

117 customer common woman, harlot (as in *AWW* 5.3.286).

117–18 bear...wit think more charitably of my judgement.

charity to my wit. Do not think it so unwholesome. Ha, ha, ha!

OTHELLO [*Aside*] So, so, so, so: they laugh that wins.

IAGO Faith, the cry goes that you shall marry her.   120

CASSIO Prithee, say true.

IAGO I am a very villain else.

OTHELLO [*Aside*] Have you scored me? Well.

CASSIO This is the monkey's own giving out. She is persuaded I will
marry her out of her own love and flattery, not out of my   125
promise.

OTHELLO [*Aside*] Iago beckons me. Now he begins the story.

CASSIO She was here even now. She haunts me in every place. I was
the other day talking on the sea-bank with certain Venetians, and
thither comes this bauble and, by this hand, falls me thus   130
about my neck.

OTHELLO [*Aside*] Crying 'O dear Cassio!' as it were. His gesture
imports it.

CASSIO So hangs and lolls and weeps upon me, so hales and pulls me.
Ha, ha, ha!   135

OTHELLO [*Aside*] Now he tells how she plucked him to my chamber.
O, I see that nose of yours, but not that dog I shall throw it
to!

CASSIO Well, I must leave her company.

IAGO Before me, look where she comes!   140

CASSIO 'Tis such another fitchew! Marry, a perfumed one.

Enter BIANCA.

What do you mean by this haunting of me?

---

119 they] F; *not in* Q1   120 Faith] Q1; *Why* F   120 that you shall] Q2; *that you* F; *you shall* Q1   123 scored me?
Well] F; *stor'd me well* Q1   124–6] Q1; *This...out / ...her / ...promise* F   127 beckons] Q1; *becomes* F
130 this] Q1; *the* F   130 and] F; *not in* Q1   130 by this hand] Q1; *not in* F   130 falls me] F; *she falls* Q1
134 hales] Q1; *shakes* F   137 O] F; *not in* Q1   141 SH CASSIO] F; *not in* Q1   141 SD] *after 140 in* F; *after 139 in*
Q1

---

118 **unwholesome** morally tainted.

119 **they...wins** Proverbial (Tilley L93).

120 **cry** rumour, report.

123 **scored me** There are three possible
meanings: (1) branded, wounded me (as in *Ant.*
4.7.12); (2) posted my name (as a cuckold) (as in
Shr. Induction 2.24); (3) made my reckoning (as in
Sonnets 122.10).

125 **love** love for me.

125 **flattery** self-flattery (leading to delusion).
Compare *TGV* 4.4.188: 'Unless I flatter with
myself too much'.

129 **sea-bank** sea-shore.

130 **bauble** worthless plaything.

137 **nose** There is probably a sexual connotation
here; see Hulme, p. 135.

140 **Before me** Upon my soul, before God.

141 **such another** A common idiom meaning
'one just like all the others'.

141 **fitchew** polecat, noted for its rank odour and
lechery. Compare *Lear* 4.6.123–4: 'The
fitchew...goes to't / With a...riotous appetite.' It
was a slang term for a loose woman; compare
Thomas Dekker and John Webster, *Northward Hoe*
(ed. W. C. Hazlitt) 1.1: 'Your captains were wont
to take their leaves of their London pole-cats (their
wenches I mean, sir).'

BIANCA Let the devil and his dam haunt you! What did you mean
by that same handkerchief you gave me even now? I was a fine fool
to take it. I must take out the work? A likely piece of work   145
that you should find it in your chamber and not know who left
it there! This is some minx's token, and I must take out the work?
There, give it your hobby-horse, wheresoever you had it. I'll
take out no work on't.

CASSIO How now, my sweet Bianca! How now, how now!   150

OTHELLO [*Aside*] By heaven, that should be my handkerchief!

BIANCA If you'll come to supper tonight, you may. If you will not,
come when you are next prepared for.   *Exit*

IAGO After her, after her!

CASSIO Faith, I must. She'll rail in the streets else.   155

IAGO Will you sup there?

CASSIO Faith, I intend so.

IAGO Well, I may chance to see you; for I would very fain speak with
you.

CASSIO Prithee, come; will you?   160

IAGO Go to; say no more.

                                 Exit Cassio

OTHELLO [*Coming forward.*] How shall I murder him, Iago?

IAGO Did you perceive how he laughed at his vice?

OTHELLO O, Iago!

IAGO And did you see the handkerchief?   165

OTHELLO Was that mine?

IAGO Yours, by this hand. And to see how he prizes the foolish woman
your wife: she gave it him, and he hath given it his whore.

OTHELLO I would have him nine years a-killing. A fine woman, a fair
woman, a sweet woman!   170

IAGO Nay, you must forget that.

OTHELLO Ay, let her rot and perish, and be damned tonight, for she
shall not live. No, my heart is turned to stone: I strike it and it
hurts my hand. O, the world hath not a sweeter creature! She

145 work] F; whole worke Q1   146 not know] Q1; know not F   148 your] F; the Q1   152 If you'll] F; An you'll
Q1   152 If you] F; an you Q1   155 Faith] Q1; Yes F   155 streets] F; streete Q1   157 Faith] Q1; Yes F
161 SD] Q1; *not in* F   162 SD] *Capell subst.; not in* F, Q1   167–8] F; *not in* Q1   171 that] F; *not in* Q1   172 Ay]
F; And Q1   174 hath] F; has Q1

143 **dam** mother. 'The devil and his dam' was
a proverbial phrase (Tilley D225).

145 **take…work** See 3.4.174 n.
145 **piece of work** story, business.
148 **hobby-horse** a loose woman. Compare *WT*
1.2.276–8: 'My wife's a hobby-horse, deserves a

name / As rank as any flax-wench that puts
to / Before her troth-plight.'
153 **you…prepared for** the next time I shall
expect you (i.e. never).
167 **Yours…hand** Note the quibble by means
of which Iago makes the common oath the literal
truth.

might lie by an emperor's side and command him tasks.   175

IAGO Nay, that's not your way.

OTHELLO Hang her, I do but say what she is: so delicate with her needle,
an admirable musician – O, she will sing the savageness out of a
bear – of so high and plenteous wit and invention –

IAGO She's the worse for all this.   180

OTHELLO O, a thousand, thousand times – and then of so gentle
a condition!

IAGO Ay, too gentle.

OTHELLO Nay, that's certain; but yet the pity of it, Iago! O Iago,
the pity of it, Iago!   185

IAGO If you are so fond over her iniquity, give her patent to offend;
for if it touch not you, it comes near nobody.

OTHELLO I will chop her into messes. Cuckold me!

IAGO O, 'tis foul in her.

OTHELLO With mine officer!   190

IAGO That's fouler.

OTHELLO Get me some poison, Iago, this night. I'll not expostulate
with her, lest her body and beauty unprovide my mind again – this
night, Iago.

IAGO Do it not with poison; strangle her in her bed, even the bed she 195
hath contaminated.

OTHELLO Good, good! The justice of it pleases; very good!

IAGO And for Cassio, let me be his undertaker. You shall hear more
by midnight.

OTHELLO Excellent good!   200
                    A trumpet [sounds within].
What trumpet is that same?

IAGO I warrant something from Venice.

---

181 O] F; *not in* QI   181 thousand, thousand] QI; thousand, a thousand F   184 Nay] F; I QI   184 O Iago] F; *not
in* QI   185 of it, Iago] F; *not in* QI   186 are] F; be QI   187 touch] F; touches QI   192 night. I'll] F; night·I'le
QI   197] QI; Good, good / …good F   198–9] QI; And…undertaker / …midnight F   200 SD] *Theobald subst.*;
A Trumpet. QI *(after 199); not in* F   202–4] I…Venice / …duke / …him F; Something…Lodovico / …him QI
202 I warrant] F; *not in* QI   202 Venice] F; *Venice* sure QI

176 your way proper course (of thought).

179 invention imagination.

181–2 gentle a condition Either (1) well born
(as in *H5* 4 Prologue 45); or (2) amiable a character
(as in *Wiv.* 1.4.139).

183 gentle kind, yielding (to men) (as in *Lucrece*
545).

186 fond over stupid about, doting on.

186 patent license (as in *AWW* 4.5.66).

187 comes near affects, harms.

188 messes pieces of meat.

192–6 Get me…contaminated Compare
Cinthio's source story: 'They were discussing
whether the Lady should perish by poison or the
dagger, and not deciding on either of them' (Bullough, VII, 250).

192 expostulate argue at length (as in *TGV*
3.1.253).

193 unprovide…mind weaken my resolution.

198 be his undertaker deal with him.

Enter LODOVICO, DESDEMONA *and* ATTENDANTS.

'Tis Lodovico. This comes from the duke. See, your wife's with
him.

LODOVICO God save you, worthy general!

OTHELLO   With all my heart, sir.   205

LODOVICO The duke and senators of Venice greet you.

[*He gives Othello a letter.*]

OTHELLO I kiss the instrument of their pleasures.

[*He opens the letter and reads.*]

DESDEMONA And what's the news, good cousin Lodovico?

IAGO I am very glad to see you, signior;

Welcome to Cyprus.   210

LODOVICO I thank you. How does Lieutenant Cassio?

IAGO Lives, sir.

DESDEMONA Cousin, there's fallen between him and my lord

An unkind breach; but you shall make all well.

OTHELLO Are you sure of that?   215

DESDEMONA My lord?

OTHELLO 'This fail you not to do, as you will –'

LODOVICO He did not call; he's busy in the paper.

Is there division 'twixt my lord and Cassio?

DESDEMONA A most unhappy one; I would do much   220

T'atone them, for the love I bear to Cassio.

OTHELLO Fire and brimstone!

DESDEMONA My lord?

OTHELLO Are you wise?

DESDEMONA What, is he angry?

LODOVICO   Maybe the letter moved him;   225

For as I think they do command him home,

Deputing Cassio in his government.

DESDEMONA By my troth, I am glad on't.

OTHELLO   Indeed!

DESDEMONA   My lord?

202 SD] *after 199 in* F, Q1   203 Lodovico. This comes] *Lodouico, this, comes* F; *Lodouico, Come* Q1   203 See] F; *and
see* Q1   205 God save you] *Saue you* F; *God saue the* Q1   206 senators] Q1; *the Senators* F   206 SD] *Rowe subst.;
not in* F, Q1   207 SD] *Capell subst.; not in* F, Q1   209–10] F; *one line in* Q1   219 'twixt my] F; *betweene thy* Q1
228 By my troth] Q1; *Trust me* F

214 **unkind breach** unnatural separation, un-
characteristic quarrel.
226 **For as** Because.

227 **government** office of command (as in *1H4*
4.1.19).
228 **on't** of it.

OTHELLO I am glad to see you mad.

DESDEMONA   Why, sweet Othello?

OTHELLO Devil!   230

[*He strikes her.*]

DESDEMONA I have not deserved this.

LODOVICO My lord, this would not be believed in Venice,
    Though I should swear I saw't. 'Tis very much.
    Make her amends; she weeps.

OTHELLO   O devil, devil!
    If that the earth could teem with woman's tears,   235
    Each drop she falls would prove a crocodile.
    Out of my sight!

DESDEMONA   I will not stay to offend you.

LODOVICO Truly, an obedient lady.
    I do beseech your lordship, call her back.

OTHELLO Mistress!   240

DESDEMONA My lord?

OTHELLO What would you with her, sir?

LODOVICO   Who? I, my lord?

OTHELLO Ay, you did wish that I would make her turn.
    Sir, she can turn, and turn, and yet go on,
    And turn again. And she can weep, sir, weep.   245
    And she's obedient; as you say, obedient,
    Very obedient – proceed you in your tears –
    Concerning this, sir, – O, well-painted passion! –
    I am commanded home – get you away!

229 mad] F, QI; *madam conj. Nicholson*   229 Why] F; How QI   230 SD] *Theobald subst.; not in* F, QI   235 woman's]
F; womens QI   238 an] QI; *not in* F   249 home] F; here QI

229 **mad** The meaning here is obscure. It may
be the counterbalance of 'wise' (224), with Othello
saying 'I am happy to see that you have so obviously
lost your mind (to speak so blatantly about your love
for Cassio).' Nicholson's suggestion that Othello is
being heavily formal ('I am glad to see you,
madam'), with F's and QI's 'mad' being an
abbreviation of 'madam' is attractive but lacks
sufficient authority for adoption.

233 **very much** outrageous.

235 **teem** with be impregnated by, spawn with
(as in *Tim.* 4.3.190).

236 **falls** lets fall.

236 **prove** Either (1) turn into; or (2) be the same
as the tears of.

236 **crocodile** Compare the proverbial saying

'crocodile tears' (Tilley C831). Hakluyt's account of
Sir John Hawkins's second voyage (1565) includes
a description of the crocodile's supposed propensity
for dissimulation: 'His nature is ever, when he
would have his prey, to cry and sob like a Christian
body, to provoke them to come to him, and then he
snatcheth at them.'

243 **turn** come back.

244–5 **turn...again** Quibbles on the meanings:
(1) come back (as in *AYLI* 2.7.162); (2) be fickle
(as in *TGV* 2.2.4); (3) go for sexual intercourse (as
in *MV* 1.3.81).

246 **obedient** yielding to whatever is asked of
her (with a sexual innuendo).

248 **painted passion** simulated emotion.

I'll send for you anon. – Sir, I obey the mandate,   250
And will return to Venice. – Hence, avaunt!

                                    [*Exit Desdemona*]

Cassio shall have my place. And, sir, tonight
I do entreat that we may sup together.
You are welcome, sir, to Cyprus. Goats and monkeys! *Exit*

LODOVICO Is this the noble Moor whom our full senate   255
  Call all-in-all sufficient? Is this the nature
  Whom passion could not shake? Whose solid virtue
  The shot of accident nor dart of chance
  Could neither graze nor pierce?

IAGO   He is much changed.

LODOVICO Are his wits safe? Is he not light of brain?   260
IAGO He's that he is; I may not breathe my censure
  What he might be. If what he might he is not,
  I would to heaven he were.

LODOVICO   What! Strike his wife!
IAGO Faith, that was not so well; yet would I knew
  That stroke would prove the worst.

LODOVICO   Is it his use?   265
  Or did the letters work upon his blood
  And new-create this fault?

IAGO   Alas, alas!
  It is not honesty in me to speak
  What I have seen and known. You shall observe him,
  And his own courses will denote him so,   270
  That I may save my speech. Do but go after,
  And mark how he continues.

LODOVICO I am sorry that I am deceived in him.

                                  Exeunt

---

251 SD] *Rowe; not in* F, Q1   254] Q1; You...Cyprus / ...monkeys F   254 SD] F, Q1; *not in some copies of* Q1
256 Is] F; *not in* Q1   256 nature] F; noble nature Q1   261 is] is: F; is, Q1   261 censure] censure. F; censure, Q1
262 be.] be: F; be, Q1   262 what] F; as Q1   267 this] Q1; his F

254 **Goats and monkeys** See 3.3.404 and n.
258 **shot...chance** Compare *Ham.* 3.1.57:
'slings and arrows of outrageous fortune'.
261 **censure** See 2.3.174 n.
262–3 **If what...were** i.e. if he is not out of his

mind, I wish to God he were (for only that would
serve to excuse his actions).
265 **use** custom (as in *MM* 3.2.126).
266 **blood** passion (here of anger).
270 **courses will denote** actions will reveal.

4.2 *Enter* OTHELLO *and* EMILIA.

OTHELLO You have seen nothing then?
EMILIA Nor ever heard, nor ever did suspect.
OTHELLO Yes, you have seen Cassio and she together.
EMILIA But then I saw no harm, and then I heard
     Each syllable that breath made up between them. 5
OTHELLO What! Did they never whisper?
EMILIA   Never, my lord.
OTHELLO Nor send you out o'th'way?
EMILIA   Never.
OTHELLO To fetch her fan, her gloves, her mask, nor nothing?
EMILIA Never, my lord.
OTHELLO That's strange. 10
EMILIA I durst, my lord, to wager she is honest,
     Lay down my soul at stake. If you think other,
     Remove your thought; it doth abuse your bosom.
     If any wretch have put this in your head,
     Let heaven requite it with the serpent's curse! 15
     For if she be not honest, chaste, and true,
     There's no man happy. The purest of their wives
     Is foul as slander.
OTHELLO   Bid her come hither; go!

                             Exit Emilia

     She says enough; yet she's a simple bawd
     That cannot say as much. This is a subtle whore, 20
     A closet lock and key of villainous secrets;
     And yet she'll kneel and pray. I have seen her do't.

           Enter DESDEMONA *and Emilia.*

DESDEMONA My lord, what is your will?
OTHELLO   Pray, chuck, come hither.

Act 4, Scene 2   4.2] *Scena Secunda.* F; *not in* Q1   3 you] F; and you Q1   8 her gloves; her mask] F; her mask, her gloues Q1   15 heaven] F; heauens Q1   17 their wives] F; her Sex Q1   18 SD] F; *after* slander *in* Q1   23 Pray] Q1; Pray you F

Act 4, Scene 2
12 at stake as the wager.
13 abuse your bosom deceive you.
15 serpent's curse 'Then the Lord God said to the serpent, Because thou hast done this, thou art cursed above all cattle, and above every beast of the field: upon thy belly shalt thou go, and dust shalt thou eat all the days of thy life' (Gen. 3.14).

17 happy fortunate.
19 bawd procuress.
20 This i.e. Desdemona.
21 closet...key concealer, locker-up. Usually in Shakespeare 'closet' refers to a room, but here it seems to mean 'chest for papers', as in *Mac.* 5.1.6.

DESDEMONA What is your pleasure?

OTHELLO   Let me see your eyes.
      Look in my face.

DESDEMONA   What horrible fancy's this?   25

OTHELLO [*To Emilia*] Some of your function, mistress:
      Leave procreants alone and shut the door;
      Cough or cry 'hem' if anybody come.
      Your mystery, your mystery! Nay, dispatch!

                                  Exit Emilia

DESDEMONA Upon my knees, what doth your speech import?   30
      I understand a fury in your words,
      But not the words.

OTHELLO   Why? What art thou?

DESDEMONA Your wife, my lord; your true and loyal wife.

OTHELLO Come, swear it; damn thyself;
      Lest, being like one of heaven, the devils themselves   35
      Should fear to seize thee. Therefore be double-damned:
      Swear thou art honest.

DESDEMONA   Heaven doth truly know it.

OTHELLO Heaven truly knows that thou art false as hell.

DESDEMONA To whom, my lord? With whom? How am I false?

OTHELLO Ah, Desdemon, away, away, away!   40

DESDEMONA Alas, the heavy day! Why do you weep?
      Am I the motive of these tears, my lord?
      If haply you my father do suspect
      An instrument of this your calling back,
      Lay not your blame on me. If you have lost him,   45
      I have lost him too.

OTHELLO   Had it pleased heaven
      To try me with affliction, had they rained
      All kind of sores and shames on my bare head,
      Steeped me in poverty to the very lips,

---

26 SD] *Hanmer; not in* F, QI   29 Nay] QI; May F   30 knees] QI; knee F   30 doth] F; does QI   32 But...words] QI; *not in* F   34–7 Come...honest] QI; *as prose in* F   39] QI; To...lord / ...false F   40 Ah] F; O QI   42 motive] F; occasion QI   42 these] F; those QI   45 lost] F; left QI   46 I] F; Why I QI   46 lost] F; left QI   47 they rained] F; he ram'd QI   48 kind] F; kindes QI

26 **Some of your function** Do your job (as brothel-keeper).

29 **mystery** trade (of bawd), as in *MM* 4.2.34.

38 **false as hell** Proverbial phrase (Tilley H398).

43 **haply** by chance.

46–52 **Had it...patience** Probably an allusion to Job.

47 **they rained** QI's reading 'he ram'd' (= rained) makes one wonder whether 'heaven' was originally 'God'.

Given to captivity me and my utmost hopes,   50
I should have found in some place of my soul
A drop of patience. But, alas, to make me
The fixèd figure for the time of scorn
To point his slow unmoving finger at!
Yet could I bear that too, well, very well;   55
But there where I have garnered up my heart,
Where either I must live or bear no life,
The fountain from the which my current runs
Or else dries up – to be discarded thence
Or keep it as a cistern for foul toads   60
To knot and gender in! Turn thy complexion there,
Patience, thou young and rose-lipped cherubin;
Ay, there look grim as hell!

DESDEMONA I hope my noble lord esteems me honest.

OTHELLO O ay: as summer flies are in the shambles,   65
That quicken even with blowing. O, thou weed,
Who art so lovely fair and smell'st so sweet
That the sense aches at thee, would thou hadst ne'er been
    born!

DESDEMONA Alas, what ignorant sin have I committed?

OTHELLO Was this fair paper, this most goodly book,   70
Made to write 'whore' upon? What committed!
Committed? O thou public commoner!

---

50 utmost] F; *not in* Q1   51 place] F; part Q1   53 The] F; A Q1   54 unmoving] Q1; and moving F   54 finger]
F; fingers Q1   54 at] F; at – oh, oh, Q1   62 thou] F; thy Q1   63 Ay, there] *Theobald;* I heere F, Q1   65 summer]
F; summers Q1   66–8] *Capell;* That…weed / …sweet / …thee / …born F; That…blowing / …fair / …thee /
…born Q1   66 weed] F; blacke weede Q1   67 Who] F; Why Q1   67 and] F; Thou Q1   68 ne'er] Q1; neuer F
71 upon] F; on Q1   72–5] F; *not in* Q1

53–4 **The fixèd…at** Othello sees himself as an
eternal object of derision, pointed at forever – like
the numbers on a clock-face, pointed at by the
hour-hand which, though moving, appears to the
human eye to be standing still. Compare *Sonnets*
104.9–10: 'yet doth beauty, like a dial-hand, / Steal
from his figure, and no pace perceiv'd'.
56 **garnered** stored.
58–61 **The fountain…gender in** The vocabulary here is from Prov. 5.15–18: 'Drink the water
of thy cistern…Let thy fountain be blessed, and
rejoice with the wife of thy youth.' This Geneva
version has a marginal note: 'God blesseth marriage
and curseth whoredom.'
58 **fountain** spring. Compare *Mac.* 2.3.98–9:
'The spring, the head, the fountain of your
blood / Is stopp'd.'

60 **cistern** cesspool.
61 **knot and gender** copulate and engender.
61 **Turn…there** Grow pale when that
happens.
64 **honest** chaste.
65 **summer flies** Compare *Lear* 4.6.112–13:
'the small gilded fly / Does lecher in my sight'.
65 **shambles** butcher's slaughter-house.
66 **quicken…blowing** come to life merely
with the depositing of larvae.
69 **ignorant** unknowing, innocent.
72 **Committed** Committed adultery. Compare
Lear 3.4.81–2: 'commit not with a man's sworn
spouse'.
72 **commoner** whore (as in *AWW* 5.3.194).

I should make very forges of my cheeks
That would to cinders burn up modesty
Did I but speak thy deeds. What committed!   75
Heaven stops the nose at it, and the moon winks;
The bawdy wind, that kisses all it meets,
Is hushed within the hollow mine of earth
And will not hear it. What committed?
Impudent strumpet!

DESDEMONA   By heaven, you do me wrong.   80
OTHELLO Are not you a strumpet?
DESDEMONA   No, as I am a Christian.
If to preserve this vessel for my lord
From any other foul unlawful touch
Be not to be a strumpet, I am none.
OTHELLO What, not a whore?
DESDEMONA   No, as I shall be saved.   85
OTHELLO Is't possible?
DESDEMONA O, heaven forgive us!
OTHELLO   I cry you mercy then:
I took you for that cunning whore of Venice
That married with Othello. You, mistress,
That have the office opposite to Saint Peter,
And keeps the gate of hell! You, you, ay, you!   90

Enter Emilia.

We have done our course; there's money for your pains.
I pray you turn the key, and keep our counsel.   *Exit*
EMILIA Alas, what does this gentleman conceive?

---

78 hollow] F; hallow QI   80 Impudent strumpet] QI; *not in* F   83 other] F; hated QI   87 forgive us] F; forgiuenesse
QI   87 then] F; *not in* QI   91 gate of] F; gates in QI   91 You...you!] F; I, you, you, you; QI   91 SD] *after 89
in* F; *after 85 in* QI

---

76 **moon** The symbol of chastity.
76 **winks** closes its eyes (as in *Cym.* 2.4.89).
77–8 **The bawdy...earth** Aeolus and Boreas
were believed to live in the caves of mountainous
Thrace (*Aeneid* I. 81–6). Compare *2H6* 3.2.88–9:
'but curs'd the gentle gusts, / And he that loos'd
them forth their brazen caves'.
77 **bawdy** i.e. because it blows promiscuously
on everybody; compare *MV* 2.6.16: 'Hugg'd and
embraced by the strumpet wind'. Othello sees even
the most promiscuous of natural forces being
shamed by Desdemona's deed.
78 **mine** cave.

82 **vessel** body. Compare I Thess. 4.3–5: 'ye
should abstain from fornication, That every one of
you should know, how to possess his vessel in
holiness and honour, And not in the lust of
concupiscence'.
87 **cry you mercy** ask your pardon.
91 **keeps...hell** Compare Prov. 7.27: 'Her [the
harlot's] house is the way unto the grave, which
goeth down to the chambers of death.'
92 **done our course** completed our business
(with sexual overtones).
94 **conceive** imagine.

How do you, madam? How do you, my good lady?   95
DESDEMONA Faith, half-asleep.
EMILIA Good madam, what's the matter with my lord?
DESDEMONA With who?
EMILIA Why, with my lord, madam.
DESDEMONA Who is thy lord?
EMILIA   He that is yours, sweet lady.   100
DESDEMONA I have none. Do not talk to me, Emilia.
I cannot weep, nor answers have I none
But what should go by water. Prithee tonight
Lay on my bed my wedding sheets, remember;
And call thy husband hither.
EMILIA   Here's a change indeed!   *Exit*   105
DESDEMONA 'Tis meet I should be used so, very meet!
How have I been behaved that he might stick
The smallest opinion on my least misuse?

Enter IAGO *and Emilia.*

IAGO What is your pleasure, madam? How is't with you?
DESDEMONA I cannot tell. Those that do teach young babes   110
Do it with gentle means and easy tasks.
He might have chid me so; for, in good faith,
I am a child to chiding.
IAGO   What is the matter, lady?
EMILIA Alas, Iago, my lord hath so bewhored her,
Thrown such despite and heavy terms upon her   115
As true hearts cannot bear.
DESDEMONA Am I that name, Iago?
IAGO   What name, fair lady?
DESDEMONA Such as she said my lord did say I was.
EMILIA He called her whore. A beggar in his drink

97] QI ; Good...madam / ...lord F   100] F; *not in* QI   102 answers] F; answer QI   104 my wedding] F; our
wedding QI   106 very meet] F; very well QI   108 least misuse] F; greatest abuse QI   108 SD] F; *after 109 in* QI
109] *Pope*; What...madam / ...you F, QI   113 to] F; at QI   116 As] QI; That F   116 bear] QI; bear it F
118 said] F; sayes QI

96 **half-asleep** i.e. stunned.
103 **go by water** be given expression by tears.
Compare *1H4* 3.1.93–4: 'a world of water
shed / Upon the parting of your wives and you';
and also 'To write in water' (Tilley W114), a
proverbial description of unavailing activity.
106 **meet** fitting.
107–8 **stick...opinion** attach the least censure.

Compare *Cor.* 1.1.271: 'Opinion that so sticks on
Martius'.
108 **least misuse** most trivial misbehaviour.
QI's 'greatest abuse' is possible.
113 **am a child to chiding** have no experience
of being upbraided.
115 **despite** abuse (as in *Cor.* 3.3.139).

Could not have laid such terms upon his callet. 120
IAGO Why did he so?
DESDEMONA I do not know; I am sure I am none such.
IAGO Do not weep, do not weep! Alas the day!
EMILIA Hath she forsook so many noble matches,
     ' Her father, and her country, and her friends, 125
     To be called whore? Would it not make one weep?
DESDEMONA It is my wretched fortune.
IAGO   Beshrew him for't!
     How comes this trick upon him?
DESDEMONA   Nay, heaven doth know.
EMILIA I will be hanged if some eternal villain,
     Some busy and insinuating rogue, 130
     Some cogging, cozening slave, to get some office,
     Have not devised this slander; I'll be hanged else.
IAGO Fie, there is no such man; it is impossible.
DESDEMONA If any such there be, heaven pardon him.
EMILIA A halter pardon him and hell gnaw his bones! 135
     Why should he call her whore? Who keeps her company?
     What place, what time, what form, what likelihood?
     The Moor's abused by some most villainous knave,
     Some base notorious knave, some scurvy fellow.
     O heaven, that such companions thou'dst unfold, 140
     And put in every honest hand a whip
     To lash the rascals naked through the world,
     Even from the east to th'west!
IAGO   Speak within door.
EMILIA O fie upon them! Some such squire he was

---

124 Hath] F; Has QI   125 country, and] Country? And F; Countrey, all QI   127–8 Beshrew...him] F; *one line in* QI   135–7] QI; A...him / ...bones / ...whore / ...company / ...time / ...likelihood F   138 most villainous] F; outragious QI   140 heaven] QI; heauens F   142 rascals] F; rascall QI   143 door] F; dores QI   144 them] F; him QI

120 **callet** slut, drab.
124 **Hath...matches** Compare Cinthio's source story: 'the Lady's relatives did all they could to make her take another husband' (Bullough, VII, 242).
127 **Beshrew** Curse.
128 **trick** delusion (as in *Ant.* 4.2.14).
129 **eternal** inveterate.
130 **busy** See 3.3.255 n.
130 **insinuating** worming into favour, wheedling (as in *1H6* 2.4.35).

131 **cogging** cheating, deceiving (as in *R3* 1.3.48).
131 **cozening** deceiving.
135 **halter** hangman's noose.
137 **form** appearance.
137 **likelihood** grounds for such an inference (as in *TGV* 5.2.43).
140 **companions** rogues (as in *Wiv.* 3.1.120).
140 **unfold** disclose, expose.
143 **within door** less loudly, more controlledly.
144 **squire** fellow.

That turned your wit the seamy side without   145
And made you to suspect me with the Moor.

IAGO You are a fool, go to.

DESDEMONA   O good Iago,
What shall I do to win my lord again?
Good friend, go to him; for, by this light of heaven,
I know not how I lost him. Here I kneel: 150
If e'er my will did trespass 'gainst his love
Either in discourse of thought or actual deed;
Or that mine eyes, mine ears, or any sense
Delighted them in any other form;
Or that I do not yet, and ever did,   155
And ever will – though he do shake me off
To beggarly divorcement – love him dearly,
Comfort forswear me! Unkindness may do much,
And his unkindness may defeat my life,
But never taint my love. I cannot say 'whore':   160
It does abhor me now I speak the word;
To do the act that might the addition earn
Not the world's mass of vanity could make me.

IAGO I pray you be content; 'tis but his humour.
The business of the state does him offence,   165
And he does chide with you.

DESDEMONA If 'twere no other –

IAGO   It is but so, I warrant.
             [*Trumpets sound within.*]
Hark how these instruments summon to supper!
The messengers of Venice stay the meat.

147 O good] Q1; Alas F   150–63 Here…make me] F; *not in* Q1   154 them in] Q2; them: or F   166 And…you]
Q1; *not in* F   167 warrant] F; warrant you Q1   167 SD] *Rowe subst.*; *not in* F, Q1   168 summon] F; summon you
Q1   169 The messengers] F; And the great Messengers Q1   169 stay the meat] staies the meate F; stay Q1

145 **seamy side without** wrong side out.
146 **suspect me** i.e. of adultery.
147 **go** to be quiet.
147–50 **O good…him** In Cinthio's source
story Disdemona asks the help of the Ensign's wife:
'Because I know that he is very friendly with your
husband, and confides in him, I beg you, if you have
learned anything from him which you can tell me,
that you will not fail to help me' (Bullough, VII,
248).
152 **discourse of thought** process of thinking.
Compare *Ham.* 4.4.36–7: 'He that made us

with such large discourse / Looking before and
after'.
153 **that** if.
154 **Delighted them** Took delight.
155 **yet** still.
158 **Comfort forswear** Let comfort abandon.
159 **defeat** destroy.
161 **abhor** Quibble on (1) disgust; (2) make into
a whore.
162 **addition** title.
163 **vanity** finery.
169 **stay the meat** wait for their meal.

Go in, and weep not; all things shall be well.   170

Exeunt Desdemona and Emilia

Enter RODERIGO.

How now, Roderigo?

RODERIGO I do not find that thou deal'st justly with me.

IAGO What in the contrary?

RODERIGO Every day thou daff'st me with some device, Iago, and
rather, as it seems to me now, keep'st from me all conveniency   175
than suppliest me with the least advantage of hope. I will indeed
no longer endure it. Nor am I yet persuaded to put up in peace
what already I have foolishly suffered.

IAGO Will you hear me, Roderigo?

RODERIGO Faith, I have heard too much; for your words and   180
performances are no kin together.

IAGO You charge me most unjustly.

RODERIGO With naught but truth. I have wasted myself out of my
means. The jewels you have had from me to deliver to Desdemona
would half have corrupted a votarist. You have told me she hath   185
received them, and returned me expectations and comforts of
sudden respect and acquaintance, but I find none.

IAGO Well, go to; very well.

RODERIGO Very well, go to! I cannot go to, man, nor 'tis not very
well. By this hand, I say 'tis very scurvy and begin to find myself 190
fopped in it.

IAGO Very well.

RODERIGO I tell you 'tis not very well. I will make myself known to
Desdemona. If she will return me my jewels, I will give over my

170 SD.1 *Exeunt Desdemona and Emilia*] F; *Exit women.* QI   172] QI; I...find / ...me F   174–9] F; Every...Iago /
...me / ...least / ...it / ...already / ...suffered QI   174 daff'st] F (dafts); doffest QI   175 me now,] F; me, thou
QI   180–1] F; Faith...words / ...together QI   180 Faith] QI; *not in* F   180 for] QI; and F   181 performances]
F; performance QI   183 With...truth] F; *not in* QI   183 my] F; *not in* QI   184 deliver to] QI; deliuer F
185 hath] F; has QI   186 expectations] F; expectation QI   187 acquaintance] F; acquittance QI   188 well] F; good
QI   189 nor] F; *not in* QI   190 By...scurvy] QI; Nay I think it is scurvy F   193 tell you] F; say QI

174 **daff'st me** dost fob me off.
174 **device** scheme, trick.
175 **conveniency** opportunity, advantage.
176 **advantage** furthering, increase.
177 **put up** accept, endure. Compare *Tit.*
1.1.432–3: 'be dishonored openly, / And basely put
it up without revenge'.
180–1 **your words...together** Proverbial:
'Great promise small performance' (Tilley P602).
185 **votarist** nun (sworn to chastity); as in *MM*
1.4.5.

186 **comforts** encouragements.
187 **sudden respect** immediate regard. Compare *Cym.* 3.5.134–6: 'She held the very garment
of Posthumus in more respect than my noble and
natural person.'
187 **acquaintance** QI's 'acquittance' (= recompense) is possible, but Roderigo seems to be
complaining that he has not even met Desdemona,
let alone received her sexual favours.
189 **go to** have sex. See Partridge, pp. 121–2.
191 **fopped** duped, cheated.

suit and repent my unlawful solicitation; if not, assure yourself I   195
will seek satisfaction of you.

IAGO You have said now?

RODERIGO Ay, and said nothing but what I protest intendment of
doing.

IAGO Why, now I see there's mettle in thee, and even from this instant   200
do build on thee a better opinion than ever before. Give me thy
hand, Roderigo. Thou hast taken against me a most just
exception; but yet I protest I have dealt most directly in thy
affair.

RODERIGO It hath not appeared.   205

IAGO I grant indeed it hath not appeared; and your suspicion is not
without wit and judgement. But, Roderigo, if thou hast that in
thee indeed, which I have greater reason to believe now than ever – I
mean purpose, courage, and valour – this night show it. If thou the
next night following enjoy not Desdemona, take me from this   210
world with treachery, and devise engines for my life.

RODERIGO Well, what is it? Is it within reason and compass?

IAGO Sir, there is especial commission come from Venice to depute
Cassio in Othello's place.

RODERIGO Is that true? Why, then Othello and Desdemona return again   215
to Venice.

IAGO O no, he goes into Mauritania and takes away with him the
fair Desdemona, unless his abode be lingered here by some
accident; wherein none can be so determinate as the removing of
Cassio.   220

RODERIGO How do you mean 'removing' of him?

IAGO Why, by making him uncapable of Othello's place – knocking out
his brains.

RODERIGO And that you would have me to do?

---

198 and] F; and I haue Q1   200 instant] F; time Q1   203 exception] F; conception Q1   204 affair] F; affaires Q1
207 in] F; within Q1   210 enjoy] F; enioyest Q1   212 what is it] F; *not in* Q1   213 commission] F; command Q1
217 takes] Q1; taketh F   221 of] Q1; *not in* F

196 **seek satisfaction** demand repayment (not
'challenge to a duel').

197 **You...now?** You have spoken your mind
then? I take this to be a question because of the
nature of Roderigo's reply. Most editors follow
Onions's interpretation: 'What you now say is true.'

198 **protest intendment** aver the intention.

203 **exception** objection.

203 **directly** straightforwardly (as in *MV*
4.1.359).

211 **engines for** plots against (as in *Tit.* 2.1.123).

212 **compass** range of possibility.

217 **Mauritania** An ancient kingdom in north
Africa which included modern Morocco and part
of Algeria – hence, the land of the Moors. See
pp. 10–14 above.

218 **abode be lingered** stay be prolonged.

219 **determinate** decisive, conclusive.

IAGO Ay, if you dare do yourself a profit and a right. He sups tonight   225
with a harlotry, and thither will I go to him. He knows not yet of
his honourable fortune. If you will watch his going thence – which
I will fashion to fall out between twelve and one – you may take
him at your pleasure. I will be near to second your attempt, and
he shall fall between us. Come, stand not amazed at it, but go along   230
with me. I will show you such a necessity in his death that you shall
think yourself bound to put it on him. It is now high supper-time
and the night grows to waste. About it!

RODERIGO I will hear further reason for this.

IAGO And you shall be satisfied.   235

Exeunt

4.3 *Enter* OTHELLO, LODOVICO, DESDEMONA, EMILIA *and*
ATTENDANTS.

LODOVICO I do beseech you, sir, trouble yourself no further.

OTHELLO O, pardon me; 'twill do me good to walk.

LODOVICO Madam, good night. I humbly thank your ladyship.

DESDEMONA Your honour is most welcome.

OTHELLO Will you walk, sir? O, Desdemona.   5

DESDEMONA My lord?

OTHELLO Get you to bed on th'instant. I will be returned forthwith.
Dismiss your attendant there. Look't be done.

DESDEMONA I will, my lord.

Exeunt [Othello, Lodovico and Attendants]

EMILIA How goes it now? He looks gentler than he did.   10

DESDEMONA He says he will return incontinent;
He hath commanded me to go to bed
And bade me to dismiss you.

EMILIA   Dismiss me?

DESDEMONA It was his bidding; therefore, good Emilia,

---

225 if] F; and if QI   225 a right] F; right QI   226 harlotry] F; harlot QI   235 SD] F; *Ex. Iag. and* Rod. QI
Act 4, Scene 3   4.3] *Scena Tertia.* F; *not in* QI   0 SD] F; *after 4.2.234 in* QI   0 SD LODOVICO, DESDEMONA] F;
Desdemona, Lodovico QI   2 'twill] F; it shall QI   8 Dismiss] F; dispatch QI   9 .SD] *Capell subst.; Exeunt.* QI; *Exit.* F
(both after 8)   12 He] QI; And F   13 bade] QI; bid F

226 **harlotry** harlot (QI's reading).
228 **fall out** occur.
232 **high** fully, quite.
232 **supper-time** i.e. the time when the
seventeenth-century Englishman ate his main
evening meal.

233 **grows to waste** is passing; but Iago may
mean literally that he is wasting time on a night
when he has so much to do.

Act 4, Scene 3
11 **incontinent** at once.

  Give me my nightly wearing, and adieu.   15
  We must not now displease him.
EMILIA I would you had never seen him.
DESDEMONA So would not I: my love doth so approve him
  That even his stubbornness, his checks, his frowns –
  Prithee, unpin me – have grace and favour in them. 20
EMILIA I have laid those sheets you bade me on the bed.
DESDEMONA All's one. Good faith, how foolish are our minds!
  If I do die before thee, prithee shroud me
  In one of those same sheets.
EMILIA   Come, come, you talk.
DESDEMONA My mother had a maid called Barbary: 25
  She was in love, and he she loved proved mad
  And did forsake her. She had a song of willow;
  An old thing 'twas but it expressed her fortune,
  And she died singing it. That song tonight
  Will not go from my mind. I have much to do 30
  But to go hang my head all at one side
  And sing it like poor Barbary – prithee, dispatch.
EMILIA Shall I go fetch your nightgown?
DESDEMONA   No, unpin me here.
  This Lodovico is a proper man.
EMILIA A very handsome man.
DESDEMONA   He speaks well.   35
EMILIA I know a lady in Venice would have walked barefoot to Palestine
  for a touch of his nether lip.
DESDEMONA [*Sings*]
   The poor soul sat sighing by a sycamore tree,
    Sing all a green willow;

---

17 I would] Q1; I, would F 19 his frowns] F; and frownes Q1 20 in them] Q1; *not in* F 21 those] F; these Q1
22 faith] Q1; Father F 23 thee] Q1; *not in* F 24 those] Q1; these F 27 had] F; has Q1 30–50 I have…not next]
F; *not in* Q1 38, 52 SD] Desdemona *sings* Q2; *not in* F 38 sighing] Q2; *singing* F

15 **nightly wearing** night-clothes.
19 **stubbornness** roughness.
19 **checks** rebukes (as in *Ant.* 4.4.31).
20 **unpin** Presumably the fastenings of her dress or hair.
22 **All's one** It doesn't matter, all right.
24 **talk** talk nonsense (as in *Mac.* 4.2.64).
25 **Barbary** A form of the name Barbara; but ironically resonant in view of the barbarian–Venetian polarity at the heart of the play.
26 **proved mad** turned out to be unfaithful (as in *AWW* 5.3.3).
28 **fortune** fate.

30–1 **I have…But** It's all I can do not.
31 **all at one side** i.e. in the traditional pose of melancholy.
33 **nightgown** dressing-gown.
34 **proper** fine, handsome.
38–54 See supplementary note.
38 **sycamore** This was the Elizabethan name for the fig mulberry. It was not traditionally associated with the forsaken in love (except perhaps by the punning 'sick-amour'); but it is in a grove of sycamore that the love-sick Romeo is found wandering by Benvolio (*Rom.* 1.1.121).
39 **willow** A proverbial emblem for the forsaken

Her hand on her bosom, her head on her knee, 40
    Sing willow, willow, willow;
The fresh streams ran by her and murmured her moans;
    Sing willow, willow, willow.
Her salt tears fell from her and softened the stones –
Lay by these. 45
    Sing willow, willow, willow –
Prithee, hie thee; he'll come anon.
    Sing all a green willow must be my garland.
    Let nobody blame him; his scorn I approve –
Nay that's not next. Hark, who is't that knocks? 50

EMILIA It's the wind.

DESDEMONA [*Sings*]
    I called my love false love, but what said he then?
    Sing willow, willow, willow;
    If I court moe women, you'll couch with moe men –
So get thee gone; good night. Mine eyes do itch – 55
Does that bode weeping?

EMILIA   'Tis neither here nor there.

DESDEMONA I have heard it said so. O, these men, these men!
Dost thou in conscience think – tell me, Emilia –
That there be women do abuse their husbands
In such gross kind?

EMILIA   There be some such, no question. 60

DESDEMONA Wouldst thou do such a deed for all the world?

EMILIA Why, would not you?

DESDEMONA   No, by this heavenly light.

EMILIA Nor I neither by this heavenly light;
I might do't as well i'th'dark.

DESDEMONA Wouldst thou do such a deed for all the world? 65

EMILIA The world's a huge thing; it is a great price
    For a small vice.

---

46 Sing...willow] *Sing Willough, &c. Willough, Willough* F   47 hie] high F   50 who is't] F; who's Q1
52–4 I called...moe men] F; *not in* Q1   55–6 So...weeping] F; Now...night / ...weeping Q1   55 So] F; Now Q1
56 Does] Q1; Doth F   57–60 I have...question] F; *not in* Q1   65 Wouldst] F; Would Q1   65 deed] F; thing Q1
66–7 The...price / ...vice] Q1; The...thing / ...vice F

lover (Tilley w403). Compare its association with Ophelia (*Ham.* 4.7.166), Viola (*TN* 1.5.268), and Lady Bona (*3H6* 3.3.228).

44 Her salt...stones Compare 'Constant dropping will wear the stone' (Tilley D618).

45 these Presumably some of her jewellery or other accessories.

47 hie thee make haste.
47 anon at once.
54 moe more.
59 abuse deceive.
60 gross kind obscene manner.
62 heavenly light i.e. of the moon.
66 price prize.

DESDEMONA   In troth, I think thou wouldst not.

EMILIA In troth, I think I should, and undo't when I had done it.
  Marry, I would not do such a thing for a joint-ring, nor for
  measures of lawn, nor for gowns, petticoats, nor caps, nor any   70
  petty exhibition. But for all the whole world! Ud's pity,
  who would not make her husband a cuckold, to make him a
  monarch? I should venture purgatory for't.

DESDEMONA Beshrew me, if I would do such a wrong for the whole
  world.   75

EMILIA Why, the wrong is but a wrong i'th'world; and having the world
  for your labour, 'tis a wrong in your own world, and you might
  quickly make it right.

DESDEMONA I do not think there is any such woman.

EMILIA Yes, a dozen; and as many to th'advantage as would store   80
  the world they played for.
          But I do think it is their husbands' faults
          If wives do fall. Say that they slack their duties
          And pour our treasures into foreign laps,
          Or else break out in peevish jealousies,   85
          Throwing restraint upon us; or say they strike us,
          Or scant our former having in despite –
          Why, we have galls, and though we have some grace,
          Yet have we some revenge. Let husbands know
          Their wives have sense like them: they see, and smell,   90

---

67 In troth] F; Good troth QI   68 In troth] F; By my troth QI   68 it] QI; *not in* F   69–70 nor for measures] F;
or for measures QI   70 petticoats] F; or Petticotes QI   71 petty] F; such QI   71 all] F; *not in* QI   71 Ud's pity]
QI; Why F   82–99 But I do...us so] F; *not in* QI

68 **undo't** make it right again.

69 **joint-ring** A finger-ring made in two
separable parts, with the joins artistically concealed.

70 **lawn** fine white linen.

71 **exhibition** allowance, gift.

71 **Ud's** God's.

73 **venture purgatory** risk being condemned to
purgatory. Emilia sees adultery as an ultimately
forgiveable sin.

80 **to th'advantage** over and above, in addition
(as in *MND* 1.1.102).

80 **store** populate.

81 **played** A quibble on (1) gambled, hazarded;
(2) copulated.

83 **duties** marital duties, sexual activity in
marriage.

84 **our** i.e. which should be ours.

84 **foreign** alien (other than their wives').

87 **scant** reduce.

87 **having** allowance (as in *Wiv.* 3.2.72); but
this, like 'duties', 'pour our treasures', 'laps',
probably has sexual overtones.

87 **in despite** out of spite.

88–99 **Why, we...us so** Compare Shylock's
very similar defence of his desire for revenge in *MV*
3.1.59–72: 'Hath not a Jew hands, organs,
dimensions, senses, affections, passions; fed with
the same food...as a Christian is? If you prick us,
do we not bleed? If you tickle us, do we not
laugh?...And if you wrong us, shall we not
revenge?...If a Jew wrong a Christian, what is his
humility? Revenge. If a Christian wrong a Jew,
what should his sufferance be by Christian
example? Why, revenge. The villainy you teach me,
I will execute.'

88 **galls** tempers or spirits to make us feel
resentment.

And have their palates both for sweet and sour
As husbands have. What is it that they do
When they change us for others? Is it sport?
I think it is. And doth affection breed it?
I think it doth. Is't frailty that thus errs? 95
It is so too. And have not we affections,
Desires for sport, and frailty, as men have?
Then let them use us well; else let them know
The ills we do, their ills instruct us so.

DESDEMONA Good night, good night. God me such uses send, 100
Not to pick bad from bad, but by bad mend!

Exeunt

5.1 *Enter* IAGO *and* RODERIGO.

IAGO Here, stand behind this bulk; straight will he come.
Wear thy good rapier bare, and put it home.
Quick, quick, fear nothing; I'll be at thy elbow.
It makes us or it mars us; think on that,
And fix most firm thy resolution. 5

RODERIGO Be near at hand; I may miscarry in't.

IAGO Here, at thy hand; be bold, and take thy stand.
[*He retires.*]

RODERIGO I have no great devotion to the deed,
And yet he hath given me satisfying reasons.
'Tis but a man gone. Forth my sword! He dies! 10

IAGO [*Aside*] I have rubbed this young quat almost to the sense,

---

100] QI; Good...night / ...send F   100 God] QI; Heauen F   100 uses] F; vsage QI   Act 5, Scene 1
5.1] *Actus Quintus. Scena Prima.* F; *Actus.* 5. QI   1] QI; Here...bark / ...come F   1 bulk] QI; Barke F   4 on]
F; of QI   7 stand] F; sword QI   7 SD] *Capell subst.; not in* F, QI   8 deed] F; dead QI   9 hath] F; has QI
11 SD] *Theobald subst.; not in* F, QI   11 quat] F; gnat QI

---

93 **sport** A quibble on (1) entertainment; (2) copulation.
94 **affection** passion.
97 **sport** See 2.1.217 n.
100 **uses** profitable habits of thought.
101 i.e. Not to learn bad ways from the evil that has befallen me, but to learn good from it.

Act 5, Scene 1
1 **bulk** a projecting part of a building. Compare

Cor. 2.1.210–11: 'stalls, bulks, windows / Are smother'd up'. For a discussion of where Roderigo concealed himself on the Jacobean public stage, see supplementary note to 5.2.0 SD. For a possible staging of this scene, see illustration 5, p. 26 above.
2 **bare** drawn, unsheathed.
4 **It makes...us** Proverbial (Tilley M48).
11 **quat** contemptible youngster; lit. a pimple or small boil (which can be irritated by rubbing). .
11 **to the sense** to the quick, raw.

And he grows angry. Now, whether he kill Cassio,
Or Cassio him, or each do kill the other,
Every way makes my gain. Live Roderigo,
He calls me to a restitution large   15
Of gold and jewels that I bobbed from him
As gifts to Desdemona.
It must not be. If Cassio do remain,
He hath a daily beauty in his life
That makes me ugly; and besides, the Moor   20
May unfold me to him – there stand I in much peril.
No, he must die. But soft, I hear him coming.

Enter CASSIO.

RODERIGO I know his gait; 'tis he. Villain, thou diest!
          [*He lunges at Cassio.*]
CASSIO That thrust had been mine enemy indeed
          But that my coat is better than thou think'st.   25
          I will make proof of thine.
          [*He wounds Roderigo.*]
RODERIGO   O, I am slain!
          [*Iago wounds Cassio in the leg and exit*]
CASSIO I am maimed forever. Help, ho! Murder, murder!

Enter OTHELLO.

OTHELLO [*Aside*] The voice of Cassio: Iago keeps his word.
RODERIGO O villain that I am!
OTHELLO [*Aside*]   It is even so.
CASSIO O help, ho! Light! A surgeon!   30
OTHELLO [*Aside*] 'Tis he. O brave Iago, honest and just,

12 angry. Now] F; angry now: Q1   14 gain] F; game Q1   16 Of] F; For Q1   19 hath] F; has Q1   21 much] F;
not in Q1   22 But soft] *conj. Dyce³; But so,* F; be't so Q1   22 hear] Q1; heard F   23 SD] *Rowe subst.; not in* F, Q1
24 mine] F; my Q1   25 think'st] Q1; know'st F   26 SD.1 *He...Roderigo] Capell subst.; not in* F, Q1
26 SD.2 *Iago...exit] Theobald subst.; not in* F, Q1   27] Q1; I...forever / ...murder F   27 maimed] F; maind Q1
27 Help] F; light Q1   28, 29, 31 SD] *not in* F, Q1   29 It is] F; Harke tis Q1

14 **makes my gain** helps me win the game. Q1's
reading 'game' merely makes literal the gambling
image.
16 **bobbed** swindled. Compare *Tro.* 3.1.68:
'You shall not bob us out of our melody.'
19 **daily beauty** regularly demonstrated
attractiveness.
21 **unfold** expose.
25–6 **my coat...thine** This may mean merely
that Cassio's coat is more substantial than Roderigo
suspected. However, the reference may be to a

metal-plated or reinforced leather undercoat worn
for protection. Hart cites James Shirley, *The
Politician* 4.5: 'were you not wounded?...I
prepared a privy coat.'
26 **I will...thine** I will put yours to the test.
27–36 This entry and commentary of Othello is
often cut or unnoticed in modern theatre productions. It is possible that at the Globe or Blackfriars
he spoke his lines from the upper acting-area. See
illustration 5, p. 26 above.
31 **brave** excellent, noble.

That hast such noble sense of thy friend's wrong!
Thou teachest me. Minion, your dear lies dead,
And your unblest fate hies. Strumpet, I come!
Forth of my heart those charms, thine eyes, are blotted;   35
Thy bed, lust-stained, shall with lust's blood be spotted.

Exit Othello

Enter LODOVICO *and* GRATIANO.

CASSIO What, ho! No watch? No passage? Murder, murder!
GRATIANO 'Tis some mischance; the cry is very direful.
CASSIO O, help!
LODOVICO Hark!   40
RODERIGO O, wretched villain!
LODOVICO Two or three groan. It is a heavy night.
These may be counterfeits: let's think't unsafe
To come in to the cry without more help.
RODERIGO Nobody come? Then I shall bleed to death.   45
LODOVICO Hark!

Enter Iago, with a light.

GRATIANO Here's one comes in his shirt, with light and weapons.
IAGO Who's there? Whose noise is this that cries on murder?
LODOVICO We do not know.
IAGO   Did you not hear a cry?
CASSIO Here, here; for heaven's sake, help me!
IAGO   What's the matter?   50
GRATIANO This is Othello's ancient, as I take it.
LODOVICO The same indeed, a very valiant fellow.
IAGO What are you here that cry so grievously?
CASSIO Iago? O, I am spoiled, undone by villains!

34 unblest] F; *not in* Q1   34 hies] highes F; hies apace Q1   35 Forth] Q1; For F   36 SD] F; *Ex.* Q1
37] Q1; What...passage / ...murder F   38 cry] Q1; voyce F   42 groan] F; grones Q1   42 It is a] Q1; 'Tis F
46 SD *Iago, with a light.*] Q1 *(after 45)*; *Iago.* F *(after 45)*   47 light] F; lights Q1   48] Q1; Who's there / ...murder F
49 We] F; I Q1   49 Did] Q1; Do F   50 heaven's] Q1; heauen F

33 **Minion** Darling (used contemptuously here to mean 'hussy'); i.e. Desdemona.
34 **unblest** i.e. because she is damned.
34 **hies** approaches swiftly.
35 **Forth of** From out.
36 **Thy bed...spotted** This is oddly inconsistent with Othello's intention to strangle Desdemona specifically not to shed her blood (see 4.1.192–7; 5.2.3–4).

37 **passage** passers-by (as in *Err.* 3.1.99).
42 **heavy** gloomy, dark (as in *Lucrece* 709).
44 **come...cry** Either (1) draw near to the place the cries came from; or (2) approach the brawling group.
48 **cries on** shouts out. Compare *Tro.* 5.5.35: 'Crying on Hector'.
54 **spoiled** ruined, finished.

Give me some help.   55
IAGO O me, lieutenant! What villains have done this?
CASSIO I think that one of them is hereabout
    And cannot make away.
IAGO   O, treacherous villains!
    [*To Lodovico and Gratiano*] What are you there? Come in,
        and give some help.
RODERIGO O, help me here!   60
CASSIO That's one of them.
IAGO   O murderous slave! O villain!
                [*He stabs Roderigo.*]
RODERIGO O damned Iago! O inhuman dog!
                [*He faints.*]
IAGO Kill men i'th'dark? Where be these bloody thieves?
    How silent is this town! Ho, murder, murder!
        [*Lodovico and Gratiano come forward.*]
    What may you be? Are you of good or evil?   65
LODOVICO As you shall prove us, praise us.
IAGO Signior Lodovico?
LODOVICO He, sir.
IAGO I cry you mercy. Here's Cassio hurt by villains.
GRATIANO Cassio?   70
IAGO How is't, brother?
CASSIO My leg is cut in two.
IAGO   Marry, heaven forbid!
    Light, gentlemen. I'll bind it with my shirt.

                    Enter BIANCA.

BIANCA What is the matter, ho? Who is't that cried?
IAGO Who is't that cried?   75
BIANCA O, my dear Cassio, my sweet Cassio!
        O, Cassio, Cassio, Cassio!
IAGO O notable strumpet! Cassio, may you suspect
    Who they should be that have thus mangled you?
CASSIO No.   80

56] QI; O…lieutenant / …this F   56 me] F; my QI   57 that] F; the QI   59 SD] *Theobald; not in* F, QI   60 here]
QI; there F   61 SD] *Rowe subst.; He thrusts him in.* Q2; *not in* F, QI   62 dog!] F; dog, – o, o, o. QI   62 SD] *Muir;
not in* F, QI   63] QI; Kill…dark / …thieves F   63 men] F; him QI   63 these] F; those QI   64 SD] *Dover Wilson;
not in* F, QI   76–7] *Capell;* O…dear Cassio / …Cassio F; *one line in* QI   76 my sweet] F; O my sweete QI
77 O, Cassio,] F; *not in* QI   79 have thus] F; thus haue QI

66 **praise** value, appraise.   is literally the case: 'the Ensign…cut the right leg
69 **I cry you mercy** Pardon me.   entirely through' (Bullough, VII, 249).
72 **My leg…two** In Cinthio's source story this   79 **mangled** wounded (as in *Rom.* 4.3.52).

GRATIANO I am sorry to find you thus; I have been to seek you.

IAGO Lend me a garter: so. O for a chair
    To bear him easily hence!

BIANCA   Alas, he faints!
    O, Cassio, Cassio, Cassio!

IAGO Gentlemen all, I do suspect this trash   85
    To be a party in this injury.
    Patience awhile, good Cassio. Come, come,
    Lend me a light. Know we this face or no?
    Alas, my friend and my dear countryman!
    Roderigo? No – yes, sure – O, heaven, Roderigo!   90

GRATIANO What, of Venice?

IAGO Even he, sir; did you know him?

GRATIANO   Know him? Ay.

IAGO Signior Gratiano! I cry your gentle pardon.
    These bloody accidents must excuse my manners
    That so neglected you.

GRATIANO   I am glad to see you.   95

IAGO How do you, Cassio? O, a chair, a chair!

GRATIANO Roderigo?

IAGO He, he, 'tis he.

      [*Enter* ATTENDANTS *with a chair.*]
    O, that's well said, the chair!
    Some good men bear him carefully from hence.
    I'll fetch the general's surgeon. [*To Bianca*] For you,
      mistress,   100
    Save you your labour. – He that lies slain here, Cassio,
    Was my dear friend. What malice was between you?

CASSIO None in the world, nor do I know the man.

IAGO [*To Bianca*] What, look you pale? – O, bear him out o'th'air.
      [*Cassio is carried off; Roderigo's body is removed*]
    Stay you, good gentlemen. Look you pale, mistress?   105

81] QI; I...thus / ...you F   82–3 IAGO...hence] F; *not in* QI   83–4 Alas...Cassio] *one line in* F, QI   86–7] F;
one line in QI   86 be] F; beare QI   86 party] F; part QI   86 injury] F; *not in* QI   87 Come, come,] F; *not in* QI
90 O, heaven] QI; Yes, 'tis F   93 your] F; you QI   98 SD] *Capell subst.; not in* F, QI   98] QI; He...he / ...chair F
98 He, he] F; He, QI   98 the] F; a QI   99 men] man F, QI   100 SD, 104 SD.1 *To Bianca*] *Johnson; not in* F, QI
102 between] F; betwixt QI   104 out o'] QI; o' F   104 SD.2] *Dover Wilson subst. after Capell; not in* F, QI
105 gentlemen] F; Gentlewoman QI

---

94 **accidents** sudden happenings.
95 **neglected** failed to recognise, ignored.
98 **said** i.e. done.
101 **Save...labour** Don't trouble yourself (by
attending to Cassio any further).

102 **malice** ill-will (to cause the quarrel).
104 **O, bear...air** 'Fresh air is ill for the
diseased or wounded man' (Tilley A93).
105 **Stay...gentlemen** F's reading suggests
that Gratiano and Lodovico start to accompany

Do you perceive the gastness of her eye?
[*To Bianca*] Nay, if you stare, we shall hear more anon.
Behold her well; I pray you, look upon her.
Do you see, gentlemen? Nay, guiltiness
Will speak, though tongues were out of use.   110

Enter EMILIA.

EMILIA 'Las, what's the matter? What's the matter, husband?
IAGO Cassio hath here been set on in the dark
        By Roderigo and fellows that are 'scaped.
        He's almost slain and Roderigo dead.
EMILIA Alas, good gentleman! Alas, good Cassio!   115
IAGO This is the fruits of whoring. Prithee, Emilia,
        Go know of Cassio where he supped tonight.
        [*To Bianca*] What, do you shake at that?
BIANCA He supped at my house, but I therefore shake not.
IAGO O, did he so? I charge you go with me.   120
EMILIA O, fie upon thee, strumpet!
BIANCA I am no strumpet, but of life as honest
        As you that thus abuse me.
EMILIA   As I? Foh! Fie upon thee!
IAGO Kind gentlemen, let's go see poor Cassio dressed.
        Come, mistress, you must tell's another tale.   125
        Emilia, run you to the citadel
        And tell my lord and lady what hath happed.
        Will you go on afore? [*Aside*] This is the night
        That either makes me, or fordoes me quite.

                                                    Exeunt

106 gastness] F; ieastures Q1   107 SD] *Rowe; not in* F, Q1   107 if] F; an Q1   107 stare] F; stirre Q1   107 hear]
F; haue Q1   109–10] Q1; Do...speak / ...use F   110 SD] Q1; *not in* F   111] Q1; Alas...matter / ...husband F
111 'Las] Q1; Alas F   111 what's] Q1; what is F   111 What's] Q1; What is F   112 hath] F; has Q1   114 dead]
Q1; quite dead F   116 fruits] F; fruite Q1   116 Prithee] F; pray Q1   118 SD] *This edn; not in* F, Q1   121 O, fie]
F; Fie, fie Q1   123 Foh! Fie] Q1; Fie F   124] Q1; Kind gentlemen / ...dressed F   127 hath] F; has Q1
128 on afore] F; on, I pray, Q1   128 SD] *Steevens²; not in* F, Q1   129 makes] F; markes Q1

Cassio and are stayed by Iago to hear his accusations
against Bianca. If Q1's 'Gentlewoman' is correct, it
is Bianca who tries to go off with Cassio and is
detained by Iago with this sarcastic mode of
address. The former is the more dramatically
plausible.
  106 gastness terror, frightened look.
  107 It is not clear what exactly Iago means here.
If F is correct: 'Nay, from the look in your eyes we
shall have a full confession shortly.' If Q1's 'an you

stir' is right, then Iago has a hold on Bianca, who
starts to struggle and is threatened by him.
  110 tongues...use men no longer had the
power to speak.
  117 know learn.
  122 honest chaste.
  124 dressed i.e. his wound bandaged.
  125 you must...tale Proverbial (Tilley T49).
  129 fordoes me quite ruins me completely.

5.2 *Enter* OTHELLO, *with a light, and* DESDEMONA *in bed.*

OTHELLO It is the cause, it is the cause, my soul:
        Let me not name it to you, you chaste stars.
        It is the cause. Yet I'll not shed her blood,
        Nor scar that whiter skin of hers than snow
        And smooth as monumental alabaster –   5
        Yet she must die, else she'll betray more men.
        Put out the light, and then put out the light:
        If I quench thee, thou flaming minister,
        I can again thy former light restore,
        Should I repent me; but once put out thy light,   10
        Thou cunning'st pattern of excelling nature,
        I know not where is that Promethean heat
        That can thy light relume. When I have plucked thy rose,
        I cannot give it vital growth again;
        It needs must wither. I'll smell it on the tree.   15
                    He kisses her.
        O balmy breath, that dost almost persuade
        Justice to break her sword! One more, one more!
        Be thus when thou art dead, and I will kill thee
        And love thee after. One more, and this the last.
        So sweet was ne'er so fatal. I must weep.   20
        But they are cruel tears: this sorrow's heavenly –

Act 5, Scene 2   5.2] *Scœna Secunda.* F; *not in* QI   0 SD] *Enter Othello, and Desdemona in her bed.* F; *Enter* Othello *with a light.* QI   10 thy light] F; thine QI   11 cunning'st] F; cunning QI   13] QI; That...relume / ...rose F   13 relume] F; returne QI   13 thy rose] F; the rose QI   15 needs must] F; must needes QI   15 it] QI; thee F   15 SD] Q2; *after 19 in* QI; *not in* F   16 O] F; A QI   16 dost] F; doth QI   17 Justice] F; Iustice herselfe QI   17 sword! One more, one more!] F; sword once more QI   19 One] F; once QI   19 this] QI; that's F

Act 5, Scene 2

0 SD For a discussion of Jacobean staging, see supplementary note; see also illustration 6, p. 36 above.

1 **It is the cause** i.e. I must keep in my mind the crime (of adultery). Compare *Lear* 4.6.109–11: 'What was thy cause? Adultery? Thou shalt not die.'

4 **that whiter...snow** her skin that is whiter than snow (Abbott 419a). Proverbial phrase (Tilley S591).

5 **monumental** i.e. like that used for tombs.

6 **else she'll...men** Othello is attempting to raise his action from being one of personal revenge to one that is for the good of society.

7 i.e. first quench this lamp, and then snuff out the life of Desdemona.

8 **flaming minister** i.e. the lamp in his hand. Compare Ps. 104.4: 'Which maketh the spirits his messengers, and a flaming fire his ministers'.

11 **cunning'st...nature** skilfully created product of nature at its most perfect.

12 **Promethean heat** i.e. the life-giving fire that the Titan Prometheus stole from heaven and gave to men.

13 **relume** light again.

13 **thy rose** F's reading is superior to QI's 'the rose' in view of 16.

17 **sword** i.e. the symbol of Justice's ability to punish.

21–2 **this sorrow's...love** Compare Heb. 12.6: 'For whom the Lord loveth, he chasteneth.'

It strikes where it doth love. She wakes.

DESDEMONA Who's there? Othello?

OTHELLO   Ay, Desdemona.

DESDEMONA Will you come to bed, my lord?

OTHELLO Have you prayed tonight, Desdemon?

DESDEMONA   Ay, my lord.   25

OTHELLO If you bethink yourself of any crime

    Unreconciled as yet to heaven and grace,

    Solicit for it straight.

DESDEMONA Alack, my lord, what may you mean by that?

OTHELLO Well, do it, and be brief: I will walk by: 30

    I would not kill thy unpreparèd spirit;

    No – heaven forfend! – I would not kill thy soul.

DESDEMONA Talk you of killing?

OTHELLO   Ay, I do.

DESDEMONA   Then heaven

    Have mercy on me!

OTHELLO   Amen, with all my heart!

DESDEMONA If you say so, I hope you will not kill me.   35

OTHELLO Hum!

DESDEMONA And yet I fear you, for you're fatal then

    When your eyes roll so. Why I should fear I know not,

    Since guiltiness I know not, but yet I feel I fear.

OTHELLO Think on thy sins.

DESDEMONA   They are loves I bear to you.   40

OTHELLO Ay, and for that thou diest.

DESDEMONA That death's unnatural that kills for loving.

    Alas, why gnaw you so your nether lip?

    Some bloody passion shakes your very frame:

    These are portents; but yet I hope, I hope   45

    They do not point on me.

OTHELLO   Peace, and be still!

DESDEMONA I will so. What's the matter?

OTHELLO That handkerchief which I so loved and gave thee,

    Thou gav'st to Cassio.

---

22 where] F; when Q1   22 doth] F; does Q1   29] Q1; Alack...lord / ...that F   29 Alack] F; Alas Q1   32 heaven]
Q1; Heauens F   33–4 Then...me] *one line in* F, Q1   35 so] Q1; *not in* F   38] Q1; When...so / ...not F   41 Ay]
F; *not in* Q1   45 I hope, I hope] F; I hope Q1   48–9 That...Cassio] Q1; That handkerchief / ...Cassio F

28 **Solicit** Pray (for forgiveness).
28 **straight** at once.
40 **They are...you** An allusion to the sin of
loving a human being more than God.

46 **point on me** presage my future. Compare
Sonnets 26.9–10: 'Till whatsoever star that guides
my moving / Points on me graciously'.
47 **matter** thing in question (disturbing you).

DESEMONA No, by my life and soul!
Send for the man and ask him.

OTHELLO Sweet soul, take heed. 50
Take heed of perjury: thou art on thy death-bed.

DESDEMONA Ay, but not yet to die.

OTHELLO Yes, presently.
Therefore confess thee freely of thy sin;
For to deny each article with oath
Cannot remove nor choke the strong conception 55
That I do groan withal. Thou art to die.

DESDEMONA Then Lord have mercy on me!

OTHELLO I say, Amen.

DESDEMONA And have you mercy too! I never did
Offend you in my life; never loved Cassio
But with such general warranty of heaven 60
As I might love. I never gave him token.

OTHELLO By heaven, I saw my handkerchief in's hand.
O perjured woman! Thou dost stone my heart,
And mak'st me call what I intend to do
A murder, which I thought a sacrifice. 65
I saw the handkerchief.

DESDEMONA He found it then;
I never gave it him. Send for him hither;
Let him confess a truth.

OTHELLO He hath confessed.

DESDEMONA What, my lord?

OTHELLO That he hath used thee.

DESDEMONA How? Unlawfully? 70

OTHELLO Ay.

DESDEMONA He will not say so.

OTHELLO No, his mouth is stopped:
Honest Iago hath tane order for't.

49–50 No...him] No...soul / ...him Q1; No...man / ...him F   50–1 Sweet...death-bed] *Capell;* Sweet... perjury / ...bed F, Q1   52 Yes] Q1; *not in* F   55 conception] F; conceit Q1   57 Then Lord] Q1; O Heauen F 58–9] F; And...too / ...Cassio Q1   63 my] F; thy Q1   64 mak'st] makest Q1; makes F   68 Let] Q1; And let Q1 68 hath] F; has Q1   70 used thee] F; vds death Q1

52 **presently** immediately.
54 **article** A legal term meaning an item in a formal indictment.
55 **conception** A quibble: (1) belief; (2) plan (I have conceived).
56 **groan withal** A quibble: (1) am distressed by; (2) am giving birth to.

59 **Offend** Sin against.
60 **warranty** allowance, permission.
63 **stone** harden, turn to stone.
65 **sacrifice** See 6 n. above.
70 **used** copulated with. See Partridge, p. 214.
73 **tane order for** arranged (as in *R3* 4.2.52).

DESDEMONA O, my fear interprets! What, is he dead?

OTHELLO Had all his hairs been lives, my great revenge   75
      Had stomach for them all.

DESDEMONA Alas, he is betrayed, and I undone.

OTHELLO Out, strumpet! Weep'st thou for him to my face?

DESDEMONA O banish me, my lord, but kill me not!

OTHELLO Down, strumpet!   80

DESDEMONA Kill me tomorrow; let me live tonight!

OTHELLO Nay, if you strive –

DESDEMONA But half an hour!

OTHELLO   Being done, there is no pause.

DESDEMONA But while I say one prayer!

OTHELLO   It is too late.

DESDEMONA O, Lord, Lord, Lord!   85

              He smothers her.

EMILIA (*Within*) My lord, my lord! What, ho! My lord, my lord!

OTHELLO What noise is this? Not dead? Not yet quite dead?
      I that am cruel am yet merciful;
      I would not have thee linger in thy pain.
      So, so.

EMILIA (*Within*) What, ho! My lord, my lord!

OTHELLO   Who's there?   90

EMILIA [*Within*] O, good my lord, I would speak a word with you.

OTHELLO Yes – 'tis Emilia – by and by. – She's dead.
      'Tis like she comes to speak of Cassio's death:
      The noise was high. Ha! No more moving?
      Still as the grave. Shall she come in? Were't good?   95

74 O] F; *not in* QI   74 interprets] F; interprets then QI   75–6] F; Had…lives / …all QI   78 Out] F; O QI   82 if] F; an QI   83 OTHELLO Being…pause] F; *not in* QI   85 SD] *Smothers her.* F; *he stifles her.* QI (*after* late *in* F *and* QI)   85] QI; *not in* F   86 SD] *at the doore* F; *calls within* QI   86] QI; My…ho / …lord F   87 noise] F; voyce QI   89–90 I…pain / …so] F; *one line in* QI   90 SD] F; *not in* QI   91 SD] *Malone; not in* F, QI   94 high] F; here QI

75 **Had all…lives** Proverbial (Tilley H30); compare 3.3.443–4.

76 **stomach** appetite, capacity.

83 **Being done…pause** Having thus started to do the deed, I cannot stop.

90 **So, so.** There was a stage tradition in the eighteenth century of Othello stabbing Desdemona at this point; and critics, supporting the stage business, have called upon medical evidence to prove that victims of suffocation or strangulation do not recover consciousness. Other critics argue that Shakespeare may have been ignorant of such medical facts or that Desdemona died from shock. In Webster's *The Duchess of Malfi* (a play obviously written under the influence of *Othello*) the Duchess is strangled and also revives to speak some words (see 4.2.237, 350, 353; ed. J. R. Brown, 1964).

93 **like** likely that.

94 **The noise was high** The uproar (created by the attack on Cassio) was loud. Some editors take this to refer to the commotion caused by Desdemona's death.

95 **Still as the grave** Proverbial (Tilley D135).

I think she stirs again. No. What's best to do?
If she come in, she'll sure speak to my wife –
My wife, my wife! What wife? I have no wife.
O insupportable! O heavy hour!
Methinks it should be now a huge eclipse 100
Of sun and moon, and that th'affrighted globe
Should yawn at alteration.

EMILIA [*Within*]   I do beseech you
That I may speak with you. O, good my lord!

OTHELLO I had forgot thee. O, come in, Emilia.
Soft, by and by. Let me the curtains draw. 105
Where art thou?

                          [*He unlocks the door.*]
                          What's the matter with thee now?

Enter EMILIA.

EMILIA O, my good lord, yonder's foul murders done.

OTHELLO What? Now?

EMILIA But now, my lord.

OTHELLO It is the very error of the moon: 110
She comes more nearer earth than she was wont
And makes men mad.

EMILIA Cassio, my lord, hath killed a young Venetian
Called Roderigo.

OTHELLO   Roderigo killed?
And Cassio killed?

EMILIA   No, Cassio is not killed. 115

OTHELLO Not Cassio killed! Then murder's out of tune,
And sweet revenge grows harsh.

DESDEMONA O, falsely, falsely murdered!

EMILIA   O Lord! What cry is that?

OTHELLO That? What?

96 best to do] F; the best Q1   98 What wife?] F; my wife; Q1   102 Should] Q1; Did F   102 SD] *Malone; not in* F, Q1   102–3 I...lord] F; *one line in* Q1   103 That] F; *not in* Q1   103 O] F; *not in* Q1   106 SD.1 *He unlocks the door.*] *Theobald subst.; not in* F, Q1   106 SD.2 *Enter* EMILIA.] F; *after 105 in* Q1   111 nearer] F; neere the Q1   113–14 Cassio...Roderigo] Q1; Cassio...killed / ...Roderigo F   113 hath] F; Has Q1   114–15 Roderigo...Cassio killed] *Capell; one line in* F, Q1   118 O Lord] Q1; Alas F

102 **yawn** gape wide (as with an earthquake).
102 **at alteration** i.e. with the change in nature brought on by Desdemona's murder.

110 **error** straying off course. See 2.3.163 n.

EMILIA Out and alas, that was my lady's voice!   120
         [*She draws the bed-curtains.*]
     Help, help, ho, help! O, lady, speak again!
     Sweet Desdemona, O sweet mistress, speak!

DESDEMONA A guiltless death I die.

EMILIA O, who hath done this deed?

DESDEMONA Nobody; I myself. Farewell.   125
     Commend me to my kind lord. O farewell!   *She dies*

OTHELLO Why, how should she be murdered?

EMILIA   Alas, who knows?

OTHELLO You heard her say herself it was not I.

EMILIA She said so; I must needs report the truth.

OTHELLO She's like a liar gone to burning hell: 130
     'Twas I that killed her.

EMILIA   O, the more angel she,
     And you the blacker devil!

OTHELLO She turned to folly, and she was a whore.

EMILIA Thou dost belie her, and thou art a devil.

OTHELLO She was false as water.

EMILIA   Thou art rash as fire to say   135
     That she was false. O, she was heavenly true!

OTHELLO Cassio did top her: ask thy husband else.
     O, I were damned beneath all depth in hell
     But that I did proceed upon just grounds
     To this extremity. Thy husband knew it all.   140

EMILIA My husband?

OTHELLO   Thy husband.

EMILIA   That she was false to wedlock?

OTHELLO Ay, with Cassio. Nay, had she been true,
     If heaven would make me such another world
     Of one entire and perfect chrysolite,
     I'd not have sold her for it.

---

120 that was] F; it is QI   120 SD] *Dover Wilson subst.; not in* F, QI   124 hath] F; has QI   126 SD] QI; *not in* F
128 heard] QI; heare F   129 the] F; a QI   131–2 O...devil] QI; *prose in* F   135–6 Thou...true] F; Thou...fire /
...true QI   135 art] F; as QI   142 Nay] QI; *not in* F

120 **Out** Used merely to emphasise 'alas'.
133 **folly** unchastity, lewdness (as in *Tro.*
5.2.18).
134 **belie** slander.
135 **false as water** Proverbial (Tilley w86).
137 **top** See 1.1.90 n.

137 **else** i.e. if you do not believe it; as in *John*
4.1.107.
140 **extremity** final punishment (a legal term).
144 **entire...chrysolite** pure and perfect
topaz. The idea echoes Desdemona's and Emilia's
discussion at 4.3.61 ff. and foreshadows the savage
at 5.2.342–4 who throws away the pearl.

EMILIA   My husband?   145
OTHELLO Ay, 'twas he that told me on her first;
    An honest man he is, and hates the slime
    That sticks on filthy deeds.
EMILIA   My husband?
OTHELLO What needs this iterance, woman? I say thy husband.
EMILIA O mistress, villainy hath made mocks with love!   150
    My husband say that she was false?
OTHELLO   He, woman;
    I say thy husband. Dost understand the word?
    My friend, thy husband, honest, honest Iago.
EMILIA If he say so, may his pernicious soul
    Rot half a grain a day! He lies to th'heart.   155
    She was too fond of her most filthy bargain.
OTHELLO Ha!
EMILIA Do thy worst.
    This deed of thine is no more worthy heaven
    Than thou wast worthy her.
OTHELLO   Peace, you were best.   160
EMILIA Thou hast not half that power to do me harm
    As I have to be hurt. O gull! O dolt!
    As ignorant as dirt. Thou hast done a deed –
    I care not for thy sword – I'll make thee known,
    Though I lost twenty lives. Help! help! ho, help!   165
    The Moor hath killed my mistress. Murder, murder!

Enter MONTANO, GRATIANO *and* IAGO.

MONTANO What is the matter? How now, general?
EMILIA O, are you come, Iago? You have done well,
    That men must lay their murders on your neck.
GRATIANO What is the matter?   170
EMILIA Disprove this villain, if thou be'st a man.
    He says thou told'st him that his wife was false.

---

146 on her] F; *not in* QI 149] QI; What...woman / ...husband F 149 iterance] F; iteration QI 150–3] F; *not in* QI 151 that] Q2; *not in* F 161 that] F; the QI 164 known] F; know QI 165 ho] F; O QI 166 hath] F; has QI 166 SD IAGO] F; Iago, *and others.* QI 169 murders] F; murder QI 170 SH GRATIANO] F; *All.* QI

---

 149 **iterance** repetition.
 150 **made mocks with** made a dupe of, played games with.
 155 **He lies to th'heart** Proverbial (Tilley T268).

 160 **you were best** it would be best for you.
 162 **to be hurt** Either (1) to endure anything you have the power to inflict; (2) a capacity to feel pain on behalf of my mistress.
 162 **gull** dupe (as in *TN* 5.1.343).

      I know thou didst not, thou'rt not such a villain.
      Speak, for my heart is full.
IAGO I told him what I thought, and told no more   175
      Than what he found himself was apt and true.
EMILIA But did you ever tell him she was false?
IAGO I did.
EMILIA You told a lie, an odious damnèd lie:
      Upon my soul, a lie, a wicked lie!   180
      She false with Cassio? Did you say with Cassio?
IAGO With Cassio, mistress. Go to, charm your tongue.
EMILIA I will not charm my tongue; I am bound to speak:
      My mistress here lies murdered in her bed.
ALL O, heavens forfend!   185
EMILIA And your reports have set the murder on.
OTHELLO Nay, stare not, masters; it is true indeed.
GRATIANO 'Tis a strange truth.
MONTANO O monstrous act!
EMILIA   Villainy, villainy, villainy!
      I think upon't, I think – I smell't – O villainy!   190
      I thought so then; I'll kill myself for grief.
      O villainy, villainy!
IAGO What, are you mad? I charge you get you home.
EMILIA Good gentlemen, let me have leave to speak.
      'Tis proper I obey him, but not now.   195
      Perchance, Iago, I will ne'er go home.
OTHELLO O! O! O!

                  Othello falls on the bed.

EMILIA   Nay, lay thee down and roar,
      For thou hast killed the sweetest innocent
      That e'er did lift up eye.
OTHELLO [*Standing up.*]   O, she was foul!
      I scarce did know you, uncle; there lies your niece,   200
      Whose breath indeed these hands have newly stopped.
      I know this act shows horrible and grim –

175] Q1; I…thought / …more F   177] Q1; But…him / …false F   181] Q1; She…Cassio / …Cassio F
182] Q1; With…mistress / …tongue F   183] Q1; I…tongue / …speak F   184–92] F; *not in* Q1
187] Q2; Nay…masters / …indeed F   193] Q1; What…mad / …home F   197 SD] Oth. *fals on the bed.* Q1; *not in* F
199 SD] *Theobald subst.; not in* F, Q1   202 horrible] F; terrible Q1

176 **apt** plausible, likely.
182 **charm** exercise a spell upon (to silence); as
in *Shr.* 4.2.58.
183 **bound** in duty bound.

190–1 **I think…so then** See 3.3.316–21 and
4.2.129–32, where Emilia seems to intuit the truth.
199 **lift up eye** i.e. to heaven in purity of spirit
and prayer.

GRATIANO Poor Desdemon, I am glad thy father's dead:
    Thy match was mortal to him, and pure grief
    Shore his old thread in twain. Did he live now,   205
    This sight would make him do a desperate turn,
    Yea, curse his better angel from his side
    And fall to reprobance.
OTHELLO 'Tis pitiful; but yet Iago knows
    That she with Cassio hath the act of shame   210
    A thousand times committed. Cassio confessed it,
    And she did gratify his amorous works
    With that recognisance and pledge of love
    Which I first gave her. I saw it in his hand:
    It was a handkerchief, an antique token   215
    My father gave my mother.
EMILIA   O God! O heavenly God!
IAGO Zounds, hold your peace!
EMILIA   'Twill out, 'twill out. I peace!
    No, I will speak as liberal as the north;
    Let heaven, and men, and devils, let them all,
    All, all cry shame against me, yet I'll speak.   220
IAGO Be wise and get you home.
EMILIA   I will not.
    [Iago draws his sword and threatens Emilia.]
GRATIANO   Fie,
    Your sword upon a woman!
EMILIA O thou dull Moor, that handkerchief thou speak'st of

203] QI; Poor Desdemon / ...dead F 205 in twain] F; at wane QI 208 reprobance] F; reprobation QI 213 that]
F; the QI 216 O God! O heavenly God!] QI; Oh Heauen! oh heauenly Powres! F 217 Zounds] QI; Come F
217–18 'Twill...north] F; 'Twill...no / ...air QI 217 'twill out. I] F; 'twill: I QI 217 peace] F; hold my peace
sir QI 218 I will speak as] F; I'le be in speaking QI 218 north] F; ayre QI 221 SD] *Rowe subst.; not in* F, QI
221–2 Fie...woman] *Capell; one line in* F, QI 223] QI; O...Moor / ...of F 223 of] F; on QI

205 **Shore...twain** The allusion is to the
Parcae, or Fates: Clotho who spun the thread of
human life and Atropos who cut it.
 206 **turn** act.
 208 **to reprobance** into a state of damnation.
 212 **gratify** reward.
 213 **recognisance** token.
 215–16 **an antique...mother** This is inconsistent with what Othello has earlier told Desdemona
(3.4.51–9). The inconsistency is probably due to
an oversight, though some editors have argued that

Othello was deliberately frightening Desdemona on
the earlier occasion.
 217 **'Twill out** Compare the phrase 'Murder
will out.'
 218 **liberal as the north** As QI's reading is 'as
the air', the meaning is presumably 'as unrestrain-
edly as the north wind blows', with perhaps also the
sense of the 'churlish chiding of the winter's wind'
(*AYLI* 2.1.7). Some editors have suggested that
Emilia is saying that she will speak with the
bluntness that characterises people from the north
of England.

I found by fortune and did give my husband,
For often, with a solemn earnestness –   225
More than indeed belonged to such a trifle –
He begged of me to steal it.

IAGO   Villainous whore!

EMILIA She give it Cassio! No, alas, I found it
And I did give't my husband.

IAGO   Filth, thou liest!

EMILIA By heaven, I do not, I do not, gentlemen.   230
O murderous coxcomb, what should such a fool
Do with so good a wife?

OTHELLO   Are there no stones in heaven
But what serves for the thunder? Precious villain!
[*Othello runs at Iago; Montano disarms him; Iago stabs Emilia from
behind and exit.*]

GRATIANO The woman falls; sure he hath killed his wife.

EMILIA Ay, ay; O, lay me by my mistress' side.   235

GRATIANO He's gone, but his wife's killed.

MONTANO 'Tis a notorious villain. Take you this weapon,
Which I have here recovered from the Moor.
Come guard the door without; let him not pass,
But kill him rather. I'll after the same villain,   240
For 'tis a damnèd slave.
                          Exeunt Montano and Gratiano

OTHELLO   I am not valiant neither,
But every puny whipster gets my sword.
But why should honour outlive honesty?
Let it go all.

EMILIA   What did thy song bode, lady?
Hark, canst thou hear me? I will play the swan   245
And die in music: [*Sings*] 'Willow, willow, willow.'

228 give] F; gaue Q1   232 wife] F; woman Q1   233] Q1; But…thunder / …villain F   233 SD] Dyce² subst.; The
Moore runs at Iago. Iago kils his wife. Q1; not in F   233 SD.2 exit] Exit Iago. Q1 (after 235); not in F   234] Q1;
The…falls / …wife F   234 hath] F; has Q1   237 you this] F; your Q1   238 here] Q1; not in F   241 SD] Exit Mont.
and Gratiano. Q1; Exit. F   244–6 What…willow.'] F; not in Q1   246 SD] Dyce; not in F, Q1

226 **belonged** was appropriate.
231 **coxcomb** fool; lit. the cap resembling a
cock's comb that professional fools wore.
232 **stones** thunderbolts (to hurl at such a
villain). Compare *Cym.* 5.5.240: 'The gods throw
stones of sulphur.'
233 **Precious** An intensifier.

242 **whipster** whippersnapper (one who is
prone to whip out his sword).
243 **honour…honesty** the reputation for
honour outlast the possession of honour itself.
245–6 **I will…music** Proverbial: 'Like the
swan, he sings before his death' (Tilley S1028).

Moor, she was chaste; she loved thee, cruel Moor;
So come my soul to bliss, as I speak true;
So speaking as I think, I die, I die.   *She dies*

OTHELLO I have another weapon in this chamber;   250
It was a sword of Spain, the ice-brook's temper.
O, here it is. – Uncle, I must come forth.

GRATIANO (*Within*) If thou attempt it, it will cost thee dear;
Thou hast no weapon, and perforce must suffer.

OTHELLO Look in upon me then, and speak with me,   255
Or naked as I am, I will assault thee.

[*Enter Gratiano.*]

GRATIANO What is the matter?

OTHELLO   Behold, I have a weapon:
A better never did itself sustain
Upon a soldier's thigh. I have seen the day
That with this little arm and this good sword   260
I have made my way through more impediments
Than twenty times your stop. But, O vain boast!
Who can control his fate? 'Tis not so now.
Be not afraid, though you do see me weaponed:
Here is my journey's end, here is my butt   265
And very sea-mark of my utmost sail.
Do you go back dismayed? 'Tis a lost fear:
Man but a rush against Othello's breast,
And he retires. Where should Othello go?
[*He goes to the bed.*]
Now, how dost thou look now? O ill-starred wench!   270

249 I die,] QI ; alas, F   249 SD] QI ; *not in* F   251 was] F ; is QI   251 ice-brook's] Ice brookes F ; Isebrookes QI ;
Innsbrucks *conj. Fortescue*   253 SD] QI ; *not in* F   255 with] F ; to QI   256 SD] *Theobald*; *not in* F, QI   262 your]
F ; you QI   264–70 Be not...wench] F ; *not in* QI   269 SD] *Dover Wilson subst.*; *not in* F, QI

251 **sword of Spain** Toledo and Bilbao were
noted for the production of fine swords.
251 **ice-brook's temper** tempered by being
plunged into ice-cold water. Spanish rivers, such as
the Tagus, being fed by melting snows were
considered to be partly responsible for the quality
of Spanish blades. Some editors have suggested that
QI's spelling 'Isebrookes' indicates that 'Innsbruck'
is intended, because the Austrian town exported fine
metal to England during the seventeenth century.
256 **naked** unarmed (as in *2H6* 3.2.234).

262 **your stop** the hindrance you constitute (as
in *Rom.* 2.2.69).
265 **butt** target (for archery), goal (as in *H5*
1.2.186).
266 **sea-mark** beacon or other landmark used
by ships to make land (as in *Cor.* 5.3.74).
266 **my utmost sail** the farthest point of my
voyage (of life).
267 **lost** wasted, idle.
268 **Man but a rush** Aim only a reed (as if it
were a spear).
270 **ill-starred** ill-fated.

Pale as thy smock! When we shall meet at compt
This look of thine will hurl my soul from heaven
And fiends will snatch at it. Cold, cold, my girl,
Even like thy chastity.
O cursèd, cursèd slave! Whip me, ye devils,   275
From the possession of this heavenly sight!
Blow me about in winds! Roast me in sulphur!
Wash me in steep-down gulfs of liquid fire!
O Desdemon! Dead Desdemon! Dead! O! O!

Enter LODOVICO, *Montano,* CASSIO *in a chair, Iago in the charge of*
OFFICERS.

LODOVICO Where is this rash and most unfortunate man?   280
OTHELLO That's he that was Othello: here I am.
LODOVICO Where is that viper? Bring the villain forth.
OTHELLO I look down towards his feet; but that's a fable.
If that thou be'st a devil, I cannot kill thee.
        [*He wounds Iago.*]
LODOVICO Wrench his sword from him.
IAGO   I bleed, sir, but not killed.   285
OTHELLO I am not sorry neither; I'd have thee live,
For in my sense 'tis happiness to die.
LODOVICO O, thou Othello, that wert once so good,
Fallen in the practice of a damnèd slave,
What shall be said to thee?
OTHELLO   Why, anything: 290
An honourable murderer, if you will;
For naught did I in hate, but all in honour.

---

271 compt] F; count Q1   274-5] *Capell;* Even...slave / ...devils F, Q1   275 cursèd,] F; *not in* Q1   275 ye] F; you
Q1   279 Dead Desdemon] F; *Desdemona* Q1   279 O! O!] F; O, o, o. Q1   279 SD] *Enter* Lodouico, Montano, Iago,
and Officers, Cassio *in a Chaire.* Q1; *Enter* Lodouico, Cassio, Montano, *and* Iago, *with Officers.* F   280 unfortunate] F;
infortunate Q1   282] Q1; Where...viper / ...forth F   282 that] F; this Q1   284 that] F; *not in* Q1   284 SD] *Rowe
subst.; not in* F, Q1   285 Wrench] F; Wring Q1   286 live] F, Q1; loue Q1 *(one copy)*   288 wert] Q1; was F
289 damnèd] Q1; cursed F   290 shall] F; should Q1   292 did I] Q1; I did F

271 **Pale as thy smock** Proverbial (Tilley   278 **steep-down** precipice-like.
C446).   283 **his** i.e. Iago's.
271 **compt** the day of Judgement.   283 **fable** i.e. that the Devil has cloven feet; as
275 **slave** i.e. himself, not Iago.   in the proverb (Tilley D252).
276 **the possession** of being haunted by.   287 **in my sense** to one who feels like me.
277-8 **Blow me...fire** Compare Claudio's   289 **in the practice** through the machinations
vision of hell in *MM* 3.1.121-5: 'To bathe in fiery   (as in *MM* 5.1.107).
floods... / To be imprison'd in the viewless   289 **slave** villain.
winds / And blown with restless violence round
about / The pendant world'.

LODOVICO This wretch hath part confessed his villainy.
　　　　　Did you and he consent in Cassio's death?

OTHELLO Ay.　　　　　　　　　　　　　　　　　　　　　295

CASSIO Dear general, I never gave you cause.

OTHELLO I do believe it, and I ask your pardon.
　　　　　Will you, I pray, demand that demi-devil
　　　　　Why he hath thus ensnared my soul and body?

IAGO Demand me nothing; what you know, you know.　　　300
　　　　　From this time forth I never will speak word.

LODOVICO What! Not to pray?

GRATIANO Torments will ope your lips.

OTHELLO　　　　　　　　　　　　Well, thou dost best.

LODOVICO Sir, you shall understand what hath befallen,
　　　　　Which, as I think, you know not. Here is a letter　305
　　　　　Found in the pocket of the slain Roderigo,
　　　　　And here another: the one of them imports
　　　　　The death of Cassio, to be undertook
　　　　　By Roderigo.

OTHELLO　　　　　O villain!

CASSIO　　　　　　　　　Most heathenish and most gross!

LODOVICO Now here's another discontented paper,　　　　310
　　　　　Found in his pocket too; and this, it seems,
　　　　　Roderigo meant to have sent this damnèd villain,
　　　　　But that, belike, Iago, in the nick,
　　　　　Came in and satisfied him.

OTHELLO　　　　　　　　　　　　O the pernicious caitiff!
　　　　　How came you, Cassio, by that handkerchief　　　315
　　　　　That was my wife's?

CASSIO　　　　　　　　I found it in my chamber;
　　　　　And he himself confessed but even now
　　　　　That there he dropped it for a special purpose
　　　　　Which wrought to his desire.

OTHELLO　　　　　　　　　　　O fool, fool, fool!

296 never gave] F; did neuer giue QI　297 your] F; you QI　298 I] F; *not in* QI　304] QI; Sir / ...befallen F
308–9 The...Roderigo] F; *one line in* QI　313 nick] QI; interim F　314 the] QI; thou F　315 that] F; a QI
317 but] it but F; it QI

294 **consent in** agree to the planning of.
300 **what...know** Proverbial (Tilley K173).
303 **Torments** Torture.
309 **gross** flagrant, monstrous (as in *Lear* 1.3.4).
310 **discontented paper** letter expressing resentment.

313 **nick** nick of time. F's 'interim' is possible, but dramatically less satisfying.
314 **Came in** Interposed.
314 **satisfied him** gave him a satisfactory explanation.
319 **wrought to his desire** worked out in accordance with his wishes.

CASSIO There is besides in Roderigo's letter   320
How he upbraids Iago, that he made him
Brave me upon the watch, whereon it came
That I was cast; and even but now he spake –
After long seeming dead – Iago hurt him,
Iago set him on.   325

LODOVICO You must forsake this room and go with us.
Your power and your command is taken off
And Cassio rules in Cyprus. For this slave,
If there be any cunning cruelty
That can torment him much and hold him long   330
It shall be his. You shall close prisoner rest
Till that the nature of your fault be known
To the Venetian state. Come, bring him away.

OTHELLO Soft you; a word or two before you go.
I have done the state some service and they know't: 335
No more of that. I pray you, in your letters
When you shall these unlucky deeds relate,
Speak of me as I am; nothing extenuate,
Nor set down aught in malice. Then must you speak
Of one that loved not wisely, but too well;   340
Of one not easily jealous but, being wrought,
Perplexed in the extreme; of one whose hand,
Like the base Indian, threw a pearl away
Richer than all his tribe; of one whose subdued eyes,
Albeit unusèd to the melting mood,   345
Drops tears as fast as the Arabian trees

---

333 him] Q1; *not in* F   334 before you go] F; *not in* Q1   338 me as I am] F; *them as they are* Q1
339] Q1; Nor...malice / ...speak F   343 Indian] Q1; Iudean F

---

322 Brave Insult, provoke. Compare *2H6*
4.10.36: 'thou wilt brave me with these saucy
terms'.

322 whereon it came because of which it
happened.

323 cast dismissed.

327 off away.

330 hold him long keep him a long time in
dying.

331 rest remain.

334 Soft you Wait a moment.

337 unlucky unfortunate, unhappy.

341 wrought worked upon.

342 Perplexed Desperately troubled, bewil-
dered (as in *Cym.* 3.4.7).

343 base Either 'low in natural rank, or in the
scale of creation' (*OED* sv *a* 8), or 'deep-coloured,
dark' (*OED a* 5; and *Tit.* 4.2.71: 'is black so base
a hue?').

343 Indian Many editors have adopted this Q1
reading, citing the numerous sixteenth-century
references to savages who did not know the value
of the precious minerals they possessed. But F's
'Iudean' has been just as strongly defended as an
allusion either to Herod's rejection of his 'jewel of
a wife', Mariamne, in a fit of jealousy, or to Judas's
betrayal of Christ. See supplementary note.

344 subdued overcome by emotion.

346–7 Drops tears...gum The reference is to
the myrrh tree and probably comes from a

Their medicinable gum. Set you down this;
And say besides that in Aleppo once
Where a malignant and a turbaned Turk
Beat a Venetian and traduced the state, 350
I took by th'throat the circumcisèd dog
And smote him thus.

He stabs himself.

LODOVICO O bloody period!

GRATIANO All that's spoke is marred!

OTHELLO I kissed thee ere I killed thee: no way but this,
Killing myself, to die upon a kiss. 355

He [falls on the bed and] dies

CASSIO This did I fear, but thought he had no weapon,
For he was great of heart.

LODOVICO [*To Iago*] O Spartan dog,
More fell than anguish, hunger, or the sea,
Look on the tragic loading of this bed:
This is thy work. The object poisons sight; 360
Let it be hid.

[The bed-curtains are drawn.]

Gratiano, keep the house
And seize upon the fortunes of the Moor,
For they succeed on you. To you, lord governor,
Remains the censure of this hellish villain:

---

347 medicinable] F; medicinall Q1   352 SD] Q1; *not in* F   355 SD] *Cam.*; *He dies.* Q1; *Dyes* F   357 SD] *Theobald*; *not in* F, Q1   359 loading] F; *lodging* Q1   360] Q1; *This...work* / *...sight* F   361 SD] *Dover Wilson subst.*; *not in* F, Q1   363 on] F; *to* Q1

conflation of two passages in Pliny's *Naturalis Historia*, 12.14–15. In one of these we are told that 'myrrh and the trees that yield it' are found 'in many quarters of Arabia...they sweat out of themselves a certain liquor called stact, which is very good myrrh'; and in another, describing a product called opobalsamum, the liquor 'issueth out of the wound...which...commeth forth by small drops; and as it thus weepeth, the tears ought to be received in wool'. Compare *The Faerie Queene*, I, i, 9: 'The Mirrhe sweete-bleeding in the bitter wound'.

348 **Aleppo** A city in Turkey, where it was a capital crime for a Christian to strike a Turk.

353 **period** conclusion.

354 **I kissed...thee** Editors who adopt F's 'Iudean' at 343 take this to be an allusion to Judas's identifying Christ by means of a kiss in the garden of Gethsemane (Matt. 26.48); but see supplementary note.

357 **Spartan dog** Spartan dogs were, according to Seneca's *Hippolytus* (trans. J. Studley, 1581), 'eager of prey'. Compare *MND* where Theseus boasts of his hounds 'bred out of the Spartan kind' (4.1.119), and Hippolyta talks of Hercules and Cadmus baying 'a bear / With hounds of Sparta' (4.1.112–14).

358 **fell** fierce, cruel (as in *TN* 1.1.21).

359 **loading** Q1's 'lodging' meaning 'sight like corn beaten down by a storm' has had some defenders.

360 **object** spectacle, that which meets the eyes. Compare *Tro.* 3.3.180: 'The present eye praises the present object.'

361 **keep** remain in.

362 **seize upon** take legal possession of.

363 **succeed on** descend to (as in *AWW* 3.7.23).

363 **lord governor** i.e. Cassio.

364 **censure** judgement, trial (as in *Cor.* 3.3.46).

The time, the place, the torture, O, enforce it!   365
Myself will straight aboard, and to the state
This heavy act with heavy heart relate.

Exeunt

367 SD] F; *Exeunt omnes.* Q1

366 **straight** immediately.   367 **heavy** sorrowful.

SUPPLEMENTARY NOTES

1.1.10 Off-capped This F reading has been defended as meaning 'stood cap in hand out of respect' and supported by reference to *Ant.* 2.7.57: 'I have ever held my cap off to thy fortunes', and *Tim.* 4.3.212–13: 'And let his very breath... / Blow off thy cap.' Q1's 'Oft-capt' has been equally strongly supported because 'to cap' could mean 'to remove one's hat as a sign of respect', particularly in contemporary academic usage. But the citation from *Cor.* 2.1.68–9, 'You are ambitious for poor knaves' legs and caps', is not really convincing as a parallel use; and White noted that 'capped' could also mean 'with one's hat on', as in Cranmer's *Confutation of Unwritten Verities* (1582): 'And this of Paul, that a man should neither pray nor preach capped, or with his head covered'.

1.1.21 almost... wife Although this is based on Italian and English proverbs, most editors have found its exact import obscure. The enormous amount of speculation may be reduced to the following points: (1) that we are intended to believe that Iago has in mind Cassio's long-standing liaison with Bianca who is intent on marrying (see 4.1.105–42); but there is no clear evidence in the play for or against the idea that Cassio knew Bianca before he landed in Cyprus; (2) that Iago is not being specific, but is referring slightingly to Cassio's obvious reputation as a ladies' man, who is liable to be snared in marriage by one of his conquests; (3) that the line is parenthetical and (reading 'fellow's' for 'fellow') is early evidence of Iago's own bitter jealousy over Emilia's supposed infidelity with Cassio; (4) that this is one of the many inconsistencies in the presentation of Cassio's character between Acts 1–2 and Acts 3–5, dealt with by N. Allen in his discussion of Shakespeare's treatment of his source in Cinthio (*S.Sur.* 21 (1968), 15). The numerous emendations of 'fair wife' (see Furness, pp. 5–10) are testimony to the inventiveness of Shakespeare scholars.

1.3.259–60 to comply... satisfaction All editors agree that some emendation of F's and Q1's 'my defunct' is needed. The conjectures are legion and are based on the following ambiguities in word usage: (1) 'young affects' can mean 'emotions typical of young people', or 'feelings which strongly influence young people', or 'newly-felt emotions (in me)'; (2) 'proper' can mean 'own', or 'peculiar', or 'legitimate', or 'personal'; (3) 'comply with heat' can mean 'satisfy eagerly', or 'gratify my sexual passion'. If 'defunct' is allowed to stand and 'my' is emended to 'me', then it is possible to see 'the young affects in me defunct' as a parenthesis in the sentence 'to comply with heat... and proper satisfaction'. If 'defunct' is emended to 'distinct' (= individual) or 'disjunct' (= separate) or 'defenced' (= guarded) or 'defect' (= defective), then the word is an adjective in apposition to 'proper' and describing 'satisfaction'.

1.3.265–6 seel... instruments This reading from F conveys a quite different metaphorical picture from Q1's 'foyles... / My speculatiue and actiue instruments'. The former depicts Cupid seeling with wantonness the eyes of Othello (like a young hawk being blinded) so that the powers of perception necessary to his position of commander will be useless. The latter has Cupid making ineffective Othello's thoughts and senses. Either of these readings is acceptable; but most editors make some amalgam of the two texts unnecessarily.

2.1.65 tire the ingener The phrase has puzzled most editors, and F's spelling 'Ingeniuer' has encouraged the wildest of speculations: e.g. 'ingenuous virtue' (Steevens), 'ingene ever' (Malone). In general, opinion is divided between two interpretations, both of which involve the interpretation of 'ingener' as a noun signifying 'artist': (1) dress or decorate the imagination of the creative artist; (2) weary or exceed the abilities of the artist attempting to praise her. Q1's 'beare all excellency' is clear, but is usually considered banal and un-Shakespearean.

2.1.284 trace I take the meaning of this F reading to be 'follow, track' (*OED* sv v^1 5) with 'for' in the sense of 'because of'. However, most editors find this interpretation unacceptable. Ridley, committed to Q1 as a copy-text, suggests that 'crush' may have 'something like the sense of "crowding" a horse at a fence – which is just what Iago is trying to do' and cites in support *2H4* 4.2.33–4: 'The time misorder'd doth... / Crowd us and crush us to this monstrous form.' By far the most common emendation is Steevens's 'trash.' (= check by weights or a cord), with Walker (NS) adopting Bailey's variant of 'leash'. Yet the meaning thus produced does not fit Iago's line of thought: while habitually he wants to slow down Roderigo's pursuit of Desdemona, here he clearly wishes to incite the now-disillusioned lover to further action. Hulme (pp. 254–7) suggests a different meaning of F's 'trace', arguing that the allusion is to 'hunger-trace', a term applied to the loss of feathers in a young hawk which has been too severely starved during training.

2.3.59–63 And let me the cannikin clink Hart cites a number of contemporary drinking songs in which cannikins and clinking figure largely, but no text or music of any original of Iago's song have come to light. Various tunes have been unearthed which fit the words well: W. Chappell set the words to a ballad air called 'Wigmore's Galliard' (*Popular Music of the Olden Time*, 1855–9, I, 190); F. W. Sternfeld thinks the lyrics best fit a tune 'Joan Sanderson' or 'Cushion Dance' of which he prefers the version in Playford's *Dancing Master* (1686) (*Music in Shakespearean Tragedy*, 1963, pp. 63, 145–6); and D. C. Greer suggests the use of the tune 'Soldier's Life', which appeared in the 1651 edition of *Dancing Master* (*Music and Letters* 43 (1962), 304–19).

2.3.76–83 King Stephen was a worthy peer This song is a version of the seventh stanza of a well-known Scottish ballad called 'Bell my Wife' or 'Tak your auld cloak about thee', of which the full text can be found in Percy's *Reliques of Ancient English Poetry*, 1765, II, no. 7, and A. Ramsay's *Tea Table Miscellany*, 1730, p. 113. No sixteenth-century musical setting is known. L. Elson (*Shakespeare in Music*, 1901, pp. 202–3) and P. Seng ('The Dramatic Function of the Songs in Shakespeare's Plays', unpublished Ph.D. thesis, Harvard University, 1955, p. 481) chose an old Scottish tune in J. Johnson's *The Scottish National Museum*, 1839, II, 258 ff., as the best setting; but F. W. Sternfeld notes that the tune was first printed in J. Oswald's *Caledonian Pocket Companion*, 1750–60, II, 29, and that a scoring for voice and keyboard accompaniment was published in R. Bremner's *Thirty Scots Songs, for Voice and Harpsicord*, 1757, I, 14 (*Music in Shakespearean Tragedy*, 1963, pp. 146–50).

3.3.124–5 They're...rule There is no agreement about the meaning of this passage. Q1's 'denotements' was defended by Malone, and adopted by Ridley, as meaning 'indications, or recoveries, not openly revealed, but involuntarily working from the heart, which cannot rule and suppress its feelings'. This, of course, necessitates also taking 'passion' as the object rather than the subject of 'rule'. F's 'dilations' is not elsewhere used by Shakespeare, but is often taken to be a Latinate usage meaning 'stops, pauses' of the kind that men of phlegmatic constitutions, who are not governed by their passions, cannot prevent occurring. Walker (NS) suggests that the word also meant 'dilatations', a word used in physiology to describe the expansions of the arteries of the heart. Johnson's emendation 'delations' (= secret accusations) is the most commonly adopted reading, despite the facts that the evidence for such a usage in Shakespeare's time is non-existent, and that Iago's pauses could hardly be described accurately as accusations. I believe the lines mean: 'These stops are the involuntary swellings of the heart in a just man who is not normally a slave of his passions.'

3.3.168–9 mock...feeds on This has occasioned an enormous amount of commentary (see Furness, pp. 175–80). Theobald's conjecture of 'make' for 'mock' makes the lines mean 'jealous people feed on the suspicions that they themselves have created'. Other editors are divided between the ideas that (1) jealousy feeds on love which it plays with and torments; (2) jealousy mockingly feeds on the heart of the man who is its victim; (3) the victim himself produces the unreal groundless suspicions which are the food that sustains jealousy.

3.3.430 shrewd doubt There is no certainty about the meaning of 'shrewd' here. Shakespeare uses it elsewhere in various ways: (1) bitter, piercing, grievous (as in *MV* 3.2.243); (2) sharp, critically penetrating (as in *Tro.* 1.2.190 and *R3* 2.4.35); (3) telling, effective (as in *AWW* 3.5.68). While any of these meanings is possible, in view of Othello's mental state at this point the first of them appears the most likely.

3.3.469–70 to obey...ever Most editors have found difficulty with the meaning of 'remorse' here; and many have attempted a solution by introducing a negative of some kind: e.g. 'Not to obey' (Pope), 'Nor to obey' (Theobald), 'without remorse' (Dover Wilson). Schmidt glosses the word as 'compunction of conscience' and Onions as 'solemn obligation', but Shakespeare nowhere else uses the word in these senses. I find no difficulty in accepting the usual Shakespearean meaning of 'pity' with Iago characteristically linking it paradoxically with 'bloody business'.

4.3.38–54 **The poor soul sat sighing by a sycamore tree** This is a version of a song well-known before Shakespeare used it and often quoted in earlier plays and poems. The fullest texts of the original can be found in Percy's *Reliques of Ancient English Poetry*, 1765, I, 199–203, and *The Roxburghe Ballads*, ed. W. Chappell, 1888, I, 171. For his version Shakespeare changed the sex of the singer and drew mainly on stanzas 1, 2, 5, 6, 7 and 11 of the original. There are three contemporary musical settings of the song in British Library Add. MS. 15117 (1616 or earlier), the Lodge Book, Folger Library (early 1570s), and the Dallis Book, Trinity College, Dublin (*c.* 1583). For detailed discussions of the texts and musical settings, see F. W. Sternfeld, *Music in Shakespearean Tragedy*, 1963, pp. 23–52, and J. H. Long, *Shakespeare's Use of Music*, 1971, pp. 153–61.

5.2.0 SD *Enter...in bed* There is no external evidence of how this scene was staged at either the Globe or Blackfriars Theatres. During the last century and at the beginning of this one, it was believed that the scene was played perhaps on an upper acting-area or, more likely, with a bed placed in an inner stage (i.e. an elaborate recessed curtained space set into the tiring-house façade at the rear of the stage). Recent scholars, however, have thrown doubt on the very existence of an inner stage, and have argued that for the climactic scene of the play to be acted without employing the main playing-area is a patent absurdity. There have been two main modern theories about how the scene was managed. L. J. Ross (*SQ* 12 (1961), 359–70) suggests that a curtained fit-up booth or pavilion, constructed before the tiring-house façade and projecting into the main acting-area, was used, this containing the bed which could be concealed when the curtains were drawn (as is ordered at 5.2.361). Moreover, this structure could also serve (1) as the 'Bulke' (Q1) behind which Iago orders Roderigo to conceal himself at 5.1.1, this word meaning in the seventeenth century literally 'a structure projecting from the front of another building'; (2) for the 'Brothel Scene' (4.2); (3) for Emilia and Desdemona to move towards for the 'Willow Scene' after the exit of Othello, Lodovico and Attendants at 4.3.10; and (4) for the opening 'discovery' of the Senate in 1.3 where the Q1 SD reads *Enter Duke and Senators, set at a Table with lights*. R. Hosley (*SQ* 14 (1963), 57–65) takes exception to this theory on the evidence he deduces from an examination of twenty-three bed scenes in plays produced between 1594 and 1642 by the Lord Chamberlain's Men or the King's Men (as the Company was known after 1603). While admitting that discovery scenes were occasionally effected at the Globe Theatre in a curtained doorway of the tiring-house façade, he believes that in *Othello* 'the bed with Desdemona lying in it is "thrust out" of the tiring-house by stage-keepers or attendant players; the bed curtains are manipulated as called for by the dialogue; and when Lodovico says, "Let it be hid" the bed, on which are now lying the bodies of Desdemona, Emilia, and Othello, is "drawn in" to the tiring-house through one of its doors' (p. 65). Hosley discounts Ross's argument for the necessity of a 'Bulke' at 5.1.1 by pointing out that F reads here 'Barke' (i.e. balke or piece of timber) which could easily refer to one of the posts supporting the stage-cover; and further suggests that the Senate scene in 1.3 is not a 'discovery' at all because *set at a Table* could equally well mean 'be seated at a table' after entrance has been made. Both of these methods of staging are clearly possible, and we do know that at least for the performance of the play at Oxford in 1610 (see p. 38 above) the bed was near enough to the audience for people to be moved by the expressions on the face of the boy actor who played Desdemona. It is also not beyond the bounds of possibility that the scene was managed differently at the Globe and Blackfriars – a difference perhaps reflected in the 'Bulke/Barke' readings of Q1 and F. See illustrations 4, 5 and 6, pp. 19, 26, and 36 above.

5.2.343 **base Indian** There were innumerable sixteenth-century travellers' tales about savages not knowing the value of the minerals they possessed, although no passage is known that contains the precise terms used in Othello's lines. Pliny discusses Indians ignorantly bartering pearls (34.17); Thomas Nashe has three of the elements in *Pierce Penniless* (1594): 'all artists for the most part are base-minded like the Indians, that have store of gold and precious stones at command, yet are ignorant of their value' (*Works*, ed. R. B. McKerrow, I, 241); and George Gascoigne's *The Steel Glass* (1575) links pearls and Moors: 'How live the Moors that spurn at glistering pearl, / And scorn the costs, which we do hold so dear?' The adjective 'base', which troubles supporters of F's reading 'Iudean', can mean either 'low in natural rank, or in the scale of creation' (*OED* sv *a* 8), or 'deep-coloured, dark' (*OED a* 5). The arguments for F's 'Iudean' being an allusion to Judas's betrayal of Christ are: (1) the use of the definite article indicates a specific person; (2) Judas was the only one of the disciples who was a Judean, with 'Iscariot' being linked in the Geneva Bible with 'the tribe of Judah'; (3) the kiss associated with Judas's identification in Gethsemane and with Othello's murder of Desdemona; (4) the obvious Biblical associations of 'pearl'; (5) Othello's and Judas's self-inflicted punishments; (6) 'base' must mean 'vile'; (7) the word 'tribe' is more appropriate for Judas than for an Indian. There seems to me to be little substance in any of these. Othello is lamenting his ignorance, stupidity, gullibility and descent to savagery, none of which is applicable to Judas. The kiss Othello gives Desdemona is hardly a sign of betrayal so much as an instinctive sexual response at odds with his mental conviction of her guilt. 'Base' does not have to mean 'vile' (see above). 'Tribe' is not always Biblical; compare Iago's lines at 3.3.177–8: 'the souls of all my tribe defend / From jealousy'. The suggestion that F's reading is a reference to the story of Herod and Mariamne is not supported by sufficient parallels to warrant much credence.

Othello is a play that has come down to us in two forms: that
(Q1) published in 1622 and that included in the First Folio (F) o
of these texts could be produced in the theatre and would be acce̶̶̶̶   ̶̶ ̶̶average
playgoer as a stage version of Shakespeare's drama, there are striking differences
between them, including an extra hundred and sixty lines or so in F, some other lines
and phrases that appear only in Q1, some fifty-three oaths only found in Q1, over a
thousand variations in vocabulary, phrasing and stage directions between the two
texts, and a wide range of variants in spelling and punctuation. There is no generally
accepted scholarly opinion about the exact relationship between the two nor about
the degree of accuracy with which either reproduces the dramatist's own manuscript
original.

The analysis of the printing-house processes that lie behind the making of Q1 and
F is necessarily technical and complicated, and that of the copy from which the texts
were set up is inescapably speculative. Subjective judgements play a necessary part
in the ordering of the surviving fragments of evidence. It is possible, however, to look
closely at each text in turn, to focus attention on the crucial differences between them,
and to outline, in relation to the discerned facts, an acceptable editorial procedure.

The 1622 quarto

Thomas Walkley entered the play in the Stationers' Register on 6 October 1621
and the next year published his quarto, which he had printed in the shop of Nicholas
Okes, with the following title page:

THE / Tragœdy of Othello, / The Moore of Venice. / *As it hath beene diuerse times acted at
the* / Globe, and at the Black-Friers, by / *his Maiesties Seruants.* / *Written by* VVilliam
Shakespeare. / [Device: McKerrow 316] / LONDON, / Printed by N.O. for *Thomas Walkley*,
and are to be sold at his / shop, at the Eagle and Child, in Brittans Bursse. / 1622.

This publication date makes it the latest of all the Shakespeare quartos. But although
it antedated the appearance of the play in F by only a year, there is no evidence that
Walkley was behaving piratically; *Othello* was but one of several plays in the repertory
of the King's Men that he published about this time without challenge from the
company, the others being Beaumont and Fletcher's *A King and No King* (1619),
Philaster (1620) and *Thierry and Theodoret* (1621). His Stationers' Register entry is
perfectly regular and was apparently unaffected by the order in the Stationers'
Court-Book on 3 May 1619 requiring that no play belonging to the King's Men was
to be printed without the company's consent. He was able to transfer his copyright
on 1 March 1628 to Richard Hawkins, who published a second quarto, which

features of F, in 1630. Moreover, it is noticeable that Jaggard and
block entry for F in the Stationers' Register on 8 November 1623 omits
along with the other plays that had earlier appeared in quarto format.
According to Hinman's[1] timetable for the printing of F, Walkley's entry must have
been made and his quarto in all probability issued before the type-setting for F had
been started. All the evidence therefore confirms that his title to the play was secure.
Obviously Walkley's permission to include *Othello* in F must have been obtained, but
the details of the arrangement cannot now be known. The short preface in Q1, 'The
Stationer to the Reader', conveys only his consciousness of being the first to give the
play to the reading public, though the mere fact of its inclusion may be interpreted
as a public assertion of his copyright:

To set forth a booke without an Epistle, were like to the old English prouerbe, A blew coat without
a badge, *& the Author being dead, I thought good to take that piece of worke vpon mee : To commend
it, I will not, for that which is good, I hope euery man will commend, without intreaty : and I am
the bolder, because the Authors name is sufficient to vent his worke. Thus leauing euery one to the
liberty of iudgement : I haue ventered to print this Play, and leaue it to the generall censure.*

Yours,

Thomas VValkley.

Q1 exists in nineteen copies, all of which are to some degree defective. Bibliographical
analysis of these[2] indicates that Okes printed them using two skeleton-formes; and
as the thirty-eight press-variants they contain appear on only one forme of each sheet
affected, it is probable that the pressman followed the systematic order of work
standard in two-skeleton books of the period: that is, a proof-sheet is pulled from
the uncorrected forme, printing is continued from this forme while the proof is being
corrected, the forme is corrected from the amended proof, a proof-sheet is pulled from
the second yet-uncorrected forme, the printing-run from the now-corrected first forme
is completed, the sheet is perfected from the corrected second forme.

The press-variants, which appear overwhelmingly in the stint of Compositor Y,
also suggest that the stop-press correction done was carried out merely to eliminate
obvious errors and without reference to the manuscript copy. However, the corrections
made on the inner forme of Sheet I would perhaps have necessitated some collation
with the manuscript, and there was probably more care exercised by the corrector
from this point to the end of the play.

The type for Q1 was set by three compositors,[3] with X setting A–F4^r, Y taking over
the composition at Iago's entrance (3.1.27) on F4^v (or perhaps at the top of F4^v) and
continuing to the end of L4^v, and Z setting Sheets M and N. The persuasive evidence
for this division consists of the three workmen's characteristic and distinctive practices
in the use of two-, three- or four-hyphen dashes, the kinds of abbreviations of proper
names in entrance and exit stage directions, the methods of setting short speeches
as a single line of type or on separate lines, the distribution of descriptive and

[1] Charlton Hinman, *The Printing and Proof-Reading of the First Folio of Shakespeare*, 1963, I, 289.
[2] See Charlton Hinman (ed.), *Othello 1622*, Shakespeare Quarto Facsimiles No. 16, 1975, pp. v–xvii; and
M. T. Jones, 'Press-variants and proofreading in the first quarto of *Othello* (1622)', *SB* 27 (1974), 177–84.
[3] See E. A. J. Honigmann, *The Stability of Shakespeare's Text*, 1965, pp. 100 ff.

imperative indications of stage action, the kinds of punctuation used in the act-divisions, the centring of first speech headings in new scenes, the variations in signatures and page-numbers, and the spread of variant spellings of frequently-used words.

The nature of the manuscript copy from which Okes set type is the subject of continuing debate. For many years perhaps the most widely-accepted theory was that of Alice Walker.[1] She argued that behind Q1 lay a manuscript of theatrical origin, possibly an early promptbook, that had been cut for acting purposes, and recopied by a scribe familiar with the play in performance, his memory of which he relied upon too frequently and so produced a contaminated version of the play. Her hypothesis rests on the discrimination of three kinds of error: (1) passages cut by the actors for practical purposes and therefore omitted from Q1 – for example, the absence of the Willow Song in 4.3 she saw as being due to the fact that the boy playing the part of Desdemona had no singing voice; (2) errors caused by compositorial carelessness such as eye-skip during the type-setting (for example, at 3.4.7–8; 4.2.72–5, 100; 4.3.57–60; 5.2.150–3); (3) 'vulgarisations' of Shakespeare's text, owed to misremembering, including Q1's 'vtmost pleasure' for F's 'very quality' (1.3.247); 'concerne' for 'import' (1.3.279); 'know' for 'warrant' (3.3.3); 'denotements' for 'dilations' (3.3.124); 'duty' for 'office' (3.4.107); 'her Sex' for 'their wiues' (4.2.17).

Other scholars, such as W. W. Greg and M. R. Ridley,[2] differed from Walker only in believing that the copy for Q1 was a transcript of rather confused and illegible foul papers, and that its errors and vulgarisations are substitutions of the kind often made by a transcriber carrying too many words in his head, which means that there is no need to postulate a book-keeper scribe contaminating the text from his memory of the play in performance.

A number of objections may be made to Walker's view of Q1. To begin with, her belief that the cuts in Q1 were motivated by theatrical considerations can be discounted. Nevill Coghill[3] has demonstrated that the playing-time saved by these 'cuts' is about ten minutes, and that if a shortened acting version was the objective then numerous other cuts could have been made without severe damage to the performance – for example, the scene with the Clown and the Musicians (3.1) which is frequently dropped in modern productions.

Furthermore, Walker's case rests upon the assumption that a single compositor set the play for Okes from a manuscript prepared by a single contaminating scribe. As we have seen, Honigmann's evidence makes it unlikely that only one man set the type for Q1; and he has also demonstrated that the copy was probably a manuscript produced by two scribes working hurriedly and simultaneously. Scribe A invariably placed his stage directions in the margin, resulting in extensive turn-over in the printed text (see fig. 1). Scribe A's preferred spellings are 'though', 'bin', 'ha'', I'le', 'Casfio', 'them'. Scribe B always centred his stage directions on his pages. Scribe B favoured the forms 'tho', 'beene', 'haue/has/hath', 'I'le/Ile/ile', 'Caffio', ''em'.

[1] Alice Walker in 'The 1622 quarto and the First Folio text of *Othello*', *S.Sur.* 5 (1952), 16–24; *Textual Problems of the First Folio*, 1953, pp. 138–61; and in NS, pp. 121–35.
[2] W. W. Greg, *The Shakespeare First Folio*, 1955, pp. 357–74; M. R. Ridley (ed.), *Othello*, 1962.
[3] Nevill Coghill, *Shakespeare's Professional Skills*, 1964, pp. 145–53, 164–202.

The very Elements of this warlike Ifle,
Haue I to night fluftred with flowing cups,
And the watch too : now mongft this flocke of drunkards,
I am to put our *Caſsio* in ſome aĉtion,
That may offend the Ifle;   *Enter* Montanio, Caſſio,
But here they come :   *and others.*
If conſequence doe but approoue my dreame,
My boate ſailes freely, both with winde and ſtreame.
Caſ. Fore God they haue giuen me a rouſe already.
Mon. Good faith a little one, not paſt a pint.

Fig. 1   Signature E4 of QI (SD setting by Compositor A)

These characteristics cannot be attributed to the compositors as they are spread throughout the text in a pattern which does not coincide with the printing-house stints.

What then can be deduced about the copy from which QI was printed? The nature and number of errors in the printed text indicate a hastily-prepared and badly-written manuscript; for many of the compositors' mistakes are due to misreading of the Secretary hand, a fact underlined by some of the proof-reader's recoveries: for example, 'Conuinced' from 'Coniured' (4.1.28); 'vnsuting' from 'vnfitting' (4.1.75); 'cunning' from 'cunuing' (4.1.87). Okes's men also were careless and introduced their own kinds of error as well as changing words in accordance with their personal predilections. Yet despite these obstructions to accurate transmission of the text, there remains some features which suggest that Shakespeare's foul papers lay behind QI.

Evidence of authorial manuscript can be found in the orthography of the QI text and in its stage directions. Both scribes and compositors tolerated to some extent certain characteristic Shakespearean spellings: 1.2.70 'gardage' (compare *Ham.* 3.4.104; *MV* 2.2.155; *TC* (Q) 4.5.253); 1.3.287 'Adue' (*Rom.* 2.2.136; *LLL* 1.2.181, 5.2.626); 3.3.146 'ghesse' (*Ado* 1.1.110; *MM* 4.4.7; *WT* 1.2.403); 3.3.371 'accumilate' (*Sonnets* 117.10); 3.4.66 'Sybell' (*Tit.* 4.1.105; *Shr.* 1.2.70); 5.2.314 'catieffe' (*Rom.* 5.1.52);[1] and the apostrophic usages 't'were, t'will, T'would, i'st, bit'h'. Doubt has rightly been cast in recent years on the practice of automatically attributing one kind of stage direction to one kind of copy, but collectively QI's directions give the impression of being authorial, the sort a dramatist might well write into his play to assist his company to visualise its production. For example, the two entrances of Brabantio in 1.1 are evocative visually – Brabantio *at a window.* (82) and *Enter* Brabantio *in his night gowne, and seruants with Torches.* (158) – as is the scene at the opening of 1.3: *Enter Duke and Senators, set at a Table with lights and Attendants.* Othello's kissing of Desdemona on his arrival in Cyprus is duly noted at 2.1.189. At key points of the action all the important stage movements are made explicit. During the drunken brawl in 2.3 we find *Helpe, helpe, within.* (127); *Enter* Cassio, *driuing in*

---

[1] For other examples see Honigmann, *Stability of Shakespeare's Text.*

Roderigo. (127); *they fight.* (137); *A bell rung:* (141); *Enter* Othello, *and Gentlemen with weapons.* (144); and in the climax of the final scene (5.2) the stage directions specify stage business that cannot accurately be inferred from the spoken text: *Enter* Othello *with a light.* (0 SD); *kisses her.* (15); *he stifles her.* (85); Emillia *calls within.* (86); Oth. *fals on the bed.* (197); *The Moore runnes at Iago. Iago kils his wife.* (233); *she dies.* (249); Cassio *in a Chaire.* (279); *He stabs himselfe.* (352).

In addition to such visualising stage directions, there are a number of unspecific entrances and exits of the kind that are also indicative of authorial copy not yet prepared for the playhouse – for example, in 1.3 *Exit two or three.* (121); ...*and the rest* (169). And there is the uncertainty about the rank and role of Montano which could presumably have originated only with the author. At his first appearance Q1 directs *Enter* Montanio, *Gouernor of* Cypres (2.1.0 SD), but neither Cassio nor Othello treats him as the former governor when they land on the island. This looks like evidence of first and second authorial thoughts comparable with the confusion about Viola's singing role in *Twelfth Night*[1] or the appearance of non-speaking 'ghost' characters in texts printed from Shakespeare's own papers (for example, the mute wife of Leonato in *Much Ado About Nothing*).[2]

The 1623 Folio

Othello appears as the ninth play in the Tragedies section of the Folio and is one of the plays that is furnished with a dramatis personae on the bottom part of the final page. It runs from signature ss3^v (page 310) to vv6^r (page 339). Compositor E set ss3^v–6^r and Compositor B was responsible for ss6^v–vv6^r. The normal order of composition by formes in F, as demonstrated by Hinman,[3] was followed in the case of *Othello*, the setting of a single quire being 3^v:4^r, 3^r:4^v, 2^v:5^r, 2^r:5^v, 1^v:6^r, 1^r:6^v. It is not always possible to be certain which of the two pages making up the forme was set first; but type-recurrence evidence does suggest that vv4^v was set before vv3^r and vv5^v before vv2^r.

Compositor E was an inexpert workman, his work stints being proofed more consistently than any other: fully half of the variants found in the Tragedies section are in the pages he set. But in *Othello* it is the latter part of the play (vv1^v–vv6^r), set by Compositor B, that contains the highest proportion of press-variants. The proof-reading of F was done by the page rather than by the forme. The corrector apparently employed one impression of the forme as a proof for one of its pages and then another impression of the same forme for the proofing of the second page. The press was stopped so that the compositor could begin correcting type of the forme being printed immediately one of its pages had been proofed, the impression of the second page being corrected while the compositor was making the changes necessary in the first.

---

[1] See the discussion of the evidence for a change in Shakespeare's intentions in J. M. Lothian and T. W. Craik (ed.), *TN*, 1975, pp. xxii–xxiii.
[2] See the discussion of the copy for the 1600 quarto of this play in A. R. Humphreys (ed.), *Ado*, 1981, p. 77.   [3] *Printing and Proof-Reading of the First Folio.*

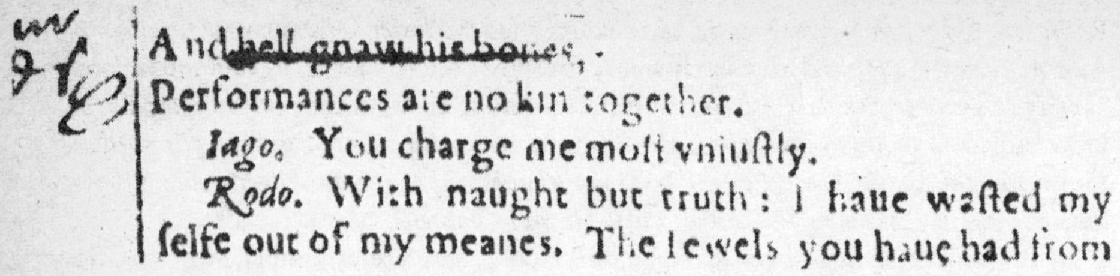

A nd hell gnaw his bones, .
Performances are no kin together.
Iago, You charge me moſt vniuſtly.
Rodo. With naught but truth : I haue waſted my
ſelfe out of my meanes, The Iewels you haue had from

Fig. 2   Head of first type-column of signature vv3ʳ of F (uncorrected version with proof-corrector's mark)

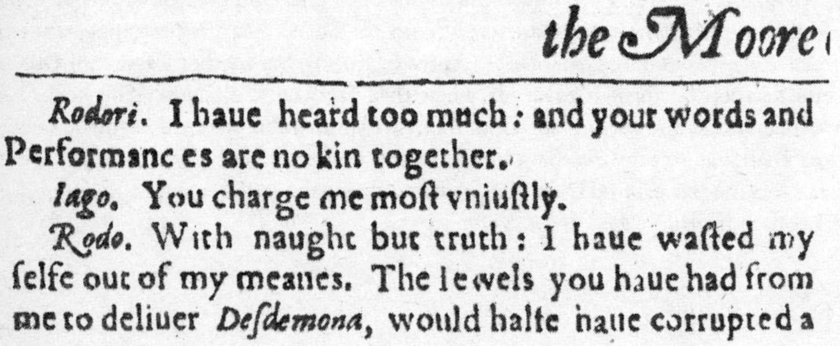

the Moore

Rodori. I haue heard too much : and your words and
Performanc es are no kin together.
Iago, You charge me moſt vniuſtly.
Rodo. With naught but truth : I haue waſted my
ſelfe out of my meanes. The Iewels you haue had from
me to deliuer *Deſdemona,* would halfe haue corrupted a

Fig. 3   Head of first type-column of signature vv3ʳ of F (corrected version)

There are seven minor press-corrections made, apparently without reference to copy, on ss3ʳ, ss4ʳ, and ss4ᵛ, necessitated by Compositor E's lack of expertise; and there are no variants due to press-correction in the quire tt. It is in the quire vv that we find the heaviest proof-correction, on vv1ᵛ, vv2ʳ, vv2ᵛ, vv3ʳ (that is, on one page of the relevant formes). This activity was almost certainly occasioned by the most remarkable press-variant in the whole of the volume, and one which has an important bearing on the vexed question of the copy used in setting type for the F text.

This variant occurs on vv3ʳ. In five of the extant copies of the Folio, one of which (Folger Library Copy 47) has an actual proof-sheet for this page bound up quite regularly as vv3ʳ:4ᵛ, there appear at the head of the first type-column the words 'And

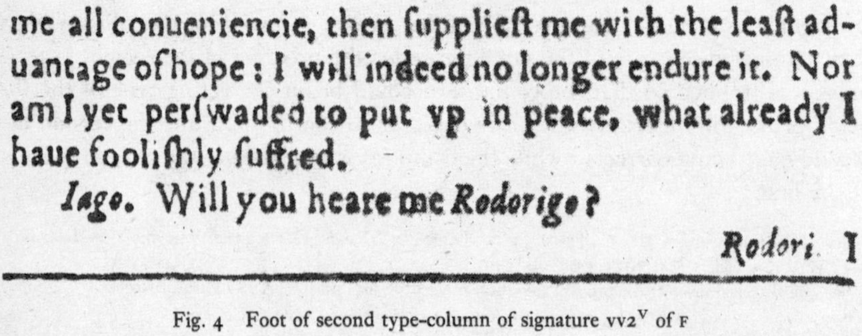

me all conueniencie, then ſupplieſt me with the leaſt ad-
uantage of hope : I will indeed no longer endure it. Nor
am I yet perſwaded to put vp in peace, what already I
haue fooliſhly ſuffred.
Iago. Will you heare me *Rodorigo ?*

Rodori I

Fig. 4   Foot of second type-column of signature vv2ᵛ of F

hell gnaw his bones', which is the latter half of Emilia's line at 4.2.135 beginning 'A halter pardon him', which in F is found twelve lines from the top of the second type-column on vv2^{v}, this column being the one that ends with '*Iago*. Will you heare me *Rodorigo*?' to which the corrected first line of vv3^{r} is the answer. Compositor B set the erroneous 'And hell gnaw his bones' after he had completed either vv4^{v}b, which ends with Othello's words 'Thy Husband knew it all.' (5.2.140) and the catchword '*Æmil.*', or vv4^{r}b, which ends with Desdemona's line 'Then Heauen haue mercy on mee.' (5.2.32–3). The remaining copies of F all have the corrected reading at the head of vv3^{r}a '*Rodori.* I haue heard too much: and your words and' (4.2.180). It is noticeable that this error and its correction occur on just those formes which Hinman suggests were set in an unusual order, that is 3^{r}:4^{v} and 2^{r}:5^{v}.

An analysis of the mistake and the related circumstances prove crucial to our understanding of the nature of the copy behind F. James Walton[1] has convincingly argued that the misreading could only have occurred if Compositor B had been setting type with several pages of manuscript laid out before him which had been cast-off and in which the words 'And hell gnaw his bones' appeared at the head of a leaf:

It is easy to suppose that Compositor B, when he saw 'And hell gnaw his bones' at the beginning of a page of manuscript, imagined that it followed directly after 'Thy Husband knew it all'...Not only does 'And hell gnaw his bones' make apparent sense when put after 'Thy Husband knew it all', but the word 'hell' occurs twice in the immediately preceding

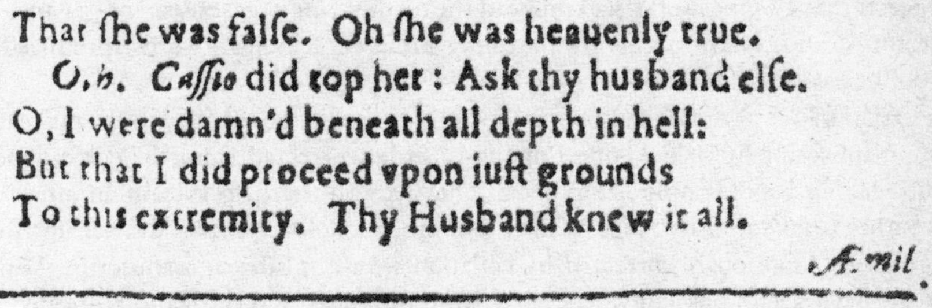

That ſhe was falſe. Oh ſhe was heauenly true.
Oth. *Caſſio* did top her: Ask thy husband elſe.
O, I were damn'd beneath all depth in hell:
But that I did proceed vpon iuſt grounds
To this extremity. Thy Husband knew it all.
Æmil

Fig. 5 Foot of second type-column of signature vv4^{v} of F

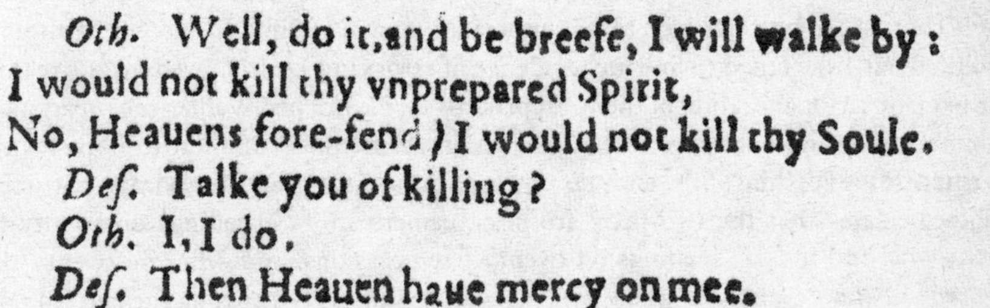

Oth. Well, do it, and be breefe, I will walke by:
I would not kill thy vnprepared Spirit,
No, Heauens fore-fend) I would not kill thy Soule.
Deſ. Talke you of killing?
Oth. I, I do.
Deſ. Then Heauen haue mercy on mee.
Oth

Fig. 6 Foot of second type-column of signature vv4^{r} of F

[1] *The Quarto Copy for the First Folio of Shakespeare*, 1971, pp. 215–27.

passage...Having set 'And hell gnaw his bones', Compositor B, we may suppose, proceeded to set the second line from the correct page of manuscript, that which began with the line with which he should have begun vv3^{r}a ('*Rodori*. I haue heard too much: and your words and').

Further reason for believing that a manuscript rather than a copy of the quarto was before the compositor is to be found in Q1 where '*Em*. A halter pardon him, and hell gnaw his bones:' appears as a single line of type eight lines from the top of signature L1^r. This makes it unlikely that Q1 could have been used as the copy for F.

There are also other variants between the two texts, not cited by Walton, which support his argument for manuscript copy for F. For example, at 1.1.153 Q1 reads 'hells paines' and F 'hell apines'; here the F version is more likely to have been the result of a compositor's misreading of a manuscript than of Q1's type. Similarly at 4.1.74 the compositor set the nonsense phrase in Q1, 'here ere while, mad', which is clearly a misreading of the correct wording that F's compositor reproduces, 'heere, o're-whelmed'. But perhaps the most suggestive error of this kind occurs at 5.1.106. Q1 gives to Iago, as he seeks to involve Bianca in the attack on Cassio, the line 'Doe you perceiue the ieastures of her eye' of which F has the correct version, 'Do you perceiue the gastnesse of her eye?' The page in Q1 on which this reading appears (L4^v) was set by Compositor Y who on 14^r set the phrase 'Ieeres, the Ibes' (4.1.80). The press-corrector, who may well have been consulting the manuscript copy in proofing the inner formes of Sheet 1, changed the words to 'geares, the gibes'. This suggests that Compositor Y had misread the manuscript's 'gastnesse' or 'gastnes' for 'gestures' and, following his own spelling preference in such words, produced the meaningless 'ieastures'.

Variants such as these (and they are many) can readily be ascribed to the misreading of a manuscript by Q1's compositors and can be corrected from the corresponding true reading by the compositors of F. They make it hard to sustain an alternative hypothesis, favoured by Alice Walker and other scholars,[1] that F was set up from a copy of Q1 laboriously corrected by collation with a theatrical manuscript. Walker, as we have seen, was convinced that Q1 reproduces a theatrically truncated and memorially contaminated version of the play, even though she admitted that all the variants between Q1 and F could not possibly have been the result of simple correction of a copy of Q1 by reference to an authoritative manuscript. In fact, as Walton has pointed out,[2] she failed to find any evidence of errors in F clearly owed to Q1's readings or to manuscript alteration of them. In place of such evidence Walker's main argument for her case rests on errors and anomalies in accidentals common to both texts, in particular the spelling of the endings of weak verbs in the preterite and past participles. She calculates that the two texts are in agreement in '-t' spellings on twenty-four occasions, and in '-d' spellings on twenty-five occasions, and differ on twenty-three occasions where Q1 has '-t' and F has '-d/-ed' spellings. By stressing the pattern rather

---

[1] For example, Fredson Bowers in *Bibliography and Textual Criticism*, 1964, pp. 158–201, and William P. Williams in 'The F1 *Othello* copy-text' (*Papers of the American Bibliographical Society* 63 (1969), 23–5), who seek to support Walker's case by analysis of Compositor E's influence in F and the nature of the F proof-reading.   [2] *Quarto Copy*, pp. 220–2.

than the number of such occurrences, she deduces that QI's compositor had already modernised a number of spellings by substituting the '-'d' ending favoured during the Jacobean period. These were preserved by F's compositor, but two out of three of the older Elizabethan spellings survived in QI and half of these were modernised by F's Jacobean compositor.

This argument cannot accommodate the evidence that three compositors and two scribes were responsible for QI. Nor is there real reason to believe in the systematic modernisation of QI; the distribution of '-t/-'d/-ed' endings is consistent with Shakespeare's own practice in Hand D of *Sir Thomas More* (*c.* 1594) and at a later date also. Furthermore, F reflects the modernising tendency characteristic of Jaggard's Compositor B who set most of the *Othello* text in the volume.

If one takes the errors of the graphic kind mentioned above and compares them with non-graphic errors – if one compares, that is, those errors that can be traced to a manuscript original with those traceable to other agencies – it appears that F preserves more of the graphic than the non-graphic errors, and does so in a proportion that is close to that in Hand D of *Sir Thomas More* but markedly different from that found in Folio plays that we know to have been set from earlier quarto copy.

Substantive variants

While we may be confident, therefore, that F, like QI, was set up from manuscript copy, it does not follow that it was set from the same manuscript. Reason for believing that it was not is yielded by a scrutiny of the substantive variants. The *Othello* variants have proved intractable to analysis and no theory of transmission yet produced has enabled an editor to make his choice of readings on purely bibliographical grounds. Scholars have contrived to leave themselves free to choose between numerous pairs of QI and F variants and to show to their own satisfaction, by the exercise of tact and judgement, that one is more 'Shakespearean' than the other. It is this persisting truth that forces us to consider the possibility that underlying QI and F there may be two Shakespearean versions of the play.

We know that in one respect at least the copy for F incorporated revisions, in that fifty-three oaths in QI are either excised or euphemised. Almost certainly these changes were made in response to the Act of 1606 against profanity and swearing in stage plays. Examination of these changes makes it clear that the task of eliminating such blasphemy was not carried out in any mechanical fashion. Certainly some oaths are simply omitted – for example, the 'Zouns' that appears in a prose passage at 1.1.109 in QI is dropped in F, as are the 'Faith' at 4.2.180, the 'Heauen' at 3.4.77 and the 'God' at 4.1.205. At other points there is the substitution of a less offensive word, such as 'troth' for 'faith' at 3.4.181 or 'Heauen' for 'God' at 3.4.73 and 4.3.100. Yet there is no consistency in such changes; for 'Faith' is also replaced by 'Why' (3.3.287), 'sooth' (3.4.92) and 'indeed' (3.4.51). There are occurrences where neither omission nor substitution was possible because of the requirements of the metre: thus at 1.1.4–6 QI's

> S'blood, but you will not heare me,
> If euer I did dreame of such a matter, abhorre me.

becomes F's

> But you'l not heare me. If euer I did dream
> Of such a matter, abhorre me.

Neither version is very satisfactory metrically, but it is at least obvious that it was the excision of 'S'blood' that caused the rearrangement.

When one examines the handling of the oaths in the two texts, one suspects that the censoring was done either by the author or a very self-confident book-keeper or printer. More importantly, it is plain that the oaths found in Q1 have very good literary or dramatic reasons for being there – that is, that they must have originated with Shakespeare himself. For example, they are a characteristic of Iago's idiom and it is noticeable that Othello starts to use them only under extreme stress or Iago's influence; which means that they are one aspect of the stylistic corruption of Othello's speech by Iago that has been traced by S. L. Bethell[1] in his article 'The diabolic images in *Othello*'.

The more extended passages in F that do not appear in Q1 are a more complicated matter. Some of these can certainly be accounted for as accidents of the printing process. For example, compositorial eye-skip is responsible for the lines omitted in Q1 at 4.2.70–6. In F at this point Othello says

> Was this faire Paper? This most goodly Booke
> Made to write Whore vpon? What commited,
> Committed? Oh, thou publicke Commoner,
> I should make very Forges of my cheekes,
> That would to Cynders burne vp Modestie,
> Did I but speake thy deedes. What commited?
> Heauen stoppes the Nose at it, and the Moone winks:

In Q1 lines 72–5 (on signature K4^r) are omitted. Obviously Compositor Y set lines 70 and 71 and then continued with line 76 because his eye caught the ending of line 75, 'What commited', which is identical with that of line 71. The omission would not be detected, for there is no correction against copy in the K gathering. Other substantial omissions probably similar to this in origin also occur, for example, at 3.4.7–8; 4.2.100; 4.3.57–60; and 5.2.150–3.

Some passages are not susceptible of such a simple mechanical explanation. Roderigo's speech at 1.1.119–39 explaining clearly to Brabantio exactly what Desdemona has done is reduced in Q1 to the first line and last three lines of the speech in F. Although lines 120 and 137 do begin with similar phrases ('If't be...' and 'If she be...') it is rather a long omission to be accounted for as an eye-skip mistake. It is also doubtful if simple accident can explain the absence in Q1 of the senator's clarifying lines about the probable reasons for the movements of the Turkish fleet at 1.3.24–30, or Othello's remarkable verse at 3.3.384–91 about his state of mind, or

---

[1] *S.Sur.* 5 (1952), 62–80.

some of the most strikingly exotic poetry in the play – those on the Pontic and the Hellespont at 3.3.454–61. The most famous of QI's mutilations is, of course, the absence of the Willow Song and its surrounding text. The lines concerned are 4.3.30–50, 52–4, and also the allusion made to the song at 5.2.244–6 by the dying Emilia.

When one considers all the longer passages in F which are not in QI, it is obvious that no single bibliographical theory about the relationship between the two texts will serve to account for all the lines affected. The idea that they were cuts made to shorten the play for performance we have seen to be palpably unacceptable, as is the notion that the Willow Song was omitted because the boy actor playing Desdemona had no singing voice – neither have most of the modern actresses who have played the role very movingly. It is striking that none of the lines absent from QI is crucial to an understanding of the action of the play. All are elaborations of effects already present in QI and can easily be defended on the grounds of the contributions they variously make to many aspects of the drama: clear exposition (1.1.120–36; 1.3.24–30), character portrayal (4.2.72–5; 4.2.150–63), psychological verisimilitude (3.3.454–61; 4.1.37–41), dramatic effect (4.3.30–50, 57–60), interconnection of images associated with the 'unnaturalness' of Desdemona's choice of a husband and the supernatural elements mixed with Othello's love, that Coghill has analysed with great subtlety[1] (1.2.65, 72–7; 1.3.60–4). Needless to say, all these anomalous passages could have come only from the pen of the author. They look more like Shakespeare's amplifications of his own text than cuts arbitrarily or purposively imposed on some original full version.

There are a few passages in QI which do not appear in F, the longest of them being four lines. Most of these (for example, 1.1.15; 1.3.199; 2.1.82; 3.1.28; 4.2.32, 166) are capable of explanation as scribal or compositorial errors. Only two QI-only sections of text are significant. The first of these occurs in the interchange between Iago and Roderigo at 1.3.359–65, which in QI reads

Iag. Go to, farewell: – doe you heare *Roderigo*?
Rod. what say you?
Iag. No more of drowning, doe you heare?
Rod. I am chang'd.   *Exit Roderigo*
Iag. Goe to, farewell, put money enough in your purse:
      Thus doe I euer make my foole my purse:

In F this appears as

Iago. Go too, farewell. Do you heare *Rodorigo*?
Rod. Ile sell all my Land.   *Exit.*
Iago. Thus do I euer make my Foole, my purse:

Clearly both versions are defective; but it is not hard to attribute both mix-ups to the printing-house.

The second section found in QI but not in F occurs during the murder of Desdemona (5.2.84–9) and is important in that it seems to imply a different staging from that found in F. QI has

[1] *Shakespeare's Professional Skills*, pp. 183–7.

> *Des.* But halfe an houre, but while I say one prayer.
> *Oth.* Tis too late.   *he stifles her.*
> *Des.* O Lord, Lord, Lord.   Emillia *calls within.*
> *Em.* My Lord, my Lord, what ho, my Lord, my Lord.
> *Oth.* What voyce is this? not dead? not yet quite dead?
>   I that am cruell, am yet mercifull,
>   I would not haue thee linger in thy paine, – so, so.

F's version is

> *Des.* But halfe an houre.
> *Oth.* Being done, there is no pawse.
> *Des.* But while I say one prayer.
> *Oth.* It is too late.   *Smothers her.*
>   *Æmilia at the doore.*
> *Æmil.* My Lord, my Lord? What hoa?
>   My Lord, my Lord.
> *Oth.* What noise is this? Not dead? not yet quite dead?
>   I that am cruell, am yet mercifull,
>   I would not haue thee linger in thy paine?
>   So, so.

In Q1's version Othello's words 'What voyce is this?' can only refer to Desdemona's exclamation and is connected with 'not dead?'; whereas in F they clearly allude to Emilia's cry offstage. As in the case of the Iago–Roderigo exchange, one suspects that the true text lies in some conflation of the two passages; the weakness of both probably deriving from the printing-house, for in Q1 the passage is spread between the bottom of signature M2^r and the top of signature M2^v, and in F across the foot of the first type-column and the head of the second type-column of signature vv4^v, a page on which there was probably some irregularity in setting.

In addition to the lines appearing exclusively in one or other of the two texts, there are many hundreds of separate variants in words and phrases. Many of these can be attributed to scribal and compositorial errors. For example, there are frequent differences in number, such as 'other' (Q1), 'others' (F) at 1.1.29; 'griefes' (Q1), 'griefe' (F) at 1.3.55; 'dores' (Q1), 'doore' (F) at 4.2.143, often amounting to a dozen differences in the space of two hundred lines. Another class of variant is of verb form: 'does' (Q1), 'doth' (F) at 4.2.30; 'takes' (Q1), 'taketh' (F) at 4.2.217; 'Has' (Q1), 'Hath' (F) at 4.2.124. A single extra word in one or other of the texts is found in many sentences; so that, for example, F supplies a second 'now' to Q1's 'Euen now' at 1.1.89 and has 'Pray you' for Q1's 'Pray' at 4.2.23, whereas it is Q1 that supplies an extra 'now' to F's 'are making the Beast with two backs' at 1.1.116 and has 'warrant you' for F's 'warrant' at 4.2.167. Simple transpositions occur throughout, such as 'all be' (F), 'be all' (Q1) at 1.1.43; 'haue we' (F), 'we haue' (Q1) at 1.3.304–5; 'her Gloues, her Mask' (F), 'her mask, her gloues' (Q1) at 4.2.8.

Many of the variant readings provide different words which convey the same meaning. For example, there is little to choose in sense between Q1's 'For be sure' and F's 'Be assur'd' at 1.2.11, or 'yond' (F), 'yonder' (Q1) at 1.2.28, or 'Introth' (F), 'By my troth' (Q1) at 4.3.68. But there are others where the sense is seriously affected and which cannot be explained by resort to any theory of printing-house origin or scribal corruption or memorial contamination. No theory of relationship between QI and F has yet been produced which enables us to choose confidently between variants like the following: 'sneake' (QI), 'steale' (F) at 3.3.39; 'Indian' (QI), 'Iudean' (F) at 5.2.343; 'reputation' (QI), 'estimation' (F) at 1.3.270; 'provulgate' (QI), 'promulgate' (F) at 1.2.21; 'enscerped to clog' (QI), 'ensteep'd, to enclogge' (F) at 2.1.70; 'scorne' (QI), 'storme' (F) at 1.3.245; 'Wring' (QI), 'Wrench' (F) at 5.2.285; 'Reprobation' (QI), 'Reprobance' (F) at 5.2.208; 'faithfull' (QI), 'truely' (F) at 1.3.122. Each word in these pairs and in many others like them in the two texts can be and have been defended as being the more 'Shakespearean' on the grounds of dramatic effect, poetic power, literary appropriateness and so on.

Editorial procedure

Such is the evidence on which we must assess the nature of the QI and F texts and their interrelationship. It is impossible in the present state of knowledge to be dogmatic, or to build on bibliographical foundations a theory of transmission which would enable us to approach with confidence a Shakespearean original of the play. Both texts are defective owing to a variety of circumstances surrounding their production; yet each is superior to the other in many respects. Clearly behind each text there lies *a* Shakespearean manuscript. The crucial question persists – was it the same manuscript?

There are a number of possible editorial paradigms, of which three are dominant: (1) that QI and F are independently, but not directly, derived from a single Shakespearean holograph; (2) that F derives from a copy of QI wholly or partly corrected from a redaction of the same Shakespearean holograph; (3) that QI and F derive from two different, but closely related, Shakespearean holographs. All three hypotheses are likely in practice to yield an eclectic text, but with differing emphases. The first allows to each text an authority dependent on the reliability attributed to its transmission. The second allows a certain precedence to QI while admitting an uncertain number of 'corrections' and 'revisions' from F. The third may or may not invite an eclectic procedure, depending upon the degree of autonomy, precedence and authority postulated of the two underlying autographs; it could even invite separate editions of F and QI *Othello*.

M. R. Ridley in his Arden edition of 1958 and Alice Walker and Dover Wilson in their New Shakespeare edition of 1957 take the second option, but with sharply differing editorial consequences. Ridley believed that by adopting QI as copy-text, reinstating 'the cuts made in it' with some 'possible revisions' from F, he could get 'as near as we are likely to get to the play as Shakespeare first wrote it, with nothing between us and him but the blunders of honest but not always skilful transcriber and compositor.'[1] Walker and Wilson assumed that F was set up from a copy of QI which had been systematically corrected from the promptbook underlying Walkley's manuscript. They therefore give priority to F when readings are evenly matched but

[1] Ridley, p. xliii.

follow Q1 where 'it appears to have preserved a reading more consonant with Shakespeare's style and dramatic intentions'.[1] Both editions are thus eclectic.

The practice adopted in the present edition is based upon the belief that Q1 and F are derived from two distinct manuscripts of equal authority, both of which have been variously corrupted in transmission, by scribes and compositors in Q1 and by editorial intervention and compositors in F. In fact, my strong impression is that what we are dealing with is Shakespeare's first version of the play (behind Q1) and his own transcription of it (behind F), during the process of making which he not only created additions for dramatic clarification or imaginative amplification but was also enticed into changes in words and phrases which appeared to him at the time as improvements on his first thoughts. This means that the text is, like its predecessors, an eclectic one; but one which has been arrived at by treating each pair of variants as a separate entity. The adoption of one variant or the other has been governed by a consideration of the known factors concerning the occurrence of the reading in each text. In some cases the choice between them was a simple one: paleographical knowledge determined the acceptance of F's 'heere, o're-whelmed' at 4.1.74, and the same kind of evidence combined with an awareness of the nature of the press-correction in Q1 demanded we read 'gastnesse' at 5.1.106. Accidental omissions which are probably the result of printing-house carelessness, such as those in Q1 at 4.2.72–5 or in F at 1.3.199, have been supplied by reference to the fuller text. At points where both F and Q1 are defective owing to compositorial error Shakespeare's probable intention has been made out from a conflation of the two texts (for example, at 1.3.359–65). The substantial passages in F which are clearly Shakespearean, the omission of which from Q1 cannot be explained on any bibliographical grounds (such as the Willow Song or Othello's speech at 3.3.454–61), have been adopted on the grounds that they were clearly written by Shakespeare at some point during the play's composition for inclusion at those moments in the action at which they occur in F. Where F and Q1 are both obviously erroneous, emendation has been made after due consideration of the suggestions made by previous scholars about the origin of the error in both texts and the most likely word or phrase required. The oaths in Q1 which were expurgated in F are a special case in that they appear to have been excised systematically as a result of external pressure and so generally need to be adopted in a modern text.

The procedure outlined above is only slightly different in result, if not in theory, from that adopted by previous editors of the play. It is when we come to think about the treatment of those hundreds of variants between Q1 and F, encompassing variations in number, alternative verb forms, and numerous different words and phrases equally appropriate and equally 'Shakespearean', that the difficulties arise. Previous editors have attempted to establish one text or the other as the primary authority by arguing that one text is based upon the other or that both have behind them a common original Shakespearean copy. But no one who has studied the Q1 and F variants can fail at least to suspect that, when all possible allowance has been made for scribal and compositorial sophistication or memorial contamination, the two texts reflect two stages of composition for both of which Shakespeare himself was responsible –

[1] NS, pp. 133–5.

particularly when one gives proper weight to Coghill's discussion of the matter and the recent support of and additions to his findings published by Honigmann.[1]

But if we accept the possibility that there are two versions of *Othello*, both by Shakespeare, what are the implications? One may conclude with Honigman[2] that 'traditional editorial principles' are 'as unsatisfactory as the traditional conflated texts' and therefore the only intellectually honest procedure for an editor to follow is to produce for the reader separate or parallel texts of Q1 and F, bibliographically purged of error, in the manner of W. W. Greg's edition of Marlowe's *Doctor Faustus* or J. C. Maxwell's of Wordsworth's *The Prelude*.[3] But the case of *Othello* is different from these, for the variants between the texts lie in the area of details rather than in design, overall intention and emphasis. Providing the editor supplies sufficient collation for the reader to reconstruct Q1 and F in the original form, he is free to offer what he thinks to be a 'best' version of the play in the full knowledge that in fact he is making a third version of it. This means, of course, that such an edition will be to some extent similar to a stage production (which is always an interpretation) or a critical essay about it. But then all modern editions of a Shakespeare play – indeed Q1 and F themselves – have always been just this.

Later seventeenth-century editions

Following the publication of the First Folio in 1623 five other seventeenth-century quartos of the play were issued: in 1630 (Q2) by Richard Hawkins, in 1655 (Q3) by William Leek, and in 1681 (Q4), 1687 (Q5) and 1695 (Q6), all by Richard Bentley. The play was also included in the later Folio reprints of 1632 (F2), 1663–4 (F3) and 1685 (F4).

None of these texts has any independent authority, although Q2 is interesting in that it was almost certainly set from a copy of Q1 which had been most carefully collated with a copy of F.[4] It includes all the passages in F not found in Q1 and follows F in the treatment of the oaths; but it also makes alterations as detailed as, for example, the changing of Q1's 'you will' (1.1.4) to F's 'you'l'; Q1's 'handkercher' (3.3.309) to F's 'Handkerchiefe'; and Q1's 'often' (3.3.99) to F's 'oft'. Yet it follows much of Q1's spelling and punctuation, reproduces its stage directions, and often prefers its readings to those of F at points that most modern editors have found controversial, such as 'beare all excellency' over F's 'tyre the Ingeniuer' (2.1.65) and 'lodging' over F's 'Loading' (5.2.359). In fact the editorial procedure followed in Q2 indicates that, only seven years after the publication of the First Folio, at least one printer considered that Q1 was not completely superseded by F, which could easily have been reproduced by Hawkins.

---

[1] 'Shakespeare's revised plays: *King Lear* and *Othello*', *The Library*, 6th ser., 4 (1982), 156–73.
[2] 'Shakespeare's revised plays', p. 173.
[3] W. W. Greg (ed.), *Marlow's 'Doctor Faustus' 1604–1616: Parallel Texts*, 1950; J. C. Maxwell (ed.), *William Wordsworth: The Prelude*, 1971.
[4] See Charlton Hinman, 'The "copy" for the second quarto of *Othello*', *Joseph Quincy Adams Memorial Studies*, 1948, pp. 373–89.

READING LIST

This list includes details of books and articles referred to in the Introduction or Commentary, and may serve as a guide to those who wish to undertake further study of the play.

Adamson, J. 'Othello' as Tragedy, 1980

Adamson, W. 'Unpinned or undone?: Desdemona's critics and the problem of sexual innocence', S.St. 13 (1980), 169–86

Alexander, N. 'Thomas Rymer and Othello', S.Sur. 21 (1968), 67–77

Allen, N. B. 'The two parts of Othello', S.Sur. 21 (1968), 13–29

Auden, W. H. 'The joker in the pack', in The Dyer's Hand, 1962

Bayley, J. The Characters of Love, 1960

Berry, R. 'Pattern in Othello', SQ 23 (1972), 3–19

Bethell, S. L. 'The diabolic images in Othello', S.Sur. 5 (1952), 62–80

Boose, L. E. 'Othello's handkerchief: "the recognizance and pledge of love"', ELR 5 (1975), 360–74

Bowers, F. Bibliography and Textual Criticism, 1964

Bradley, A. C. Shakespearean Tragedy, 1904

Bullough, G. Narrative and Dramatic Sources of Shakespeare, VII, 1973

Carlisle, C. J. Shakespeare from the Greenroom, 1969

Clemen, W. The Development of Shakespeare's Imagery, 1951

Coghill, N. Shakespeare's Professional Skills, 1964

Coleridge, S. T. Coleridge's Shakespearean Criticism, ed. T. M. Raysor, 2 vols., 1930

Cook, A. J. 'The design of Desdemona: doubt raised and resolved', S.St. 13 (1980), 187–96

Curtis, J. R. 'Reason and love in Othello', SQ 24 (1973), 188–97

Dean, W. 'Verdi's Otello: a Shakespearean masterpiece', S.Sur. 21 (1968), 87–96

Eliot, T. S. 'Shakespeare and the stoicism of Seneca', in Selected Essays, 1932

Elliott, G. R. Flaming Minister, 1953

Empson, W. ' "Honest" in Othello', in The Structure of Complex Words, 1951

Everett, B. 'Reflections on the sentimentalist's Othello', CQ 3 (1961), 127–39

Gardner, H. The Noble Moor (British Academy Lecture), 1956
    'Othello: a retrospect, 1900–67', S.Sur. 21 (1968), 1–11

Granville-Barker, H. Prefaces to Shakespeare, 4th ser., 1945

Greg, W. W. The Shakespeare First Folio, 1955

Hazlitt, W. Characters of Shakespeare's Plays, 1817

Heilman, R. B. Magic in the Web, 1956

Hinman, C. The Printing and Proof-Reading of the First Folio of Shakespeare, 2 vols., 1963

Holloway, J. *The Story of the Night*, 1961

Honigmann, E. A. J. *The Stability of Shakespeare's Text*, 1965

  'Shakespeare's revised plays: *King Lear* and *Othello*', *The Library*, 6th ser., 4 (1982), 156–73

Hosley, R. 'The staging of Desdemona's bed', *SQ* 14 (1963), 57–65

Hunter, G. K. *Shakespeare and Colour Prejudice* (British Academy Lecture), 1968

Hyman, S. E. *Iago: Some Approaches to the Illusion of his Motivation*, 1970

Johnson, S. *Samuel Johnson on Shakespeare*, ed. W. K. Wimsatt, 1960

Jones, Eldred. *Othello's Countrymen*, 1965

Jones, Emrys. *Scenic Form in Shakespeare*, 1971

Jones, M. T. 'Press-variants and proof-reading in the first quarto of *Othello* (1622)', *SB* 27 (1974), 177–84

Jorgensen, P. *Shakespeare's Military World*, 1956

Knight, G. W. 'The *Othello* music', in *The Wheel of Fire*, 1930

Leavis, F. R. 'Diabolic intellect and the noble hero', in *The Common Pursuit*, 1952

Matthews, G. M. 'Othello and the dignity of man', in *Shakespeare in a Changing World*, ed. A. Kettle, 1964

Morozov, M. M. 'The individualization of Shakespeare's characters through imagery', *S.Sur.* 2 (1949), 83–106

Muir, K. *The Sources of Shakespeare's Plays*, 1977

Ridley, M. R. (ed.). *Othello*, 1958

Rosenberg, M. *The Masks of Othello*, 1961

Ross, L. 'The use of a "fit-up" booth in *Othello*', *SQ* 12 (1961), 359–70

Rymer, T. *The Critical Works of Thomas Rymer*, ed. C. Zimansky, 1956

Schwartz, E. 'Stylistic impurity and the meaning of *Othello*', *SEL* 10 (1970), 293–314

Sisson, C. J. *New Readings in Shakespeare*, II, 1956

Spivack, B. *Shakespeare and the Allegory of Evil*, 1958

Spurgeon, C. *Shakespeare's Imagery*, 1935

Stanislavski, C. *Stanislavski Produces 'Othello'*, 1948

Sternfeld, F. W. *Music in Shakespearean Tragedy*, 1963

Stewart, J. I. M. *Character and Motive in Shakespeare*, 1949

Stockholder, K. S. '"Egregiously an ass": chance and accident in *Othello*', *SEL* 13 (1973), 256–72

Stoll, E. E. *'Othello': An Historical and Comparative Study*, 1915

Tynan, K. *'Othello': The National Theatre Production*, 1967

Walker, A. 'The 1622 quarto and the First Folio text of *Othello*', *S.Sur.* 5 (1952), 16–24

  Textual Problems of the First Folio, 1953

Walker, A., and J. Dover Wilson (ed.). *Othello*, 1957

Walton, J. *The Quarto Copy for the First Folio of Shakespeare*, 1971

West, R. 'The christianness of *Othello*', *SQ* 15 (1964), 333–43

Williams, P. 'The FI *Othello* copy-text', *Papers of the American Bibliographical Society* 63 (1969), 23–5

Wilson, H. S. *On the Design of Shakespearean Tragedy*, 1958